Frank Camorra is chef and owner of the acclaimed MoVida restaurants in Melbourne and Sydney. Spanish-born but raised in Australia, a trip back to his birthplace in 2000 inspired him to share his love of Spanish food. And so his stable of critically acclaimed and much-loved tapas bars and restaurants was born. Hidden down a gritty and graffiti-ed Melbourne laneway, MoVida was an instant hit, leading to MoVida Next Door and MoVida Aqui. Then came MoVida Sydney, along with venues at Melbourne and Sydney airports. Frank has co-authored four previous books: *MoVida*, *MoVida Rustica*, *MoVida Cocina* and *MoVida's Guide to Barcelona*.

◄────►

An award-winning food writer, **Richard Cornish** is senior features writer for *The Sydney Morning Herald* and *The Age's Good Food* lift-outs, and is the writer and creator of its popular 'Brain Food' column. He has co-written four previous books on Spanish food with Frank Camorra and is co-author of *Phillippa's Home Baking*. Richard lives in Melbourne with his partner, fashion designer Tiffany Treloar, daughters Ginger and Sunday, and a rambling vegetable garden.

This book is dedicated to the chefs, cooks, housewives, fishermen, butchers, hunters, foragers, nuns and food writers of Andalusia who shared these important traditional recipes with us so they will never be lost or forgotten.

Frank Camorra & Richard Cornish

MOVIDA SOLERA

A celebration of Andalusian food and culture

Photography by Alan Benson

CLEARVIEW

CONTENTS

INTRODUCTION

◄━►

The Andalusian sun seemed to be forcing its way through the cracks under the door of the old bodega. Great shafts of sunlight were punching through the gloom and bouncing off the pale sandy floor stacked with black sherry barrels, flooding the cathedral-like space with a soft golden glow. The owner of the sherry bodega, an 80-year-old widow, explained to me that sherry was first poured into barrels here 180 years ago. Every year since then a little sherry has been racked into the barrels below and some new sherry poured in the barrels on top. Almost two centuries on, that original sherry, although greatly diluted, still has an influence on the sherry being bottled each year. My hostess quietly explained that the *solera* system of maturing sherry could serve as an allegory for the food of this part of southern Spain: 'What we eat today is a blend of all the different cultures that over the years have lived in this part of the world long before we drew our first breath.'

Home to the original Iberian tribes and the early civilisations of the Tartessos, Phoenicians, Greeks, Romans, Visigoths, Moors and Jews, Andalusia has been invaded by Napoleon's army and ravaged by the Spanish Civil War. The departure point of Christopher Columbus's voyages to the Americas, it was also where the riches of the New World arrived in Europe. Its landscapes comprise mountain ranges and fertile valleys, historic and ancient cities, swathes of modern coastal development and isolated rural communities; it is swaddled by the warm waters of the Mediterranean and buffeted by the cold, rich waters of the Atlantic Ocean.

This book is a collection of traditional Andalusian recipes, and they reflect all of this. Like the sherry *solera*, the food of Andalusia builds on the past and mixes in new influences. There are the ancient indigenous ingredients, such as seafood, pork, beef, goat, herbs, honey and vegetables. To these are added the foods of the conquerors and visitors: the olives and grapes of the Romans; the saffron, spice, rice and citrus of the Moors; and the tomatoes, potatoes, chillies and peppers from the New World. Uncovering the origins of Andalusian food can feel like an archaeological dig, with millennia of layers in each dish.

The word *solera* shares the same Latin root as *suelo*, the Spanish word for 'earth' or 'ground'. The word has many other meanings: the foundation of a wall or building, the hearth of an oven, the bottom grindstone in a mill, the base of a channel, the 'mother' wine used in sherry making. It also means 'the traditional customs and uses of things'. A fitting title, then, for this celebration of the food, wine, culture and people of Andalusia.

Although I was born in Barcelona, I am Andalusian. Both sides of my family come from Córdoba and nearby towns. I was brought up on oranges, rice, cod, tomatoes, prawns, peppers, olive oil and jamón, the culinary leitmotifs that pervade Andalusia. We moved to Australia when I was four, but Mum continued to feed our family on dishes made from these foods. As often as I can I return to visit my home country.

Despite having lived and worked in Córdoba as a young chef, and travelled through Andalusia several times since, there were parts of the region that have

remained a mystery to me. For this book I covered almost 10,000 kilometres through Andalusia's eight provinces, namely Seville, Huelva, Cádiz, Málaga, Córdoba, Jaén, Granada and Almería, accompanied by co-writer Richard Cornish and photographer and trained chef Alan Benson. Also joining us was Catalan food journalist Cesc Castro. As a Catalan, Cesc provided not only the objectivity that someone from down south may not bring to the project, but also has a sympathetic understanding of the importance of food and wine to all Spanish culture.

What we found on our journey was that although in some places local culinary traditions had given way to the mainstream national Spanish cuisine, there was still an incredibly robust pride in regional dishes. Before I started this project I had no idea that people in the mountains of Jaén made their own pasta. I was only vaguely aware of the *Malagueño* practice of preserving pork in lard (using a method similar to French confit), or that some of the best cheese in the country comes from the lush meadows of Cádiz's Sierra de Grazalema.

Our research was painstakingly done in the bars, restaurants, markets, fairs, monasteries, museums and home kitchens of Andalusia. The result is an exploration of the gastronomic history and legacy of the region, as told through the stories of the scores of cooks, chefs, housewives, fisherman, butchers, peasants and nuns of Andalusia we met, talked, ate and drank with, and who so generously shared their unparalleled hospitality and delicious recipes with us. The food in this book is presented with the deepest respect and gratitude to all the people who have contributed. The recipes were given in good faith that they would be presented in context, and in the hope that they will be cooked and enjoyed in true Andalusian style, perhaps with a glass of sherry, wine or beer, but always with family and friends. They are recipes that demand a good appetite and a convivial sense of enjoyment.

MOVIDA'S GUIDE TO ANDALUSIA

At the end of each chapter you will find the details of all the restaurants, bars and shops mentioned or photographed, so if you feel inspired to explore Andalusia and its food for yourself you can follow in my footsteps.

Generally my days in Andalusia go something like this: I check out the local markets in the morning, grab a quick breakfast in a bar and perhaps take in a gallery before returning for a siesta after lunch. From there, the activities of the afternoon meld into evening, and all too soon I find it's well after midnight and bed engulfs my over-indulgences. This means I have never placed too much importance on where I stay, and as long as I am a short walk or taxi ride from the action, I am happy. You, however, may be more discerning, or less, so when planning your trip, remember that things change all the time, and check out places carefully before making a booking.

Remember too that while vegetarianism is becoming more understood in the north of Spain, it is still considered heretical across much of jamón-eating Andalusia ...

The Guadalquivir shimmers in the early evening light as the sun lowers itself into the golden plains on the horizon. It's spring in Seville, and already the heat of summer can be felt on puffs of wind that rake across the river. *Sevillanos* make the most of the last of the mild weather; older couples promenade along the banks of the river, while younger couples jog and powerwalk. The sun disappears, sending the sky into a riot of gold, mauve and pale blue, and causing the halo of the streetlamps to arc up in a warm shade of yellow. A cruise ship lets out a blast of its horn as it steams off, heading the 80 or so kilometres back down the river to the Atlantic. Named Guadalquivir ('great river') by the Arabs, this waterway is the lifeblood of large swathes of Andalusia, connecting cities to the Atlantic and providing water to irrigate crops.

The Guadalquivir was once truly great. During Roman times, it was a deep navigable river from the Atlantic to Córdoba further upstream. In the lower reaches, its waters would flood across a broad delta, nourishing the wetlands of the Doñana, a great and wild wetland. With the discovery of the New World, Seville became a safe and protected inland port where the wealth of the Aztecs and Incas was unloaded. This was also the first place recorded in Europe, where tomato is mentioned as part of the cuisine. From the sixteenth century all the gold and spoils of the conquistadors and colonists passed through the city's Casa de Contratación, Spain's national customs house where taxes were levied for the Crown. With this newfound wealth and status, Seville became the powerhouse of Spain's Golden Age, a period when Spain was the military and cultural powerhouse of the globe. The city built upon its Roman, Arab and Jewish foundations, literally – the bell tower of the Catedral de Santa María de la Sede is constructed upon the former minaret of the city's mosque. The cathedral is also home to the remains of Christopher Columbus, making it a place for pilgrims of religion and exploration alike.

Seville is also the administrative centre of Andalusia, and in many ways has the urbane feel of the national capital Madrid, blending conservative elements with its own avant-garde sensibility. Here you'll find some of the oldest bars in Andalusia, as well as restaurants offering the most cutting-edge modernist cuisine. Like Madrid, Seville doesn't have the same breadth of indigenous dishes as other provincial centres in Andalusia. What it does offer, though, is one of the largest old towns in Europe, unscarred by the carnage of twentieth-century wars, and dotted with Word Heritage-listed buildings. Seville's intact Jewish quarter and small neighbourhood plazas are planted with bitter orange trees – and in spring the fragrance of their blossom, mingled with the aromas of cooking, makes this one of the most joyous cities to wander around.

HUEVOS ROTOS

BROKEN EGGS

SERVES 4

You'll find this rich and satisfying combination of eggs, jamón and potatoes across Spain, eaten as a cheap and filling evening meal. The name itself refers to the way you eat the dish, breaking the runny egg yolks to create an impromptu dressing for the potatoes. This is a classic case of getting what you pay for. If you use the best free-range eggs, some really good jamón and the finest potatoes, you'll end up with a meal to be proud of; one to share and enjoy with a good bottle of oloroso, or even a tempranillo. This version was photographed at El Manolo Mayo restaurant, in Los Palacios y Villafranca.

1.2 kg waxy potatoes, peeled and cut into 1 cm thick chips
sea salt
1 litre olive oil, for deep-frying, plus 100 ml extra
8 eggs
12 slices jamón, cut into three

1 Place the chips in a bowl and cover with cold water, then add a teaspoon of salt. Leave to stand in a cool place for 1 hour.

2 Drain the chips well, then pat dry between two clean tea towels.

3 Pour the olive oil for deep-frying into a heavy-based saucepan or flat-bottomed wok and heat to 170°C or until a cube of bread dropped into the oil browns in 15 seconds.

4 Working in two batches, deep-fry the chips for 10 minutes or until well-browned and crisp. Use a slotted spoon to remove them from the oil, then drain on paper towel and season well with salt.

5 Pour the extra 100 ml olive oil into a large frying pan and place over medium heat. Break 2 eggs at a time into the pan and fry for 1–2 minutes or until the whites are set but the yolks are still runny. Transfer the fried eggs to a plate. Cook the remaining eggs and season with salt.

6 Divide the chips evenly between the plates, then top with fried eggs and slices of jamon. (The idea is to break the eggs with your knife and fork and let the yolk cover the chips.)

PIMIENTOS ASADOS

ROASTED CAPSICUM SALAD

SERVES 4

This is a stock-standard dish you'll find across Spain, served as a snack in bars or a *ración* in restaurants. This version comes from Restaurante Alhucemas, just outside Seville, where they serve it with sherry vinegar aged for 25 years in oak. The capsicums can be roasted in an oven, as described below, or over a barbecue grill, glowing coals or even the flame of a gas stove. This dish goes well with fish, lamb, chicken and anything barbecued.

4 large red capsicums (peppers)
150 ml extra virgin olive oil
2 teaspoons sea salt
40 ml aged sherry vinegar
1 white onion, finely diced

1 Preheat the oven to 200°C/180°C fan.

2 Place the capsicums on a baking tray, drizzle with 40 ml of the olive oil and sprinkle with 1 teaspoon of the salt. Roast in the oven for 30 minutes or until the flesh is soft and the skin is brown and blackened. (Alternatively, cook over a charcoal barbecue until the skin has blackened and the flesh is soft.)

3 Place the roast capsicums in a bowl and cover with plastic film. When the capsicums are cool enough to handle, peel off the skin, then remove and discard the stem and seeds, reserving the juices. Cut the flesh into thin strips and return to the bowl, along with any juices. Sprinkle with the remaining teaspoon of salt and add the remaining olive oil and the sherry vinegar. Cover with plastic film and refrigerate for several hours.

4 Spread the capsicum on a serving dish, then garnish with the onion and dress with the juices from the bowl. Serve chilled with other tapas or as an accompaniment to grilled fish or meats.

BUÑUELOS DE BACALAO

SALT COD FRITTERS

MAKES 24

There are a handful of bars in Seville's Plaza del Salvador, a small square opposite the baroque Iglesia del Salvador, or Church of the Saviour. I head here every time I am in town – for the bars, not the church. They now know me, not by name but by reputation: the big Australian chef and his ever-hungry crew. I come here for the delicious *buñuelos de bacalao*. Deep-fried yet light, fishy yet meaty, they are a good way to use up the lesser parts of the cod.

350 g salt cod fillet
600 ml milk
75 g butter
½ brown onion, finely diced
2 garlic cloves, finely diced
3 fresh bay leaves
100 g plain flour
3 eggs
1 tablespoon chopped chives
1 tablespoon chopped
   flat-leaf parsley
finely grated zest of 1 lemon
1 litre olive oil, for deep-frying
sea salt

1 Wash the excess salt off the salt cod fillet, then place in a large bowl. Cover with water and leave to soak for 36 hours, changing the water three times.

2 Place the milk and the drained cod in a small saucepan over medium heat. Simmer for 10 minutes or until the cod is cooked. Transfer the cod to a plate and leave until cool enough to handle. Remove and discard the skin and any remaining small bones, and break the flesh into flakes. Reserve the milk.

3 Melt the butter in a heavy-based saucepan over medium heat. Add the onion, garlic and bay leaves and cook for 6 minutes or until the onion is soft and translucent. Add the flour and cook, stirring with a wooden spoon, for 2 minutes or until the flour begins to colour. Pour in the reserved milk a little at a time, mixing it into the flour. Once all the milk has been added, cook the sauce for 10 minutes, stirring continuously, until it is as thick as soft polenta and the flavour of the raw flour has been cooked out. Add the flaked cod to the pan and stir in well, then remove from the heat.

4 Break in the eggs, one at a time, mixing them in well, then stir in the herbs and lemon zest. Pour the mixture into a shallow baking tray and leave to cool before covering with plastic film and chilling in the refrigerator for 3 hours.

5 Pour the olive oil into a heavy-based saucepan or flat-bottomed wok and heat to 170°C or until a cube of bread dropped into the oil browns in 15 seconds.

6 Remove the salt cod mixture from the refrigerator. Take a heaped tablespoon of the mixture and push it off the spoon into the oil with your finger. Working in batches of 6 fritters at a time, deep-fry the fritters for 3 minutes or until golden, crisp and cooked through.

7 Remove with a slotted spoon and drain on paper towel. Season with salt and serve hot.

FIDEOS NEGROS CON ALMEJAS

PASTA COOKED IN SQUID INK WITH CLAMS

SERVES 4-6

Miguel Palomo used to be a car salesman, and when he lost his job at the age of 50, he went to work for another car yard. He lasted a day. 'I did what came naturally and started cooking,' says the laconic chef. People thought he was mad, cooking in one of the less salubrious parts of town. But his simple, pared-back and incredibly delicious food brought the diners in, and now he is one of the most-respected chefs in the province. Miguel concentrates on the quality of the produce, and uses five fresh squid ink sacs for this dish, but for consistency we suggest you use the squid ink available in sachets or jars from specialist food stores and Italian grocers. His restaurant Alhucemas is in Sanlúcar la Mayor, just outside of Seville.

900 g clams
1½ tablespoons squid ink
350 ml garlic mayonnaise
  (see page 380)
1.2 litres fish stock
  (see page 380)
40 ml olive oil
sea salt
500 g Spanish fideos or thin
  spaghetti, broken into
  2–3 cm lengths
extra virgin olive oil,
  for drizzling

1 Wash the clams under cold running water and place in a bowl. Cover with cold water and a good pinch of salt. Leave to stand for 30 minutes then, using your hands, lift the clams into another bowl. Cover with fresh water and add a pinch of salt. Repeat three times – this encourages the clams to purge themselves of sand.

2 Mix ½ teaspoon of the squid ink into the garlic mayonnaise until it is completely mixed through. Set aside.

3 Pour the fish stock into a *perol* (see page 380) or wide heavy-based saucepan and bring to a simmer over high heat, then add the remaining squid ink, olive oil and a pinch of salt. Reduce the heat to medium and simmer for 5 minutes. Add the pasta to the stock and cook for 10 minutes, stirring occasionally.

4 Drain the clams and add them to the pan, then cover and simmer for 5 minutes. Shake the pan occasionally, lifting the lid to stir once or twice, until the pasta is soft and the clams have opened.

5 Spoon the pasta and clams onto plates and serve with a dollop of garlic and squid ink mayonnaise and a drizzle of extra virgin olive oil.

SEPIA A LA PLANCHA

GRILLED BABY CUTTLEFISH

SERVES 4–6

In Spain you can buy tiny cuttlefish that are so young they haven't grown a cuttlebone, and so small they don't need cleaning. Spanish cooks lay them onto the screaming-hot slab of steel known as *la plancha* and sear them until the flesh is just set and the outside glazed with heat. While you're unlikely to find cuttlefish that small here, you can still replicate the delicious marinade and cooking method with larger cuttlefish or calamari. If they are any larger than half the size of a playing card, they will require cleaning and cutting into bite-sized morsels.

1.2 kg small cuttlefish
3 garlic cloves, peeled
handful of flat-leaf
    parsley leaves
60 ml olive oil
1 tablespoon vegetable oil
sea salt
juice of 1 lemon
extra virgin olive oil,
    for drizzling

1 Unless you are using baby cuttlefish, they will need cleaning. Ask the fishmonger to clean the cuttlefish for you – or, to do this yourself, pull the tentacles from the body, then discard the tentacles and guts. Pull the body open and remove the cuttlebone and any remaining guts. Pull away the wings and discard, then peel off any remaining skin. Rinse the cuttlefish under cold running water, then drain well.

2 Chop the garlic and parsley together on a chopping board, then place in a bowl with the olive oil and mix well. Add the cuttlefish and stir to coat, then cover with plastic film and refrigerate for 1 hour.

3 Heat the flat grillplate of a barbecue to very hot. Pour on the vegetable oil and, using a cloth or several layers of paper towel, carefully wipe over the grill.

4 Lay the cuttlefish evenly on the grillplate and cook for 2 minutes on one side. Season well with salt and half of the lemon juice. Turn the cuttlefish over, season again with salt and the remaining lemon juice, and cook for a further 2 minutes or until browned, firm and cooked through. (Alternatively, cook the cuttlefish in a heavy-based frying pan over high heat.)

5 Serve the cuttlefish warm, with a drizzle of extra virgin olive oil and a little more salt.

RICE

A flamingo is running its beak through the still water. It's early in the day, yet the eagles have found rising columns of air to circle and soar around. Small oaks and pines cling to the thin sandy soil of the dunes. From the crest of the dune, you can see wilderness stretching to the horizon, while in the other direction is an expanse of bland, flat farmland that was first planted with rice in the 1920s. A brutal concrete village straddles a small mound in the flooded rice fields. Called Isla Mayor, this was once 'the big island' that rose above one of the largest wetlands of Europe, fed by the waters of the Guadalquivir.

Rice came to Spain with the Arabs, who also introduced the irrigation needed to grow it. Along with wheat, it became a staple, a durable food that could be stored for a considerable period, making it a tradable commodity. Rice sits at the heart of the Spanish culinary repertoire. It is cooked in the home at least once a week, yet is still served in restaurants. What is important to understand is that paella is not the national rice dish – it is just one way of cooking rice. Paella is most popular on Spain's Levantine Coast, although cheap frozen paellas are defrosted and served in tourist haunts across the Iberian peninsula. Most of the rice served in Spain is simply *arroz*, a rich, sometimes soupy dish much like a dairy-free *risotto* containing fish or meat. Rice is also cooked with milk, sugar and flavourings to make the simple dessert of *arroz con leche*.

Huge tracts of land in Spain are devoted to growing rice. Some of the rice fields are hundreds of years old and are still managed using the same methods introduced by the Arabs. Then there are great swathes of flat land, where rice is farmed in much the same way as it is in Australia. Here in the province of Seville, Isla Mayor sits at the centre of the largest rice-growing region in the old world. When the fields are flooded, this little town is again surrounded by water as far as the eye can see, reminiscent of a time when this part of Spain was wild marshland.

ARROZ con CANGREJOS de RÍO

RICE WITH FRESHWATER CRAYFISH

SERVES 4

When you cook rice in Spain, you cook it with the ingredients closest to you. In the 1920s, when the ancient wetlands of the Guadalquivir downstream of Seville were drained for rice farming, the indigenous crayfish were soon replaced with their more aggressive North American cousins. The rice growers of Isla Mayor make the most of these invasive, yet tasty crustaceans by pulling them out of the irrigation channels and making them the centrepiece of this rich, soupy rice dish. Australian yabbies, marron or other freshwater crayfish are all perfect for this dish.

1 kg small freshwater crayfish, such as marron, red claw or yabbies
100 ml extra virgin olive oil
1 garlic bulb, cut in half
80 ml brandy
1 × 440 g tin chopped tomatoes
sea salt
3 ripe tomatoes
2 white onions, diced
2 garlic cloves, finely chopped
½ red bird's eye chilli, finely chopped
3 fresh bay leaves
½ large red capsicum (pepper), finely chopped
250 g Calasparra rice

1 Prepare the crayfish by grasping the head in one hand and the tail in the other, then remove the head by twisting and pulling at the same time. Peel the tails by taking kitchen scissors and cutting the underside of the shell on both sides. Pull away the shell, remove the tail meat and refrigerate until required. Reserve the heads and shells.

2 Pour 40 ml of the olive oil into a *perol* (see page 380) or wide heavy-based saucepan and place over high heat. When the oil is hot, add the garlic bulb and crayfish shells and cook, stirring occasionally, for 7–8 minutes or until the garlic is browned and the shells are a rich ruby colour. Pour in the brandy, scraping the base of the pan with a wooden spoon to deglaze. Add the tinned tomatoes and cook for a minute before adding 1.7 litres of water. Bring to the boil, then reduce the heat and season with salt. Simmer gently for 30 minutes, skimming off any impurities from the surface. Strain through a sieve set over a bowl, pressing down on the shells to extract as much juice and flavour as possible.

3 Cut the tomatoes in half and grate the cut side against a cheese grater over a bowl to pulp the flesh. Discard the skin.

4 In the rinsed-out pan, make a *sofrito* by adding the remaining olive oil and placing over low–medium heat. When the oil is hot, add the onion with a pinch of salt and cook for 10 minutes, stirring occasionally, until soft and translucent. Stir in the garlic, chilli and bay leaves and cook for 2 minutes. Add the capsicum and cook for 15 minutes or until soft. Add the tomato pulp and continue cooking for 15 minutes, stirring occasionally, until the *sofrito* has reduced to a jam-like consistency.

5 Puree the *sofrito* with a stick blender (or in a food processor) then stir in the crayfish stock. Bring to the boil, then reduce to a low simmer and sprinkle in the rice. Stir it in, then simmer gently for 15 minutes, stirring occasionally. Add the crayfish tail meat and cook for 2 minutes or until just done. Remove from the heat and stand for a few minutes, then take the *arroz* to the table and serve straight from the pan.

ARROZ con PATO

RICE WITH DUCK

SERVES 4

Wild ducks breed in the Doñana National Park, southwest of Seville, and then come to the rice fields of Isla Mayor to glean the rice left from the harvest. Those unlucky enough to cross the hunters' line of sight end up in this rich, soupy rice dish. Whether you make this with wild or farmed duck, make sure you roast the duck to a rich golden colour, and use the aromatics from the cavity to flavour the stock.

1 × 2 kg duck

sea salt

½ brown onion, cut into quarters

1 garlic bulb, broken into cloves but not peeled

6 sprigs thyme

300 ml red wine

60 ml olive oil

2 white onions, finely diced

2 garlic cloves, finely chopped

2 tablespoons chopped thyme

½ red capsicum (pepper), finely diced

250 g Calasparra rice

freshly ground black pepper

1 Preheat the oven to 210°C/190°C fan.

2 Remove the neck and wings from the duck and rinse the cavity under running water. Season the cavity with salt, stuff it with the brown onion, garlic and thyme sprigs, then rub the skin all over with salt. Place the duck, wings and neck on a wire rack set over a roasting tin and roast for 1½ hours or until well browned and cooked through (when a skewer is inserted into the meatiest part of the bird, near the leg joint, the juices should run clear). Remove the duck from the oven, but leave the oven on. When the duck is cool enough to handle, use a large sharp knife to cut the duck in half through the breastbone.

3 Remove the onion, garlic and thyme from inside the duck and place in a clean roasting tin, along with the wings and neck. Cut off the legs, then separate the drumsticks from the thighs. Using a cleaver or the heel of a large knife, cut the thigh into two pieces. With your hands, pick the rest of the meat and skin away from the carcass in large morsels. Set aside the legs, meat and skin. Add the carcass to the roasting tin and roast for 30 minutes or until well browned.

4 Transfer the contents of the tin to a large heavy-based saucepan, add the red wine and bring to the boil over high heat. Pour in 1.7 litres of water and return to the boil, then reduce the heat and simmer for 30 minutes. Strain the stock into a bowl and discard the solids.

5 Now make a *sofrito* by pouring the olive oil into a *perol* (see page 380) or wide heavy-based saucepan and placing over medium–high heat. When the oil is hot, add the white onion with a pinch of salt and cook for 10–12 minutes or until lightly browned. Add the garlic and thyme and cook for 2 minutes, then add the capsicum, reduce the heat to medium and cook for 15 minutes or until soft.

6 Add the stock to the *sofrito* and bring to a simmer, then sprinkle in the rice, add the duck legs, meat and skin, and season with salt and pepper to taste. Stir, then simmer gently, stirring occasionally, for 18 minutes or until the rice is done – the grains should still be slightly firm in the middle. Ladle into bowls and serve immediately.

POLLO EN PEPITORIA

CHICKEN IN SAFFRON, EGG AND ALMOND SAUCE

SERVES 4

Never judge a nation's cuisine by its restaurant menus. Chicken is a dish of the Spanish home, so Spaniards don't expect to see it on the menu when they are eating out. Traditionally this dish would have been cooked with an older bird, perhaps one from the backyard, but these days Spaniards head to the market and buy a beautiful plump bird – complete with head and feet, which are added to the pot to create a richer dish. Serve with loads of crusty bread to soak up the sauce.

1 × 1.5 kg free-range,
  corn-fed chicken
1 × 150 g piece jamón bone
  or 100 g jamón serrano
4 garlic cloves, roughly chopped
12 black peppercorns
good pinch of saffron threads
few flat-leaf parsley stalks
sea salt
100 g blanched almonds
4 hard-boiled egg yolks
juice of 1 lemon

1 First, cut the chicken into 12 pieces – ask the butcher to do this for you, if you like. To do it yourself, cut the wings off the chicken where they join the breast, leaving a good morsel of breast meat on the bone. Cut off the wing tip, then cut the wings in half at the next joint. Use kitchen scissors to cut out the backbone, then cut the chicken in half along the cartilage between the two breasts. Cut off the legs, then separate the drumsticks from the thighs. Using a cleaver or the heel of a large knife, cut the thigh into two pieces. Cut the breasts in half.

2 Pour 1.5 litres of water into a large heavy-based saucepan and bring to a simmer over high heat. Add the chicken pieces, jamón bone or jamón, garlic, peppercorns, saffron and parsley stalks. Season with a pinch of salt and bring to the boil, then reduce the heat to a simmer and cook for 1 hour, skimming off any impurities that rise to the surface. Discard the parsley stalks and remove the jamón bone; when it is cool enough to handle, crumble any shreds of meat off the bone back into the pan.

3 Place the almonds in a heavy-based frying pan over medium heat and toast for 6–8 minutes or until browned; watch them carefully, as they can easily burn. Place the almonds in a mortar and pound with the pestle to the consistency of breadcrumbs. Add the egg yolks with a pinch of salt and pound to a paste – this is called the *majada*.

4 Return the pan to medium heat and bring back to a simmer. Add the lemon juice and stir through the *majada*. Season with salt to taste, then simmer for a further 10 minutes. Serve hot.

EL PAN DE CADA DÍA

DAILY BREAD

▶

The bread is better in Andalusia these days. I remember when I first went back, over 20 years ago now, to find bread that was white, hard and flavourless. It was a shame, because bread is served with every meal to sop up the sauce on the plate. In earlier, more frugal days, a simple, one-pot dish became a family meal with the addition of a loaf of bread to fill people up. Baker Fidel Pernía, from Masa Bambini bakery in Seville's old town, explains: 'We used to have good bread in Spain, but as economics took over, bread changed incrementally over the years, eventually becoming so cheap to make that it is no longer bread. It is unhealthy for you.'

Fidel is determined to change that, though. He is part of the new wave of Spanish bakers reverting to time-honoured methods of baking, using the previous day's dough as a starter and long ferments to develop flavours. Down a little street, not far from the Guadalquivir, the site for his bakery was chosen for its climate, being located in the most humid part of the city. Fidel remembers the traditional way with bread: 'Mum bought bread once a week. First it was bread with a meal, the next day it was fried for breakfast in olive oil and sprinkled with sugar, then the next day *migas*, the following day *salmorejo*, and so on.'

Fidel was working in a bank as a statistician when the urge to bake became overwhelming, but the transition from banker to baker wasn't easy. His first doughs tasted good but failed to rise, then they rose but didn't taste that good. He now makes the Andalusian favourite of *molletes* bread rolls (see page 210). 'I was taught to make them by an old baker who was passing by when I first started baking,' he says. 'He could smell the dough fermenting and he walked in with rheumy eyes. He told me that his father had been a baker who didn't want his son to work the long hard hours – but he had watched his father at work and secretly practised the same actions,' continues Fidel. 'The man then moved north to Barcelona to become a famous bullfighter, but had come back to Seville to retire. And when he began handling the dough, the memories flooded back. His eyes filled with tears and he automatically knew how to form these little rolls. He stayed with me and taught me so much. A bullfighter who learned to move from a baker, and a baker who learned to move from a bullfighter!' he adds with a laugh.

Bar and restaurant
El Rinconcillo
was founded in 1670

PRIMAVERA EN SEVILLA

SPRING IN SEVILLE

A huge arch fills the early evening sky. Lit with thousands of light bulbs, it glows gold against the darkening blue heavens. Hanging from it are tens of thousands of lanterns that bathe the fairground in soft, colourful light and illuminate the promenading crowds, who have come to eat, drink, dance and sing well into the night and, for some, into the next morning. This is *La Feria*.

Every April, the city lurches into a week of bacchanalian celebration, when hundreds of *casetas* or marquees are erected on the fairground on the other bank of the Guadalquivir. At the back of each marquee is a small kitchen where plates of tapas are prepared, perhaps fried fish, perhaps tortilla, but more likely *pinchitos morunos*, spiced lamb skewers (see page 41). The spectacle is the crowd itself, clothed in Andalusian traditional costume. The women look stunning, dressed in body-hugging flamenco dresses, the men walking proudly beside them sporting their *traje corto* (a short jacket) along with tight trousers and riding boots. The children dress in diminutive versions of the same. It is as much an exposition of local culture as it is a party. This rather beautiful display of humanity is juxtaposed with La Calle del Infierno, or Hell

Street, on the other side of the *Feria* – hectares of theme-park rides and teenagers drinking *rebujitos*, a potent mix of dry sherry and lemonade.

The *Feria de Abril* kicks off with a street parade of traditional horses and carriages, which also signals the start of the spring bullfighting season. Seville's bullring is the oldest in Spain, with construction beginning in the early 1700s. However, the banning of bullfighting by King Carlos III in the late 1700s halted the building work, and it was only after his reign ended that the stadium was completed – the result is a mélange of different styles unified by its gold and red ochre colouring. The bullfighters make their way into the ring through a phalanx of fans. Bullfighters are revered in Spain, their artful heroics when pitted against a tonne of angry bull making them demi-gods. While there is no escaping the barbaric fact that no bull makes it out of the bullring alive, there is the chance the bullfighter may not either. So, despite the ecstatic adoration that surrounds them, bullfighters seem oblivious to the festivities, instead carrying with them a dark cloud of fatalism and certain aloofness. Perhaps they know they may be closer to heaven than the clamouring masses around them.

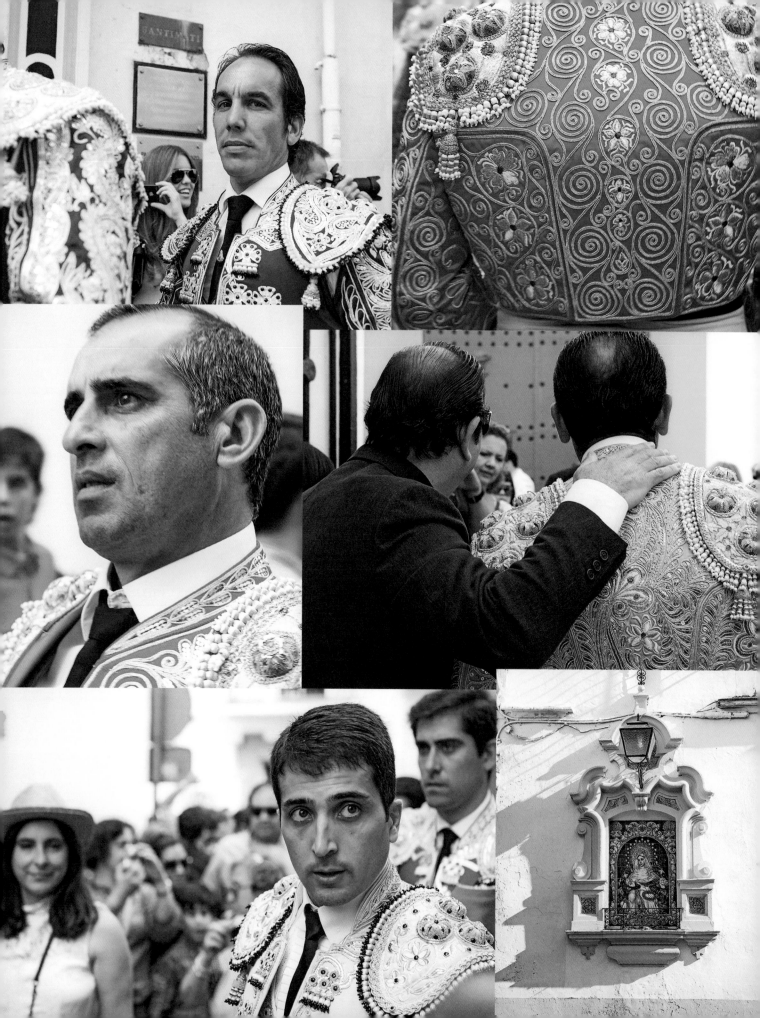

PINCHITOS MORUNOS

SEVILLE FESTIVAL LAMB SKEWERS

MAKES 20

The first time I arrived in Seville as a 20-year-old, I remember the gypsies cooking lamb skewers in the city's laneways, turning morsels of marinated meat over glowing beds of coals. A quarter of a century on, the chaos of street food and small hawkers' stalls seems to have been largely swept away, but you can still find a *pincho*, and his smaller brother *pinchito*, served hot at the Seville *Feria*. This version, from Restaurante Alhucemas, is one of the best.

1 kg lamb rump, skin off

½ teaspoon freshly ground black pepper

1 teaspoon ground cumin

½ teaspoon Keen's mild curry powder

½ teaspoon ground ginger

½ teaspoon freshly grated nutmeg

⅛ teaspoon ground turmeric

pinch of hot Spanish paprika

½ brown onion, finely sliced

2 garlic cloves, finely chopped

1 tablespoon chopped flat-leaf parsley

200 ml olive oil

1 teaspoon fine salt

sea salt

1 Use a sharp knife to trim the lamb rump of sinew and silverskin, then cut into 1 cm cubes. Place the meat in a glass or ceramic bowl and add all the remaining ingredients except the sea salt, then mix well. Cover with plastic film and refrigerate for at least 12 hours to marinate.

2 Preheat a barbecue grill to medium–high.

3 Thread the lamb onto 20 metal skewers, using about 5 pieces of lamb for each one. Place the skewers on the grill and cook for 10–12 minutes, turning occasionally.

4 Remove from the grill, season with sea salt and leave to rest for a few minutes, covered loosely with foil. Serve hot.

BUÑUELOS DE LAS GITANAS

GYPSY DOUGHNUTS

MAKES 12

Before the Seville *Feria* a group of local women do their hair, put on make-up and get into their best dresses to make *buñuelos*. The women, who belong to a gypsy catering firm called La Mama Dolores, stand in a line. One takes the sticky yeast dough and, with wet hands, pats it out into flat cakes with a hole in the centre. She slides them into the hot oil and her sister then swirls each one with a stick, the centrifugal force spinning it out into a doughnut shape. Her aunt removes the cooked *buñuelos* and slides them onto a rod to drain. Other family members take the money and serve up piping-hot pots of drinking chocolate for dunking. I suggest you follow the lead of the gypsy women and have a few people around to help you make these.

14 g dried yeast
250 g bread flour
pinch of salt
1 tablespoon caster sugar
1 litre olive oil, for deep-frying
2 tablespoons white sugar

1 Pour 250 ml of lukewarm water into a bowl, then add the yeast and leave to stand for a few minutes in a warm place until frothy.

2 Meanwhile mix the flour, salt and caster sugar in a large bowl. Add the yeast mixture and use a wooden spoon to work the dough for 5 minutes, to develop the gluten – you should see rubbery strands starting to appear in the dough as you work it. When it is ready, it should be the consistency of a very thick batter or very wet dough

3 Cover the bowl with plastic film and leave in a warm place for 30 minutes or until roughly doubled in size.

4 Pour the olive oil into a heavy-based saucepan or flat-bottomed wok and heat to 170°C or until a cube of bread dropped into the oil browns in 15 seconds.

5 Fill a large bowl with warm water and place it next to the stove. Wet your hands with water from the bowl and shake off the excess, being careful not to splash it into the hot oil. Break off a piece of dough at a time (approximately 40 g or the size of a golf ball) and slap it between your palms, working quickly to flatten it. Use your finger to make a hole in the middle, then slip the doughnut gently in the oil, taking care as it may splatter. Slip the end of a long-handled wooden spoon into the doughnut's hole and spin around to shape the doughnut. (If you have a frying partner, get them to do this while you carry on patting out the pieces of dough and placing them in the oil.)

6 Deep-fry the doughnuts for about 2 minutes on each side, or until browned and cooked through. Remove and drain on paper towel.

7 Dust the doughnuts with sugar while still warm, then serve with hot chocolate.

LOS MODERNOS

THE MODERNISTS

By a whitewashed courtyard in the old Jewish quarter of Utrera, a town 30 minutes from Seville, is a little tapas bar called Besana. Here chefs and cooking teachers Mario Ríos and Curro Sánchez Noriega have taken the DNA of traditional Andalusian cooking and spliced it with the scientific cooking championed by the likes of Ferran Adrià, of El Bulli fame. The portions are small, as are the prices – in a post-GFC world, this allows diners of all economic circumstances to sit and dine together.

The headlong rush to modernism in Spanish cuisine has had less impact in the south of the country. Andalusia is by nature a conservative place, which sees any explorations of modernist cooking tempered by a strong connection to the land, or indeed the sea, as exemplified by chef Ángel León at Aponiente (see page 160), in neighbouring Cádíz province. Further along the coast, in the city of Huelva, modernist chef Xanty Elías pushes the envelope with a first course of 'nothing', simply a bowl of air and a spoon coated in licorice-root gel. Here he combines the classic ingredients of his home province, mainly seafood and Ibérico pork, with others that have been transformed using food science, such as the reproductive organs of a cuttlefish served with a rich bisque emulsion and 'beach sand' made from olive oil, bread, garlic and sea algae. Heading along the coast in the other direction, José Carlos García has an exclusive dining room in Málaga looking out over the city's port, where his kitchen crew cook for just six tables (see page 218) and dishes include a minimalist version of gazpachuelo, the traditional fisherman's soup or stew.

But Andalusia's most famous modernist would have to be Dani García, a chef who has had a string of successes playing with different formats, from his fast-and-fun Manzanilla tapas bars to his seasonal fine-dining restaurant on the Mediterranean in Marbella. Here he plays with people's preconceptions, making foie gras look like an almond in its shell, or forming beef tendon into a prawn-shaped delicacy.

Back at Besana, the chefs send out little dishes that pack a punch way beyond their low price point: sweetbreads with shiitake mushrooms and goat's cheese sauce; roasted suckling pig with cabbage; marinated champignons with a creamy mushroom sauce; candied almonds and broken pieces of crunchy olive-oil biscuit. 'Every young chef in Spain wants to be in the vanguard,' says Noriega, referring to the wave of food modernism that has swept the nation in the first years of the new century. 'But here in Andalusia, the prevailing attitude among young chefs is that we can still move ahead while taking pride in our heritage and applying our skills and respect to our wonderful products from the land and sea, to make them even more special.'

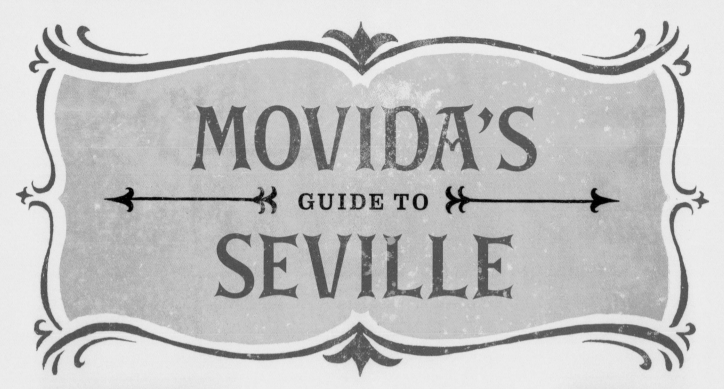

MOVIDA'S
GUIDE TO
SEVILLE

El Rinconcillo ♟ ✕

Calle Gerona 40, Seville; tel 954 22 31 83
www.elrinconcillo.es

I like old bars. And this one dates back to
1670. With its worn stone floor and carved
wooden bar and painted carved woodwork
this is one of the prettiest bars in Spain.
It is the place where the locals bring
visitors. It's old-fashioned, so expect a
refreshing *caldo*, chicken and jamón broth
or, in spring, the house speciality of *revuelto
Rinconcillo*, a salad of freshly cooked
prawns with asparagus and broad beans.

Restaurante Los Cuevas ♟ ✕

**Calle Virgen de la Huerta 1 & Calle
Salado, Seville; tel 954 27 80 42**
www.loscuevas.com

Look for the red-painted windows then
come inside and pull up a stool and join
the *Sevillanos* at the bar. Have a *montadito*,
a little toasted roll filled with chorizo,
tinned mackerel or *pringá*, the yummiest
bits of reheated stew. Try the grilled
vegetables too – the boss grows his own
vegetables in his kitchen garden in
a nearby town.

Convento de Madre de Dios ✕

Calle San José 4, Seville; tel 954 21 78 22

In the corner of the tile-lined vestibule
of this convent is a *torno*, or revolving
wooden cylinder. You approach it, place
your money in the *torno*, say a prayer and
order from an assortment of sweets and
pastries handmade by the nuns on the
other side of the *torno*. Here they specialise
in oven-baked *empanadillas* stuffed with
tuna and angel hair (strands of candied
melon) flavoured with *aguardiente*,
a grappa-like spirit.

Pastries are placed in '*el torno*' by nuns

Taberna La Goleta

Mateos Gago 20, Seville

It's the wooden fridge, tiny bar, nano W.C. and rough wines that make this hole-in-the-wall worth visiting. Cheap, fun and very characterful.

Bodega Santa Cruz 'Las Columnas'

Calle Rodrigo Caro 1, Seville; tel 954 21 16 94

A busy bar in the Santa Cruz district of the old town, this place is dominated by and named after the columns out front. There's a lot of tourist traps around these parts, but the food here is more than passable. Go for the rabbit cooked with potato and garlic, or the pork loin cooked with sweet wine.

Bar Restaurante Casa Manolo

Calle San Jorge 16, Triana, Seville; tel 954 33 47 92

In a suburb famous for its ceramics, just across the Guadalquivir from Seville's old town, is this traditional bar serving very good *espinacas con garbanzos*, spinach and chickpeas, and *menudos*, a dish of tripe and chorizo cooked in paprika, wine and a *sofrito* redolent of clove and nutmeg.

Masa Bambini

Calle Huelva 6, Seville; tel 685 47 85 78

This bakery is making a name for itself with its artisanal sourdough breads and pastries. Come here for really good *regañás*; the hard, salty biscuits served with many meals and tapas were originally made to provision the sea voyages which set sail from Seville for the New World. Head for the bright-red door and the aroma of fermenting yeast and baking bread.

Confitería la Campana

Calle Sierpes 1 & 3, Seville; tel 954 22 35 70

The Royal Warrant proudly hangs in the window of this pastry shop: *Proveedor de la Real Casa. Sevillanos* like a bit of pomp. Come for a coffee and pastry, perhaps a madeleine (see page 298), here made with a hint of lemon zest. Sit in the square and baptise your madeleine in a cup of hot chocolate. There are also beautiful ornate tin gift boxes of pastries for sale.

Corral del Rey

Corral del Rey 12, Seville; tel 954 22 71 16
www.corraldelrey.com

Located in the old-town neighbourhood of Barrio de la Alfalfa, just 5 minutes' walk from the cathedral, the former seventeenth-century Casa Palacio has been restored and converted into a small private boutique hotel: central and stylish, with a luxurious price tag to match.

Hotel Amadeus

Calle Farnesio 6, Seville; tel 954 50 14 43
www.hotelamadeussevilla.com

Comfortable and affordable accommodation in the historic Jewish quarter. The décor is conservative and plush, with a leitmotif reflecting the owners' love of classic music.

Petite Palace Marqués Santa Ana

Calle Jimios 9–11, Seville; tel 954 22 18 12
www.petitpalacemarquessantaana.com

Comfortable, affordable and centrally located hotel in a quiet street, with a pleasant terrace overlooking the city.

Las Casas de la Judería

Calle Santa María la Blanca 5, Seville; tel 954 41 51 50
www.casasypalacios.com

This small hotel built around a patio offers beautifully appointed rooms with period furniture in a good location a short walk from the cathedral.

Puerta Catedral

various central locations in Seville; tel 954 21 69 12
www.puertacatedral.com

Moderately priced studios and apartments for short stays and holidays.

Restaurante Alhucemas

Avenida del Polideportivo 4, Sanlúcar La Mayor; tel 955 70 38 24

Unpromisingly located on a main road by a sporting complex, in a satellite town to the west of the city, is this excellent restaurant serving minimalist versions of Andalusian classics. Be enticed by a dish of roasted red peppers dressed with 25-year-old aged sherry vinegar (see page 12), perfect baby cuttlefish quickly seared on the grill (see page 20) or pasta cooked in squid ink (see page 18), all made with the very best ingredients direct from the market. It is worth the trip.

Manolo Mayo 🍷 ✗

Avenida de Sevilla 29, Los Palacios y Villafranca; tel 955 81 10 86
www.manolomayo.com

This classic Andalusian restaurant and hotel was founded in 1963, in a small town on the outskirts of Seville. Popular for its large and lively lunch service, the *huevos rotos*, egg, jamón and chips (see page 10), is both massive and excellent. The Mayo family is also known for their excellent rice dishes.

Restaurante Estero 🍷 ✗

Avenida Rafael Beca 6–11, Isla Mayor; tel 954 77 73 89
www.restaurantestero.com

After a morning bird spotting in the Dehesa de Abajo, a wildlife refuge in the forest on the edge of the Guadalquivir wetlands, head to this town filled with brutal Franco-era architecture – you have to experience one while you're in Spain – and dine on excellent rice dishes in the middle of Europe's largest rice-growing district. Try the *arroz con pato*, soupy rice made with wild duck (see page 27).

Besana Tapas 🍷 ✗

Calle Niño Perdido 1 acc, Utrera; tel 955 86 38 04
www.besanatapas.com

This small modern bar is housed in a former synagogue in Utrera, the Spanish home of breeding bulls and training bullfighters. The portions are small, but so are the prices. The kitchen is tiny too, 'so the market is our pantry', say the chefs, a young duo who combine tradition and modern techniques, with delicious results.

Hacienda de San Rafael

Carretera N-IV km 594, Las Cabezas de San Juan; tel 954 22 71 16
www.haciendadesanrafael.com

Once part of a thriving olive estate, the Hacienda has been restored and converted into an exclusive hideaway. This is exquisite accommodation if you want to combine a few nights in the Spanish countryside with some sightseeing – it is located midway between Seville and Jerez de la Frontera.

Manuel gives his donkey an affectionate scratch behind the ears. A worker in a family jamón butchery, he spends his days tending the pigs and having silly conversations with his donkey. A romantic, he still talks about the days when the only way between the villages of Huelva, deep in the great oak forest of *la dehesa*, was on the back of a mule.

Perched between the Atlantic coast and the mountains of the Sierra de Aracena, with its western edge bordering Portugal, Huelva is not a province that has captured the global imagination. Yet it is one of the most beautiful parts of the nation, where the people nurture and enjoy their strong sense of identity.

The capital city sits on the low-lying flats of the Odiel River, which once upon a time formed a vast delta with the great Guadalquivir. Held by many to be the site of the fabled lost kingdom of Tartessos, it was known as Onuba to the Phoenecians, a name that stuck under the Greeks and then the Romans – even today the city's residents are known as *Onubenses*. Much of the ancient, classical and renaissance city of Huelva was destroyed by the tsunami that followed the 1755 Lisbon earthquake, and many of today's notable buildings date from the late nineteenth century, when the British company Rio Tinto was mining the hills of the province for copper. The Río Tinto, or Red River – which gave the company its name – still cuts a rusty red swathe through the province. Across the Río Tinto estuary from the capital is Moguer, where Christopher Columbus, nearing the end of his fundraising campaign, garnered the last of his finance from wealthy landowners before he set sail on his 1492 voyage of discovery. Columbus's statue stands in Huelva city square, his hand forever pointing west, towards the Americas.

Isla Cristina, the province's main fishing port, lies closer to the Portuguese border, on the shores of what was once an island surrounded by ancient wetlands. Here are caught perhaps the world's best prawns, which grow fat and sweet on the rich, intermingling waters of the Atlantic and the run-off from the wetlands of Huelva and Cádiz provinces. Inland, the rolling hills of the central plains are home to a fine wine industry, where brandy is distilled and a local speciality, *vino de naranja* (wine infused with orange), is made. To the north east, the town of Jabugo, nestled in a fold of the Aracena mountains and surrounded by oak trees – the source of the acorns on which the jamón pigs feed – has become a hub of jamón processing. Small jamón butchers dot the ranges, bringing much-needed employment to the region.

Back in the Sierra de Aracena village of Corteconcepción, Manuel stands under the shade of a cork oak, the bark of which has been harvested to make corks for wine. Around him a herd of fat black pigs are rooting about for acorns and grubs. 'In many ways Huelva is as it was many years ago,' he says. 'Change is happening here, but not as fast as the rest of Spain. We are lucky because, hopefully, we can change for the better, and keep the best of the past.'

ESPÁRRAGOS TRIGUEROS CON ALCACHOFAS Y JAMÓN

WILD ASPARAGUS WITH ARTICHOKES AND JAMÓN

SERVES 4-6

Every spring, out on the edge of the vast holm oak forest that covers the Sierra de Aracena, pockets of wild asparagus emerge between the rocks. Called *trigueros*, they are thinner than a pencil but more aromatic than farmed asparagus. You sometimes see similar asparagus growing around old towns in rural Australia and on the banks of the River Murray but when I can't find any, I substitute some fine-stemmed new-season's asparagus. Fried with artichokes and dressed with fine *lonchas* of jamón, this simple recipe comes from Restaurante Jose Vicente in Aracena.

It's important to cook the artichokes straight after cleaning them, rather than keeping them in acidulated water in the usual way to stop them discolouring, as any moisture clinging to the artichokes would make the hot oil spit dangerously. Just remember to keep a watchful eye on the oil as it heats and turn it down if it gets too hot.

5 bunches wild asparagus
   or thin asparagus
6 large globe artichokes
1 litre olive oil, for deep-frying
sea salt
8 long slices of jamón, cut into
   5 cm × 2.5 cm size pieces

1 Wash and drain the asparagus, then remove any woody parts by bending the spears – they will break where the tough stem gives way to the tender part of the spear.

2 Pour the olive oil into a heavy-based saucepan or wok and heat to 170°C or until a cube of bread dropped into the oil browns in 15 seconds.

3 Meanwhile, prepare the artichokes by cutting off the lower stems, leaving about 3 cm. Peel the stem with a sharp knife. Using a sharp, serrated knife, cut off the top 3–4 cm of the artichokes. Peel away the outer leaves until you get to the softer, paler leaves. Cut each artichoke in half, then use a paring knife to remove any furry choke from the centre. Cut each half into three even-sized wedges.

4 Carefully add the artichoke wedges to the hot oil and deep-fry, turning occasionally, for 7–8 minutes or until cooked through – the heart should be tender when pierced with the tip of a knife. Remove with a slotted spoon, drain on paper towel and season well with salt.

5 Place the asparagus in the hot oil and cook for 4–5 minutes or until lightly browned and soft. Remove with a slotted spoon, drain on paper towel and season well with salt.

6 Place the artichoke wedges on a serving plate, cover with asparagus and dress with sliced jamón. Serve warm.

JAMÓN

Domingo Eíriz Martín stands in a great cathedral-like *secadero*, or drying room. Hanging from the ceiling above his head are hundreds of legs of jamón, all around the halfway mark in their two-year transformation from the world's best-fed pigs to some of the world's best jamón. 'For 200 years we have been making jamón here in Corteconcepción,' says Domingo, one of the co-owners. 'But before I let you taste my jamón, first you must see my pigs,' he says, smiling broadly. On a hill behind the *secadero* is a herd of perhaps the happiest pigs I have seen. Those not grazing for acorns under the oak trees or sunning themselves are wallowing in a muddy patch by a dam.

Domingo's family specialises in making jamón ibérico de bellota – jamón made from an indigenous breed of Spanish pig whose diet is enriched with acorns foraged in the oak forests known as *la dehesa*. Their pigs are slaughtered at over two years of age, after two seasons of feasting on acorns. Their hindquarters are salted for roughly a day per kilo, then cleaned and left to dry and mature in the surprisingly humid air that blows in from the coast. Over the next two years micro-flora, various moulds and bacteria transform the meat, while the salt protects it from putrefaction.

The resulting jamón is incredibly delicious – and is sold direct to the public at prices a quarter of what one would pay in Madrid. But the real beauty of a visit here to buy direct from the farm gate is that you get to taste all the other smallgoods produced by the family: cured loin, chorizo and the nuggety-looking *morcón* (a fat-cured pork sausage redolent of smoked paprika).

Jamones are cured in *secaderos*
for up to 48 months

COQUINAS

PIPPIES COOKED IN FINO SHERRY

SERVES 4–6

The fishermen stand at the bar, beer in hand. They have been at sea since most of us were still in bed. The seas have been calm, the conditions favourable and their catch generous. In this small tile-lined bar by the docks at Isla Cristina, they finish their day at noon with a small celebratory feast of fresh prawns and cockles. Cockles are known as *chirlas*, and here are cooked with a simple sauce of garlic, olive oil, flour and sherry, then finished with chopped parsley. You can use cockles, small clams or pippies to make this – just remember to serve it with crusty bread, as the dish is more about the sauce than the shellfish. This version was inspired by the *chirlas* served at Abuelo Mañas at Isla Cristina.

2 kg pippies (or similar
   shellfish)
sea salt
40 ml extra virgin olive oil
3 garlic cloves, finely chopped
1 tablespoon plain flour
120 ml fino sherry
200 ml fish stock (see page 380)
2 fresh bay leaves (optional)
1 tablespoon roughly chopped
   flat-leaf parsley

1 Wash the pippies under cold running water and place in a bowl. Cover with cold water and a good pinch of salt. Leave to stand for 30 minutes then, using your hands, lift the clams into another bowl. Cover with fresh water and add a pinch of salt. Repeat three times – this encourages the pippies to purge themselves of sand.

2 Pour the olive oil into a *rondeau* (see page 383) or large deep saucepan and place over medium heat. When the oil is hot, add the garlic and fry gently, stirring, for 1 minute until the garlic is cooked but not coloured.

3 Add the flour to the pan, stir in well and cook for a minute, stirring constantly. Pour in the sherry, scraping the base of the pan to deglaze. Add the fish stock and bay leaves (if using), bring to a simmer and cook for a minute until the sauce thickens a little.

4 Add the pippies and stir, then increase the heat to high and cover with a lid. Cook the pippies for 5–6 minutes or until they are all open, shaking the pan occasionally to encourage them to open. (Sometimes pippies fill with sand and won't open, so discard any unopened ones.)

5 Stir in the parsley and season with salt to taste, if necessary – be careful, as the pippies will already be salty.

6 To serve, place the pippies on a large plate and spoon over plenty of the sauce.

CHOCOS EN AMARILLO

CUTTLEFISH IN SAFFRON SAUCE

SERVES 4-6

The cuttlefish at the Isla Cristina fish market come straight from the boats, still writhing in their blue boxes. *Los chocos*, or cuttlefish, are part of people's identity here – in fact, locals are sometimes called *chocos* because they eat so much of them. One of the popular and more rustic ways of eating cuttlefish is to cook the intact cuttlefish directly over glowing coals, *chocos sucios*, the internal organs discarded just prior to eating but not before they have imbued the cuttlefish with an amazingly intense flavour of the sea. This more refined version from Restaurante Portichuelo, in Huelva, braises the cuttlefish in an aromatic sauce of wine, garlic and saffron with a handful of peas added for textural contrast.

3 large cuttlefish, about
   600 g each
2 large waxy potatoes,
   such as nicola
60 ml extra virgin olive oil
1 large onion, finely chopped
3 fresh bay leaves
sea salt
3 garlic cloves, finely chopped
1 tablespoon plain flour
130 ml fino sherry
pinch of saffron threads
freshly ground black pepper
100 g frozen peas
juice of ½ lemon

1 Ask the fishmonger to clean the cuttlefish for you. Alternatively, hold the tentacles of the cuttlefish in one hand and the body in the other and pull. Discard the tentacles and guts, then pull the body open. Remove the cuttlebone and any remaining guts and discard. Pull away the wings and discard. Peel off any remaining skin and rinse under cold water. Cut into 2 cm pieces.

2 Peel the potatoes and cut into very rough 2 cm cubes using the 'click' method (see page 379).

3 Pour the olive oil into a *rondeau* (see page 383) or large deep saucepan and place over medium–high heat. Add the onion and bay leaves with a pinch of salt and reduce the heat to medium. Cook for 10 minutes or until the onion is soft and translucent, then add the garlic and cook for another minute. Add the cuttlefish and cook, stirring every now and again, for 3–4 minutes or until the cuttlefish start to turn opaque. Sprinkle over the flour and mix in well with a wooden spoon. Pour in the sherry, scraping the base of the pan to deglaze. When the sherry starts to bubble, stir in 900 ml of water, and bring back to a simmer.

4 Meanwhile, in a small heavy-based frying pan, toast the saffron for a minute or so over medium heat until you just start to smell the aroma. Add a couple of tablespoons of the simmering sauce to the saffron, swirl it around, then tip the contents of the frying pan back into the pan with the cuttlefish.

5 Add the potato to the pan and season with a teaspoon of salt and a pinch of pepper. Simmer gently for 50 minutes until the cuttlefish and potato are tender. Add the peas and simmer for another minute or until tender, then stir in the lemon juice and serve.

MARISCOS A LA MARINERA

SEAFOOD FISHERMAN'S STYLE

SERVES 4-6

Where's there's a fisherman there's a fish dish. Around the nation, Spanish fishermen have a way of cooking whatever turns up in their nets to feed the crew, most often a braise of seafood with onions, peppers, a few spices and tomatoes. The quantities and exact recipe changes from region to region, but the concept stays the same. This dish comes from a bar in Isla Cristina, Abuelo Mañas, where I watched fishermen favourably critique the quality of the fish used – one of the things I really appreciate in Spain is how passionate food producers are about what they grow or catch.

160 ml olive oil

1 brown onion, diced

sea salt

2 garlic cloves, chopped

1 green bull horn capsicum (pepper) or ½ green regular capsicum (pepper), finely diced

1 red bull horn capsicum (pepper) or ½ red regular capsicum (pepper), finely diced

6 large ripe tomatoes, peeled and chopped

1 tablespoon sweet Spanish paprika

1 medium-sized calamari, cleaned (see page 20), or ask the fishmonger to do this

6 raw prawns

600 g bass grouper fillets

2 garlic cloves, finely chopped.

120 ml dry white wine

60 ml brandy

300 g clams, purged (see page 62)

2 tablespoons roughly chopped flat-leaf parsley

extra virgin olive oil, for drizzling

1 Pour 100 ml of the olive oil into a heavy-based saucepan and place over medium–high heat. When the oil is hot, add the onion with a pinch of salt and cook for 10 minutes, stirring occasionally, until soft and translucent. Stir in the garlic and cook for a minute more. Add the capsicums and cook for 10 minutes or until soft. Reduce the heat to low–medium and stir in the tomato, paprika and a good pinch of salt. Cover and cook for 40 minutes, stirring occasionally – the sauce should be fairly juicy.

2 Meanwhile, rinse the calamari well, then cut the body into 1 cm rings and the tentacles into 5 cm lengths. Cut the fish into 6 pieces.

3 Remove the pan from the heat and blend the sauce into a rough puree using a stick blender.

4 Pour the remaining 60 ml olive oil into a 30 cm paella pan or large frying pan and place over high heat. When the oil is hot, add the calamari and prawns, season with salt and cook for 2 minutes, turning occasionally, until lightly browned. Remove the calamari and prawns and set aside. Add the fish, season with salt and cook for 1 minute on each side to brown. Add the garlic to the pan and cook for a minute or so until it begins to brown; do not let it burn.

5 Pour in the wine and brandy, scraping the base of the pan to deglaze. Return the calamari to the pan, then stir in the pureed sauce and 200 ml of water. When the sauce is bubbling, season with salt and reduce the heat to medium, then simmer for a further 6 minutes or until the fish is almost cooked through. Add the clams and prawns and cook for 3–4 minutes until the clams have opened and the fish is cooked through.

6 Sprinkle with the chopped parsley and drizzle with a little extra virgin olive oil, then place the pan in the middle of the table and serve straight away.

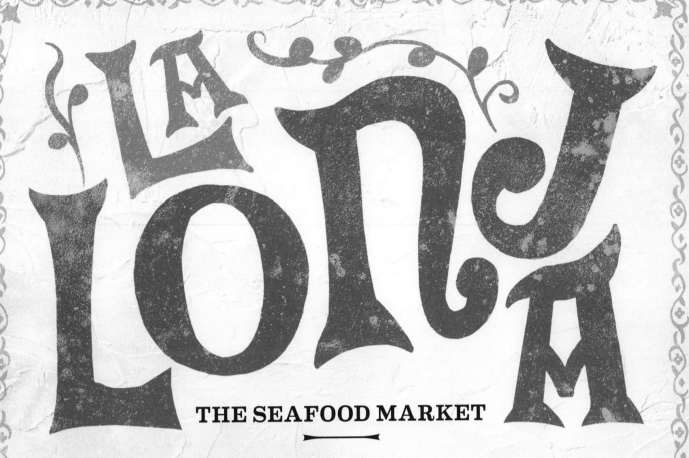

THE SEAFOOD MARKET

Having heard about the amazing seafood of Isla Cristina for as long as I can remember, I had great expectations for this famous fishing port near the Portuguese border. Once an island in the middle of a vast wetland, millennia of drainage and silt buildup have seen this rough and rugged port marooned on a low lying stretch of coast.

It wasn't the warmest welcome I have ever experienced, however. There was high excitement as word passed around that the boats were entering the harbour. But as the fishing boats pulled alongside the wharf, I was met with angry looks from the fishermen. With pen in hand, taking notes, and a camera slung around my neck, they assumed I was either an official from the fisheries department in Madrid or an EU inspector from Brussels. So when they understood I was an Australian chef, it became like a party on the pier! With stubby cigarettes hanging from the corners of their mouths, fishermen held up the freshest

boquerones (white anchovies) and *urtas* (banded snapper), still-squirming cuttlefish, octopus that suckered onto their arms and box after box of the most delicious *gambas blancas* (white prawns).

They ushered me into *la lonja*, a great shed that was part fish auction and part gladiatorial arena, with rows of fishmongers and restaurateurs engaged in a fast and furious electronic Dutch auction, all hoping to get the best of the catch for the best price. At one point, over a box of particularly delicious-looking prawns, the auctioneer false-footed, causing one bidder to stand up and scream acrimoniously at all and sundry. For a good five minutes, *la lonja* was bought to a halt by the ensuing chaos of other bidders shouting and shoving with their claims and counter-claims. The result was settled. The buyer got his prawns, and the fisherman got a good price. And I learnt never to underestimate how passionate the Spanish are about their seafood . . .

LONJA DE ISLA, S. L.
Cofradía de Pescadores y Asociación
de Armadores de Isla Cristina

LONJA DE ISLA, S. L.
Cofradía de Pescadores y Asociación
de Armadores de Isla Cristina

LONJA DE ISLA, S. L.
Cofradía de Pescadores y Asociación
de Armadores de Isla Cristina

GAMBAS A LA ISLEÑA

'HOW TO COOK PERFECT PRAWNS'

SERVES 4–6

The white prawns of Isla Cristina are famous throughout Spain. Francisco Moreno, chef and owner of Hermanos Moreno, explains why: 'Here the sweet waters from the *marismas* mix with the rich cold water of the Atlantic,' he says, referring to the wetlands of the extensive Doñana National Park nearby. And they are seriously good. Partly because of where they come from, but also because they are so very, very fresh, caught just offshore daily. The other secret is this cooking method. The only thing that could improve on these perfect prawns is a glass of ice-cold beer or fino sherry.

200 g rock salt
ice cubes
600 g super-fresh, medium-
    sized raw prawns (about 18)
sea salt

1 Pour 3 litres of water into a large saucepan, add the rock salt and bring to the boil over high heat.

2 Meanwhile, fill a large bowl with iced water.

3 Add the prawns to the boiling water and simmer for 2 minutes or until the prawns change colour and become firmer around the base of the head.

4 Using a sieve, remove the prawns from the pan and arrest the cooking by plunging them into the iced water. Leave to cool for 2 minutes, then drain well.

5 Arrange the prawns on a plate, sprinkle with sea salt and serve straightaway.

PATATAS ALIÑADAS CON CABALLA

WARM POTATO SALAD WITH MACKEREL

SERVES 4-6

They grow great potatoes in the sandy soil along the Atlantic coast of Huelva. While such ground might seem thin and infertile at first glance, the method of organic composting and crop rotation practised here has seen potatoes from *las dunas* grown and harvested for hundreds of years. What the Spanish love about them is *el sabor de yodo*, or the flavour of iodine, that plants grown by the sea pick up. Simply matched with tinned mackerel, this is a lovely dish to serve as a snack or shared plate.

**1 kg waxy potatoes,
such as nicola
sea salt
2 small white salad onions,
very finely diced
3 tablespoons chopped chives
1 clove garlic, finely chopped
60 ml olive oil
2 × 125 g cans mackerel
in oil, drained
extra virgin olive oil,
for drizzling**

1 Scrub the potatoes thoroughly under cold running water. Place in a large saucepan, cover with water and add a pinch of salt. Bring to the boil over high heat, then reduce the heat and simmer for 35 minutes or until the potatoes are cooked through. Drain well and leave until cool enough to handle but still warm, then peel and place in a large bowl.

2 Add the onion, chives, garlic, olive oil and 2 teaspoons of salt to the warm potatoes. Crush with a fork to break the potatoes into small and medium chunks and mix well.

3 Spread out the potato salad on a plate and lay the mackerel on top. Drizzle over a little extra virgin olive oil before serving.

COSTILLAS DE IBÉRICO

ROASTED PORK RIBS

SERVES 4-6

At his eponymous restaurant in Aracena, chef José Vicente roasts whole rib cages of pork until the flesh is crisp and the connective tissue soft, sweet and sticky. This is a dish that celebrates the flavour of the meat: no rubs, marinades or glazes, just the taste of the pork eaten from the bone in your hands. José uses ribs from the indigenous ibérico pigs (after the legs have been supplied to the nearby jamón butchers) – and, while this recipe cooks ribs from any pig to perfection, it's worth seeking out rare-breed animals at farmers markets and speciality butchers for their superior flavour.

1.5 kg pork ribs in one piece – ask for a whole uncut rib cage
2 tablespoons sea salt, plus extra to serve
60 ml olive oil

1 Preheat the oven to 130°C/110°C fan.

2 Place the ribs in a very large roasting tin. Season both sides with the salt, drizzle with the olive oil and rub all over with your hands.

3 Place the ribs, curved side up, into the tin and pour in 500 ml of water.

4 Place in the oven and roast for 2 hours, then turn the ribs over and continue roasting for another 1½ hours. Turn once more and roast for another 30 minutes; by now the flesh should be crisp and a deep golden brown.

5 Remove from the oven and leave to rest for 5 minutes.

6 To carve, separate the ribs by cutting between them with a sharp knife. Place on a serving plate, sprinkle with more salt and serve straightaway.

PRUEBA DE MATANZA CON PATATAS PANADERA

FRESH CHORIZO WITH BAKER'S POTATOES

SERVES 4-6

Every town in the Sierra de Aracena has a *gandinguera*. She is the woman who keeps in her head the recipes for all the different *embutidos* or smallgoods that are made on the day of the slaughter – *la matanza*. 'Every pig slaughtered is different,' says Señora Dori Moya, the *gandinguera* for the village of Linares de la Sierra. 'And every family likes their chorizo just so. Some like more salt, paprika or herbs.' To make sure every sausage is just right, a little of the mixture is fried off before it is stuffed into the skins: called *la prueba*, this delicacy is eagerly awaited by the hungry and expectant family and friends who have gathered to help butcher up the pig. *La prueba* has become so popular that it has become a dish enjoyed all year round, often served with *patatas panadera*, or slow-cooked baker's potatoes.

700 g pork shoulder, off the
    bone, skin removed
1 tablespoon sweet smoked
    Spanish paprika
pinch of ground cloves
1 tablespoon ground cumin
1 teaspoon freshly ground
    black pepper
2 garlic cloves, finely chopped
1 teaspoon dried oregano
sea salt
160 ml olive oil
4-6 eggs
thyme sprigs, to garnish

BAKER'S POTATOES

2 potatoes, washed and peeled
50 ml olive oil
2 garlic cloves, skin on

1 Leaving the fat on, cut the pork shoulder meat into about 1 cm cubes, trimming it of gristle. Place the meat in a bowl and add the paprika, cloves, cumin, pepper, garlic, oregano, a pinch of salt and 60 ml of the olive oil and mix well. Cover with plastic film and refrigerate for 12–24 hours.

2 For the baker's potatoes, cut the potatoes into 1 cm thick slices. Place in a heavy-based frying pan with the olive oil and garlic, cover with a lid and slowly cook over low heat for about 30 minutes, stirring occasionally, until the potatoes are soft. Remove from the heat, leave covered and set aside.

3 To cook the pork, pour 60 ml of the olive oil into a large frying pan and place over very high heat. When the oil is hot, add all the pork and the marinade at once. Fry, turning continuously, for 8–9 minutes, or until the pork is lightly browned and cooked through. Take off the heat.

4 Pour the remaining olive oil into a frying pan and place over medium heat. Fry the eggs, one per person, a few at a time, until the white is cooked but the yolk is still runny.

5 To serve, place a few slices of potato on each plate, cover with the pork, then top with a fried egg. Sprinkle with salt and garnish with thyme sprigs.

LA MATANZA

'SLAUGHTER DAY'

Juan Márquez welcomes us into his living room. He is old and virtually deaf, but radiates a warmth that almost conceals his frailty. His granddaughter Laura tenderly eases him back into the chair after he stands to greet me.

Juan was once the town *matachín*, the one responsible for dispatching and dismembering the pigs for the whole community. 'I began when I was still a boy,' he says, as he recalls how it all started. 'I was always interested in watching the old *matachín* as he worked, and would help him salting down the pig afterwards. Then one day when I was 14, he took me aside and quietly said, "Now it is your turn".' With his frail hands, Juan rests his fingertips on his heart: 'I love animals. I realised then that it was my responsibility not only to provide families with meat and smallgoods to feed them over the long cold winters, but I was also chosen to be the one person in the village to make sure the pigs did not needlessly suffer.'

Juan goes on to describe how the pigs were raised in sties just outside the village, where they were fed on grains and kitchen scraps, foraged wild greens, acorns and anything else that would fatten a pig. The beast would be slaughtered quickly, the blood collected to make *morcilla*, then split in half and left to cool quickly on the cold cobblestones of the streets, in the chill mountain air. From there he would work with the *gandinguera*, or guardian of the traditional recipes, and together they would break the pig down: the hindquarters for whole leg jamón, often sold to a wealthy person from the city; the front legs cured into *paleta* (shoulder jamón); and the rest of the animal turned into sausages to last the season: chorizo, *morcilla* and *morcón*.

La matanza, or 'slaughter day', was always considered a festive day. 'All the village had so much fun,' he says, with a hint of chagrin. 'Except me. And the pig even less.'

PUCHERO DE MATANZA

PIGGY HOT POT

SERVES 6

When a pig is killed, all the family and their neighbours get together to share both the workload and the spoils. With all those mouths to feed on *la matanza* ('slaughter day'), a hearty stew is made, using up bits and pieces of the pig. Just what's needed to feed a crowd on a cold winter's day, this is a meal of several acts, in which the rich stock is served as a soup, followed by a plate of hot, soft chickpeas that were cooked in the stock, and then a plate of the meat and smallgoods. You may need to get your butcher to order in all the piggy bits. That said, Asian butchers tend to stock these lesser-loved cuts. *Morcilla* is available from specialist food stores and Spanish delis.

Another classic way of serving this is called *pringá*. Take some chickpeas, some meat, some fat, a little stock and squash it together with the back of a fork. This is a great filling for *molletes*, or rolls (see page 210), to make *bocadillos*, either eaten as is or toasted.

This recipe comes from chef Luismi López of Restaurante Arrieros, in the hilltop town of Linares de la Sierra.

600 g dried chickpeas

500 g pork neck

400 g pork belly, skin off, bone removed

600 g pork ribs

400 g pork face or jowl (substitute pork skin if unavailable)

1 × 400 g piece pork spine bone or leg bone

1 × 120 g piece salt-cured pork belly, such as pancetta

1 × 140 g piece jamón serrano

280 g raw chorizo sausages

280 g *morcilla* sausages

900 g potatoes, peeled and cut into 3 cm cubes using the 'click' method (see page 379)

1 Soak the chickpeas overnight, then drain and rinse under cold running water.

2 Bring 5 litres of water to the boil in a stockpot or large saucepan over high heat. When it is boiling, add all the ingredients except the *morcilla* and the potatoes. Return to a simmer, then reduce the heat and simmer gently for 2½ hours, regularly skimming away any scum that rises to the surface of the stock.

3 Add the potatoes to the pot and top up the stock with more water until it reaches its original level. Return to the boil over high heat, then reduce the heat to medium and simmer for a further 30 minutes.

4 Remove from the heat. Transfer 600 ml of the *puchero* stock to a saucepan and bring to a simmer over medium heat. Add the *morcilla* and simmer for 5 minutes or until cooked through.

5 Remove the pork bones from the stockpot and discard. Lift out the pieces of meat and chorizo and place on a large plate or platter. Cut the *morcilla* and chorizo into 1 cm thick slices and add to the meat.

6 To serve, ladle out bowls of the stock and serve as a soup for the first course. Next, spoon the chickpeas and potatoes into the same bowls. Finally, bring the meat to the table and invite people to help themselves. Serve with thick slices of bread, if you like.

EL COCINERO

THE CHEF

Luismi López stands in the dining room of his hilltop restaurant. From the outdoor balcony, the hillside drops away to a steep, wooded valley. Straddling the banks of the river are the town's *huertas*, or kitchen gardens. On the other side is a forest of holm oaks and chestnut trees, the start of the *dehesa*, Spain's massive oak forest in which pigs are fattened on windfall acorns.

Twenty years ago, Luismi was living the high life, working as a photographer in the city. But he was born in the village of Linares de la Sierra, a town where women still gather in the square around the old fountain to wash their laundry. His father had been the town *matachín* after Juan Márquez (see page 81), and had instilled in him the importance of collecting, preparing and eating the food of the region. Eventually, the call of his hometown was too much. Luismi returned to Linares de la Sierra

with his wife, and worked towards creating a dining space in a converted farmhouse on the old mule trading route that ran through the village. He named his restaurant after this ancient track, Arrieros.

Today he is known around the world, his restaurant recommended by European restaurant guides and the *New York Times*. Not that there is a hint of pretence about the man. 'Sometimes people find my food too simple,' he says, 'but to me, it is honest.' His dishes may be rustic, but his grilled goat's cheese on bread with fresh thyme and honey is profoundly beautiful and wonderfully tasty. He has no trouble following this with a dish of beef carpaccio and shaved frozen foie gras. Luismi is able to keep one foot firmly planted in the food culture of his home village but is not afraid to use the toes of the other to test the waters of gastronomic trends.

PESTIÑOS DE MIEL

OLIVE OIL AND FENNEL PASTRIES IN HONEY

MAKES 24

Sweets and pastries treats have been served from the splendid counter at Confitería Rufino since 1875. Owner Pilar Rodríguez stands proudly in front of the carved wooden displays and mirrored cabinets filled with eel-shaped sweets made of marzipan and others made with egg yolks and walnuts cooked in sugar. But one of her biggest sellers are honey-glazed *pestiños*, little folds of short pastry just rolled and deep-fried. In some parts of Andalusia, they are simply dusted with icing sugar. In other parts they are sprinkled with sesame seeds, and in Cádiz are made with sherry. They were once only made for Holy Week and Christmas but are now often made all year around.

500 g plain flour, plus extra
   for dusting
1 tablespoon fennel seeds
pinch of cumin seeds
pinch of sea salt
200 ml olive oil
200 ml dry white wine
500 g mild-flavoured honey
500 g white sugar
1 litre olive oil, for deep-frying

1 Sift the flour into a stainless steel bowl. Place the fennel, cumin and salt on top of the flour, but resist the temptation to mix them in.

2 Heat the 200 ml of olive oil in a small heavy-based saucepan over medium heat until very hot. Pour the hot oil over the flour and spices in the bowl, then immediately pour in the wine, taking care to avoid getting splashed by the oil. Mix well with a wooden spoon to form a smooth dough, but be careful not to over-work it or the pastry will toughen. Roll the pastry into a ball and cover with plastic film, then leave to rest for an hour.

3 Roll out the pastry on a cool well-floured benchtop until it is about 2–3 mm thick. Cut into discs using an 8 cm crinkle-edged round pastry cutter (or a jar lid about 8 cm in diameter). Brush the edge of half of each pastry disc with cold water, then bring the opposite edge over until slightly overlapping and pinch together to hold in place. Place the *pestiños* on a lightly floured tray or plate.

4 Place the honey and sugar in a small heavy-based saucepan with 100 ml of water and bring to a simmer over medium heat, stirring to dissolve the sugar. Reduce the heat to low–medium and simmer for 5 minutes or until it thickens a little. Keep warm.

5 Pour the olive oil for deep-frying into a heavy-based saucepan or wok and heat to 170°C or until a cube of bread dropped into the oil browns in 15 seconds.

6 Working in batches, fry the *pestiños* for 2–3 minutes, turning occasionally, until crisp and brown. Using a slotted spoon, remove and drain on a wire rack set over a double layer of paper towel. While they are still warm, bathe the *pestiños* in the honey syrup, then leave on the rack to drain and set for 20 minutes.

7 Serve at room temperature with hot coffee or Spanish brandy.

PASTELERÍA

THE PASTRY SHOP

For me, a *pastelería* is like a jewellery store of sweet treats: little temples to the cult of sugar. Sugar arrived in Spain with the Moors, and the Andalusians are particularly fond of the sensation of sweetness, their sweet tooth evident in dishes like fried eggplant finished with sugar syrup and lamb cooked with honey.

Traditionally, pastries were often associated with specific religious festivals, but are now made all year round. Even in the smaller villages, you'll find a *pastelería* – usually run by a husband and wife team, with the husband head-down baking at the back while the wife tends the counter and charms the customers. After lunch, particularly on weekends, locals will come to buy a box of post-prandial cakes and biscuits. The *pastelería* in Aracena is one of my favourites, a beautiful little shop with painted carved wooden doors and windows, and display cabinets dating back to 1875. I love their little *borrachos* ('drunkards'), rolls of sponge soaked in sugar syrup and brandy.

The beautiful town of Aracena is known for
the quality of the light and the purity of the air

TURRÓN HELADO CON CASTAÑAS

NOUGAT ICE CREAM WITH CHESTNUTS

SERVES 6–8

The plazas and squares of towns in the Sierra de Aracena are punctuated by orange trees that perfume the streets with their blossom in spring. The towns themselves are then ringed by *huertas* or kitchen gardens with apple, pear and fig trees. Before the gardens give way to the wilds of the *dehesa*, or oak forest, there is a band of chestnut trees that provides a welcome drop of chestnuts just before winter. In days gone by, the chestnuts were mostly ground into flour to make bread and cakes. But with their mealy nuttiness, chestnuts are also delicious candied. This recipe makes quite a large batch, as they keep well for up to 6 months in the fridge if stored in a jar covered with syrup.

At José Vicente, a traditional restaurant in Aracena, sweet chestnuts are served with a silky nougat ice cream. You will need an ice cream machine for this recipe – and a trip to your favourite Spanish deli or specialist food shop for the soft Spanish nougat.

875 ml pouring cream
200 g soft nougat, broken into
    small pieces
8 egg yolks
175 g caster sugar

CANDIED CHESTNUTS

800 g fresh chestnuts
500 g caster sugar
zest of 2 lemons, in long strips
1 vanilla bean, split lengthways

1 For the candied chestnuts, take each chestnut and, using a small sharp knife, make a cross-shaped incision in its flat base. Bring a large saucepan of water to the boil, add the chestnuts and blanch for 3 minutes. Remove the pan from the heat but leave the chestnuts in the water. When the chestnuts are cool enough to handle, peel away the outer shell and brown inner membrane and wipe each chestnut clean.

2 Place the sugar, lemon zest and vanilla in a heavy-based saucepan with 1 litre of water. Bring to the boil over high heat and cook for 5 minutes, then add the peeled chestnuts. Return to the boil, then reduce the heat to medium and simmer for 20 minutes. Remove from the heat and leave to cool in the syrup.

3 Meanwhile, for the ice cream, pour the cream into a heavy-based saucepan and bring to the boil over medium heat. Add the nougat and whisk until it has dissolved in the cream, then remove from the heat and allow to cool for 1–2 minutes.

4 Place the egg yolks and sugar in a heatproof bowl and stir until the sugar has dissolved. Add a little hot cream and mix well, then stir in the rest of the cream. Transfer the mixture to a clean saucepan and place over low–medium heat. Cook, stirring with a wooden spoon, for 5–6 minutes or until it is thick enough to coat the back of a spoon. Pour into a clean heatproof bowl and leave to cool before churning in an ice-cream machine according to the manufacturer's instructions.

5 Serve a few chestnuts each with a scoop or two of ice cream.

MOVIDA'S ⟶ GUIDE TO ⟵ HUELVA

Ciquitrake 🍷✕

Calle Rascón 21, Huelva; tel 959 25 69 58

This modern bar and smart dining room in the centre of the city has a real sense of fun. Chef Carlos Ramírez plays with ideas to make some really tasty dishes like a coki salado, a small ice-cream cone filled with a tartare of fish and aioli. He is also well known for his tuna tartare served with the famous local strawberries.

El Mercado del Carmen 🍷✕🏠

Avenida de la Ría 2, Huelva; tel 959 28 36 80 www.mercadodelcarmen.com

Just because it isn't historic and rustic doesn't mean that the new Mercado del Carmen isn't one of the best in Spain, with over 180 stalls selling meat, smallgoods, fruit and veg, and some of the best seafood in Europe.

Restaurante Azabache 🍷✕

Calle Vázquez López 22, Huelva; tel 959 25 75 28 www.restauranteazabache.com

With its pastel décor and cream-coloured slatted wooden walls, Azabache feels a little dated and stilted, but the classic Spanish food is full of flavour and finesse. What's more, the chef understands the local love for cuttlefish – here served sweet, soft and sticky.

Restaurante Portichuelo 🍷✕

Calle Vázquez López 15, Huelva; tel 959 24 57 68 www.restauranteportichuelo.com

Next to the classic white theatre in a small square, you'll find old-school hospitality and classic Huelva cuisine under the guidance of restaurateur Manuel Gómez Costa, who runs this brick-and-wood-lined bar and dining room like clockwork. His *'obligatorios' revueltos* – egg with jamón, green capsicum, onion and potato – are, well, obligatory. Other offerings include five different cuttlefish dishes and the most delicious chickpea stew.

Acánthum 🍷✕

**Calle San Salvador 17, Huelva;
tel 959 24 51 35
www.acanthum.com**

Named after the decoration on top of the
Corinthian columns, to represent the
transition from simplicity to elaboration,
this contemporary restaurant offers clever,
tasty food. Xanty Elías is a modernist
chef who plays with his Andalusian roots,
serving the likes of a cuttlefish hamburger,
or perhaps cuttlefish roe blended with
a sauce made of its liver.

La Lonja de Isla 🍷✕🏠

**Muelle Martínez Catena, Isla Cristina;
tel 959 33 16 70
www.lonjadeisla.com**

If you are the type of person who would
visit Tokyo's Tsukiji fish market, then
consider going to La Lonja de Isla, the
cooperative fish market on the wharf at
Isla Cristina, to watch the fleet come in
and the catch being unloaded. Take a seat
in the raked arena and observe the robust
and entertaining fish auction below. Entry
is free – but be aware that this is a working
port, and the workers don't take kindly to
people standing in their way.

Abuelo Mañas 🍷✕

**Avenida Padre Mirabent 33, Isla Cristina;
tel 679 93 21 93**

Raul Mañas has been cooking in his
family restaurant by the seafood market
for 40 years. He is famous for his tuna
dishes, pippies or *coquinas* (see page 62)
and or fisherman's-style sea bass (*corvina
marinera*). A bit rough around the edges it
may be, but the reason you're here is to eat
the freshest seafood alongside the fishermen
who caught it.

Bodeguita Los Raposo 🍷✕

Calle Fuente 60, Moguer; tel 959 37 12 81 www.bodeguitadelosraposo.es

Many people come to this town to explore the history of Christopher Columbus, and to visit
the Santa Clara Monastery, where Columbus spent his first night after returning from the
Americas. Nearby is this traditional, rustic tavern, serving simple dishes typical of the area.
Just take a menu card, tick what you want and hand it over to the bartender.

Bar Hermanos Moreno 🍷✕

**Avenida Padre Mirabent 39, Isla Cristina;
tel 959 34 35 71**

A pleasant enough workaday bar by the
wholesale fish market, where the famous
white prawns are perfectly cooked and the
beer is ice-cold.

Bar Hermanos Rivero 🍷✕

**Avenida Padre Mirabent 34, Isla Cristina;
tel 959 34 35 08**

A very rustic and authentic fishermen's bar
specialising in a few seafood dishes. Try the
cockles.

Winemakers Montserrat and Begoña Sauci

José Vicente 🍷✕

**Avenida de Andalucía 53, Aracena;
tel 959 12 84 55**

A seasonal menu dictated by the bounty
of the Sierras is served for lunch here
(and dinner by appointment). Expect great
ibérico pork, including slow-roasted ribs,
perhaps a mushroom and potato omelette
and traditional vegetable dishes, all served
in a homely but very professional old-school
dining room.

Confitería Rufino ✕

**Constitución 3, Aracena; tel 959 12 81 21
www.confiteriarufino.com**

Since 1875 Aracena locals have been
coming to this cute pastry shop just off
the main square, its interior lined with
elaborate wooden-framed glass cases. Try
their *borrachos*, rolls of sponge soaked in
syrup and topped with caramelised vanilla
crème pâtissière.

Jamones Eíriz ✕

**Calle Pablo Bejarano 43,
Corteconcepción; tel 959 12 00 19
www.jamoneseiriz.com**

Take a drive along country lanes as they
wind through holm oak forests and wild
pastures until you come to the little village
of Corteconcepción. By the town's open-air

laundry wells is one of the most delightful
jamón makers in the region. Let the Eíriz
family take you on a tour, where you can
get up close and personal with the pigs, and
learn how their jamón and smallgoods are
produced. Their excellent jamóns offer very
good value for money.

Restaurante Arrieros 🍷✕

**Calle Arrieros 2, Linares de la Sierra;
tel 959 46 37 17
www.arrieros.net**

A rustic yet stylish dining room with a
stone fireplace, where truly beautiful and
delicious food is served. The meal might
start with a carpaccio of beef with shaved
foie gras or perhaps a simple piece of toasted
bread with herbs and goat's cheese, followed
by a fat piece of salt cod or a Spanish
hamburger made from the juiciest, tastiest
ground neck meat from an ibérico pig.

Panadería Belén
Martín Domínguez 🛍

**Calle Larga 12, Linares de la Sierra;
tel 959 46 37 31**

At this village bakery with a wood-fired
oven in a small village in the hills, they
work with both sourdough and yeast to
make good-quality rustic bread. As baker
Juan Ramos says, 'I have baked every day
for 30 years, and every day it is different
because I have to change what I do with
the weather.'

Bodegas Sauci 🍷

**Calle Doctor Fleming 1, Bollullos Par del
Condado; tel 959 41 05 24
www.bodegassauci.es**

They make more than sherry in Andalusia,
and the *vino de naranja* (orange wine) made
here by the Sauci sisters, Montserrat and
Begoña, is protected by a DO designation.
In a village outside Huelva, where the
family settled after the grapevine disease
phylloxera wiped out their business in
France, they macerate dried orange rind
in flavourless grape spirit before adding it
to wine which is then matured in a solera
system. Come for tours and cellar door sales.

Bodega Luis Felipe 🍷

**Calle Palos de la Frontera 14,
La Palma del Condado; tel 959 40 07 43
www.bodegasrubio.com**

Makers of excellent Spanish brandy who
offer cellar door sales and tours, this is
a proud brandy house known for its fine
spirits and conservative style.

The fishmonger puts the finishing touches to his display. The freshest fish from the Atlantic: hake, john dory and a selection of prawns have been perfectly positioned on a bed of ice and dressed in especially made suits to portray the nation's prime minister and his council of ministers. This is the market in Cádiz, and it's *Carnaval*. In this festival, the *Gaditanos* (as residents of the city are known), take to the streets to perform seditious sketches and poke fun at authority, making good use of their sharp wit, for which they are famous across Spain.

Walk the streets of Cádiz and you follow the same network laid out by the Phoenicians, long before the Romans invaded. Before the Phoenicians, the ancient Iberian civilisation of the Tartessos built cities on the hills rising above the vast wetlands of the Guadalquivir as it makes its way to the Atlantic.

South of the city, a small sandy promontory called Cabo de Trafalgar watches over the site of a famous sea battle that the British claimed as one of their greatest victories at sea. A little further south, not far from the mouth of the Barbate River, the towns of Barbate and Zahara de los Atunes still employ the *almadraba*, an ancient method of trapping fish in a maze of nets. Once common along this stretch of the coast, there are now just a handful of practitioners of this arcane fishing method and it is used only for catching tuna. Despite the soaring prices commanded by this prized fish, it is still popular here, and in Cádiz you'll find it served many ways, from simply cooked on the grill to simmered in a rich onion sauce to make *atún encebollado* (see page 133).

Inland from Cádiz is Jerez de la Frontera, a more sedate and urbane city after which sherry was named. Along with the port towns of El Puerto de Santa María and Sanlúcar de Barrameda, it forms the triangle of the D.O. (*Denominación de Origen*) Jerez–Xeres region. Beyond the central plains lies the Sierra de Grazalema, a spine of mountains running north to south that were once home to Berbers from North Africa, who established the string of hill settlements that today we know as the *Los pueblos blancos*, or 'the white villages'.

From the squares and patios of these whitewashed hilltop towns and villages, the views stretch as far as the disputed British territory of Gibraltar, a rocky outcrop known in the ancient world as one of the Pillars of Hercules, with an outcrop on the other side of the strait at Jebel Musa in Morocco completing the monumental duo.

But it is the sea that defines this province. With coasts bordering both the Atlantic and Mediterranean, Cádiz has always been a pervious frontier, a place that has seen the exchange of ideas, objects and customs from all around the Mediterranean and across the Atlantic, in peace and in war. This eons-old flow of humanity has left indelible marks on the landscape, people and food.

LA CALETA

GAZPACHO DE PEPI

PEPI'S GAZPACHO

SERVES 4

Pepi Navarro is a cook in one of Vejer de la Frontera's lovely old bars. She showed me how to make Andalusia's famous cold soup using a wooden mortar and pestle, a culinary artform that requires both patience and stamina. Starting with the garlic and salt, Pepi pounds each ingredient in the bottom of the pestle. She uses a little bread to stop the juices from splashing out and lets the pureed cucumber and tomato work their way up the sides of the mortar, so they don't get over-worked and lose their texture. She also adds a little of the cucumber skin for a fresh note and a hint of pleasing bitterness. This gazpacho is so deliciously refreshing; to me, it is like a wet salad. If you have a large wooden mortar and pestle, give it a try (just remember that you'll need to chop the ingredients quite finely), or simply use a blender.

4 very ripe tomatoes, peeled
2 white salad onions, peeled
1 long cucumber
1 green bull horn capsicum
    (pepper) or ½ green regular
    capsicum (pepper)
50 g two-day old bread,
    without crusts
1 small garlic clove
4 large mint leaves
2 teaspoons sea salt
40 ml extra virgin olive oil
40 ml sherry vinegar
700 ml chilled water

1 Cut the tomatoes and onions into quarters. Peel the cucumber, reserving two strips of peel, then cut the flesh into large pieces. Remove the stem and seeds from the capsicum and chop into large pieces.

2 Place the bread in a shallow dish and cover with cold water, then leave to soak for 1 minute. Squeeze the bread in your hands to remove most of the water.

3 Place the tomato, onion, cucumber, capsicum, bread, garlic, mint and reserved cucumber skin in a blender and blend to a rough, thick puree. Add the salt, olive oil and sherry vinegar and blend briefly, then add the chilled water and blend until the gazpacho is almost smooth but still retains some texture.

4 Serve immediately.

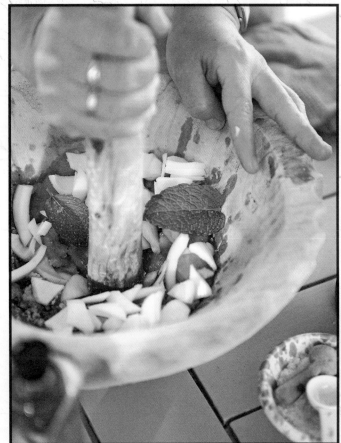

La feria in the hilltop town of Vejer de la Frontera

SOPA GRAZALEMA

FRESH MINT AND BREAD SOUP

SERVES 4

Up in the Sierra de Grazalema is the little 'white village' of Grazalema. In the centre of town is a restaurant called Cádiz el Chico that specialises in the traditional dishes of the mountains: venison roasted in the wood oven, great dishes of roasted lamb and a tart made with acorn flour. Chef Loli Gómez suggests you start with the town's eponymous soup, a nourishing and incredibly tasty mix of *puchero* stock, a little chorizo and egg, all thickened with a little bread and seasoned with fresh mint. It is excellent with a glass of rustic red wine.

1.6 litres *puchero* stock
 (see page 82) or
 chicken stock
1 tablespoon extra virgin
 olive oil
150 g raw chorizo, cut into
 5 mm thick slices
1 × 120 g piece jamón serrano,
 cut into 1 cm cubes
4 large slices sourdough bread,
 cut in half
2 hard-boiled eggs, peeled
 and roughly chopped
8 mint leaves

1 Pour the stock into a medium-sized saucepan and place over medium heat to warm.

2 Meanwhile, in a heavy-based frying pan, heat the olive oil over medium heat and fry the chorizo on each side for 60–90 seconds or until browned. Remove the pan from the heat and stir in the jamón, just to warm it through.

3 Toast the bread until lightly golden.

4 Place two pieces of bread in each of four large soup bowls. Divide the chorizo, jamón and sliced egg evenly between the bowls. Roughly tear two mint leaves into each bowl, then pour in 400 ml of the hot stock. Serve straight away.

LOS PUEBLOS BLANCOS

THE 'WHITE VILLAGES'

Little more than a cluster of whitewashed buildings tightly packed around a small patch of relatively flat ground that is the town square, Grazalema is tucked into a fold of the high sierras. An old waterwheel for the town's mill stands motionless in the clear waters of the Río Guadalete. Here the roads are tight and winding, paved over donkey tracks between the 'white villages' that dot the sierras: El Bosque, Arcos de la Frontera and Bornos, to name a few. Like Grazalema, most of the 'white villages' were established in Roman times, when the fertile high valleys were grazed by sheep raised for wool. Berbers settled the area during the Moorish period, building towns threaded with tight laneways and large open squares. Now they are rustic rural retreats, offering cool respite from the heat of the coast and the vestiges of arcane trades, such as Phoenician-era salt pans and Grazalema's cloakmakers. The 'white villages' are also repositories of ancient recipes. Despite their proximity, the food of each village is subtly different, reflecting variations in the surrounding landscape, where wild foods are harvested, as well as the way crops and animals are grown and raised.

The white village of Grazalema is home
to traditional rural industries.

ENSALADA DE REMOLACHA

BEETROOT SALAD WITH FENNEL AND CUMIN

SERVES 6

Fennel and cumin seeds are a classic Andalusian flavour combination. Traditionally, you might find these spices used to flavour a carrot salad. But as chefs gain the confidence to explore their heritage without trashing it, safe in the knowledge that these flavours naturally go together, we are seeing great dishes like this appear on menus – dishes that will become the classics of the future. This version is from Casa Varo in Vejer de la Frontera. Use small to medium-sized beetroot, as they will be more tender, and the best-quality fennel and cumin seeds you can find.

5 medium-sized beetroot,
    washed
2 small brown onions
1 garlic bulb
1 teaspoon fennel seeds
1 teaspoon cumin seeds
1 tablespoon finely
    chopped mint
juice of 1 lemon
100 ml extra virgin olive oil
40 ml white wine vinegar
sea salt

1 Preheat the oven to 200°C/180°C fan.

2 Wrap each beetroot in foil. Place on a baking tray with the onions and garlic (both still in their skins) and bake for 40 minutes or until the onions and garlic are cooked through. Remove the onions and garlic from the tray and leave to cool. Continue baking the beetroot for another 40 minutes or until cooked through, then remove and leave to cool.

3 With a sharp knife, peel the beetroot and cut into 3–4 mm thick slices, then cut into 1 cm wide strips. Place in a bowl. Peel the onions, then cut into thin strips and add to the bowl. Cut the top off the garlic head and squeeze all the roasted garlic pulp from the skins into the bowl with the beetroot and onion.

4 Place a small heavy-based frying pan over medium heat and toast the fennel and cumin seeds for 1–2 minutes or until lightly browned and the kitchen is filled with the aroma of the spices. Place the seeds in a mortar and pestle and lightly pound to break them up a little. Add to the beetroot, along with the chopped mint.

5 In a small bowl, mix the olive oil, lemon juice and white wine vinegar. Season with sea salt and toss through the beetroot salad.

6 Serve at room temperature.

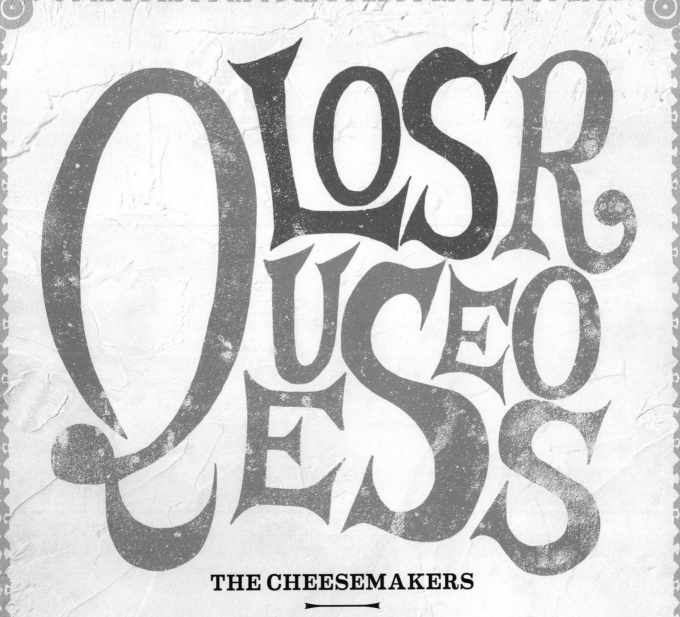

THE CHEESEMAKERS

►◄

'When you spend your life eating grass, you become selective,' says Carlos Ríos, cheesemaker at Payoyo in the town of Villaluenga del Rosario. He is referring to the herds of goats and sheep grazing on the rocky pastures below the summit of Mount Navazo Alto, taking their pick from the wild herbs such as fennel, mallow and chamomile that grow among the grass. 'The animals will graze on certain parts of some wild plants to cure themselves of parasites,' he says. 'Good cheese always starts with healthy animals grazing on good pastures.' When we pass a plantation of broad beans, it is proudly pointed out that these are grown for the animals to eat, not humans!

Up here they are particularly proud of their indigenous breed of sheep, *Merina de Grazalema*, the milk of which makes the richest, most delicious semi-cured cheese. This same milk is sometimes blended with goat's milk to create a cheese with a long, lingering aftertaste and a lovely savoury punch. Andalusians are not generally known for their cheesemaking – partly because pasture is limited to the sierras, and partly because much of the delicious cheese is still consumed locally.

QUESO DE OVEJA Y ANCHOAS

SHEEP'S CHEESE AND ANCHOVIES

SERVES 4

Up in the Sierra de Grazalema, a cheese cooperative called Payoyo makes a wonderfully fresh-tasting and beautifully sharp matured sheep's cheese. It has a lingering savouriness that just won't quit. Combined with the best Cantabrian anchovies, it is incomparable. Although it will surely only be a matter of time before this cheese is available in Australia, until then consider making this using another matured sheep's cheese, such as manchego, or even Australian goat's cheese.

This goes perfectly with beer or a small glass of chilled fino sherry, just as it is served at Casa Varo in Vejer de la Frontera.

2 slices firm sourdough bread
250 g semi-cured sheep's cheese
1 × 50 g tin Spanish anchovies

1 Cut the bread into fingers. Slice the cheese into thin wedges about the same size as the anchovy fillets.

2 Drain the anchovies, then lay an anchovy fillet on each finger of bread and top with a wedge of cheese. Serve at room temperature.

CROQUETAS de PUCHERO

RICH CROQUETTES OF LEFTOVERS

MAKES 18

Making croquettes is the Spanish way of turning leftovers into delicious, salty deep-fried snacks. They are also the test of a good bar. If the cook can get their *croquetas* right, everything else seems to fall into place. The base is generally a thick bechamel sauce infused with fresh bay leaves and mixed with whatever needs using up. This could be the scrag ends from a fillet of salt cod, the last bits of jamón left on the bone or some grated pieces of cheese. The mixture is then rolled in breadcrumbs and left in the fridge to set, before being deep-fried. In this instance we are using some leftover *puchero*, the classic Andalusian stew (see page 82), but you could just as easily make this with leftover cooked meat from the Sunday roast.

1 onion, peeled but left whole
2 fresh bay leaves
4 cloves
1 litre milk
120 g butter
100 g plain flour, plus extra
    for dusting
470 g mixed meat from
    puchero (see page 82) or
    other leftover cooked meat
    or fish, finely chopped
large pinch of freshly
    grated nutmeg
sea salt
600 g breadcrumbs
3 eggs
olive oil, for deep-frying

1 Take the onion, lay the bay leaves over its surface, pushing the cloves in like drawing pins to hold them in place. Put the onion into a medium-sized saucepan, pour in the milk and place over medium heat. When the milk comes to a rapid simmer, remove from the heat immediately and set aside.

2 Meanwhile, melt the butter in a heavy-based saucepan over medium heat. Sprinkle over the flour and mix well with a wooden spoon to make a roux. Cook the roux for 5 minutes, stirring constantly – it should be a smooth and silky paste.

3 Using a ladle, add the warm infused milk a little at a time, mixing each ladleful into the roux before adding the next and stirring constantly to make a thick sauce. Stir in the chopped meat, nutmeg and 1 teaspoon of salt, mix well and continue to cook over medium heat, stirring regularly, for 30 minutes. When the sauce is ready, it should have a consistency similar to mashed potato and the raw flour flavour should be completely cooked out. Remove from the heat and pour into a shallow container (avoid scraping out any residue that has stuck to the base of the pan, as this may discolour the sauce). Cover with baking paper and refrigerate for several hours until cold and set.

4 To shape the croquettes, weigh out 60 g of the mixture (roughly a heaped tablespoon). Using well-floured hands, roll into a log about 5 cm long with flat, not tapered, ends. Place on a tray or plate and continue shaping all the mixture into croquettes with floured hands.

5 Spread the breadcrumbs over a plate or small tray. Crack the eggs into a bowl and beat with a fork. Dip the croquettes into the egg wash, letting the excess drain off, then roll in the breadcrumbs to coat completely. Place the croquettes on a clean tray or large plate lined with baking paper and allow to set again in the fridge for about an hour.

6 Heat the olive oil in a heavy-based saucepan or wok to 170°C or until a cube of bread dropped into the oil browns in 15 seconds.

7 Deep-fry the croquettes in batches of about six at a time for 2–3 minutes or until brown and crisp on the outside and hot on the inside. Remove gently with a slotted spoon and drain on paper towel. Season with salt and serve straightaway.

TORTILLA DE PATATAS

POTATO TORTILLA

SERVES 4

Potato tortillas are stock-standard Spanish fare, perhaps even the national dish. Cheap, nourishing and delicious, they can be cut into wedges, impaled with a fork and served with a beer, or sliced and placed between two halves of a crusty bread roll. Some bars specialise in making great, fat 5-kilo tortillas as big as a gorilla's head, but this recipe makes a more manageable-sized tortilla. One of the best I've ever had was at Bar el Guitarrón de San Pedro in Jerez de la Frontera, a flamenco bar run by a Catalan woman. The secret is to stop cooking the tortilla before it completely sets in the middle, so it is meltingly soft and moist.

1 litre olive oil, plus 60 ml extra

1.2 kg desiree potatoes, peeled and cut into 1 cm cubes

1 large brown onion, diced

sea salt

10 large eggs

1 Heat the olive oil in a wide heavy-based saucepan until just warm, then add the potato and onion. Cook over low–medium heat for 20 minutes – the oil should be just gently bubbling, not frying, so the potato becomes soft but does not brown at all. Drain the potato and onion, season with salt and allow to cool slightly.

2 Beat the eggs with a teaspoon of salt in a large bowl, then add the potato and onion and gently mix together.

3 Pour the extra 60 ml olive oil into a 27 cm non-stick frying pan and place over high heat. When the oil is very hot, pour in the potato and egg mixture and mix well with a spatula for 30 seconds, then reduce the heat to medium. Use your spatula to break up the potato a little, then run it around the sides of the tortilla to form a rounded edge. Cook for another 3–4 minutes.

4 Choose a heatproof plate large enough to completely cover the pan and place it over the top. Holding it firmly in place, invert the pan so the tortilla is turned out onto the plate, cooked-side up. Carefully slide the tortilla back into the pan, uncooked-side down, then cover with the plate and cook for 3–4 minutes. When it is done, the tortilla should be only lightly browned and not quite cooked through in the centre.

5 Remove the plate that was acting as a lid and place a clean plate that fits generously over the pan on top. Holding it firmly in place, invert the pan to turn the tortilla out onto the plate. Cover with plastic film for 15 minutes to allow the residual heat to complete the cooking.

6 Cut into slices and serve at room temperature.

A cobbled stroll on a warm Jerez night

ALCACHOFAS DEL BAR JUANITO

ARTICHOKES IN OLIVE OIL

SERVES 4

There is a bar in the heart of Jerez de la Frontera called Bar Juanito, whose chefs have been using this recipe to cook artichoke hearts in olive oil with onions, garlic and breadcrumbs since they first opened their doors in 1943. The bitter compound normally associated with artichokes, cynarin, is disarmed through the cooking process. Not only does this render the artichokes luxuriously soft, but it also makes them a wonderful foil to a crisp fino sherry. The key to the dish lies in choosing good-sized artichokes and trimming them well, sculpting away the harder petals with a small, sharp knife and an attitude of minimalism.

juice of 1 lemon
8 large artichokes
4 small white onions, diced
6 garlic cloves, diced
300 ml extra virgin olive oil
100 g two-day-old bread, grated
large handful of roughly
    chopped flat-leaf parsley
sea salt and freshly ground
    black pepper

1 Half-fill a bowl with water and add the lemon juice. Use a paring knife to peel and trim the outer layers of the artichokes, leaving only the heart. Place in the acidulated water to stop them from discolouring.

2 Drain the artichokes and place in a stockpot or large saucepan, along with the onion and garlic. Cover with about 1.3 litres of cold water, then add the olive oil, grated bread and parsley, and season with salt and pepper. Bring to a slow simmer over medium heat and cook for 20 minutes until the artichokes are soft and the dish is aromatic.

3 Transfer the artichokes and some of their cooking juices to a bowl and serve straight away.

GAMBAS con BABETAS

PRAWNS WITH BRAISED PASTA

SERVES 4–6

The Spanish eat pasta. Not a lot, but when they do, they cook it in a *sofrito*, a thick jam-like sauce of onions and tomatoes – in this case, combined with a fish stock and prawns. While in other parts of Spain this kind of dish may be called *fideos*, here it is known as *babetas*, and was traditionally produced to sustain sailors on long sea voyages. It is made in a similar way to paella: by slowly cooking down the *sofrito*, then adding the pasta. Try using old-fashioned macaroni or short lengths of a ribbon pasta such as linguine. This recipe comes from Restaurante El Ventorrillo del Chato, at an old coach stop on the outskirts of Cádiz.

4 ripe tomatoes
80 ml extra virgin olive oil
700 g raw prawns, peeled
    and deveined
sea salt
3 white salad onions,
    finely diced
3 garlic cloves, chopped
3 fresh bay leaves
2 green bull horn capsicums
    (peppers) or 1 green regular
    capsicum (pepper), finely
    diced
1 litre fish stock (see page 380)
200 g linguine, broken into
    2.5 cm lengths

1 Cut the tomatoes in half and grate the cut side against a cheese grater over a bowl to pulp the flesh. Discard the skin.

2 In a 30 cm heavy-based shallow saucepan or deep frying pan, heat 1 tablespoon of the olive oil over high heat and fry the prawns for 1 minute on each side. Season with salt. Remove the prawns from the pan and set aside.

3 In the same pan, make a *sofrito* by adding the remaining olive oil and placing over low–medium heat. When the oil is hot, add the onion with a pinch of salt and cook for 15 minutes, stirring occasionally, until soft but not browned. If the onion begins to colour, reduce the heat. Stir in the garlic and bay leaves and cook for 2 minutes. Add the capsicum and cook for 15 minutes or until soft. Add the tomato pulp and continue cooking for 15 minutes, stirring occasionally, until the *sofrito* has reduced to a jam-like consistency.

4 Heat the stock in a small saucepan, then pour into the pan with the *sofrito*. Turn the heat up to high and bring to the boil. Season with salt, add the pasta and bring back to a simmer, then reduce the heat to medium and cook for 10 minutes, stirring occasionally.

5 Add the prawns to the pan and cook for another 5 minutes until the pasta is done. Serve immediately.

ATÚN

TUNA

At the end of spring, Atlantic bluefin tuna, having grown fat in the rich cold waters of the Atlantic Ocean, return to the Mediterranean Sea to breed and spawn. Off the shores of Barbate, fishermen lay nets in the shallow water like a labyrinth of fences leading to a central enclosure, and every year some of the tuna get caught in the maze. This method of fishing, which dates back to pre-Roman times, is called *almadraba*, and is considered one of the most sustainable in the world.

From here, any tuna that is not shipped straight to Japan is taken to the nearby *fábrica de conservas y salazones*, a conserving and salting factory. Every part of the tuna is used. The fat belly or *ventresca* is slowly cooked in oil to make confit and preserved in jars or tins, while the flank is cured, sometimes in lard. The roe, cured and given a little touch of annatto, is known as *huevas de atún*. One of the most important products made from tuna in this province is *mojama*: the *lomo* (loin) is salted and then hung in cages to dry naturally in the *viento de levante*, the dry winds that blow in from the east across the sierras. During this time, beneficial moulds and yeasts grow on the outside of the *mojama*, changing its flavour and texture. Like jamón, it is this essential blend of salt, wind, micro-flora and time that transforms this prized red flesh into something greater and more delicious than the sum of its parts.

ATÚN ENCEBOLLADO

TUNA COOKED IN ONION AND SHERRY SAUCE

SERVES 4-6

The first tuna of the season is always given to the Virgen del Carmen, says chef José Melero from Restaurante El Campero. In the fishing town of Barbate, he has turned a seaside tavern into Spain's equivalent of Fergus Henderson's landmark London restaurant St John. Except here the nose-to-tail is all about tuna: 'There are 24 cuts of tuna,' he says. His cuisine is exceptionally respectful to the flavour of the fish, with most cuts presented very, very simply. One of the region's classic dishes is *atún encebollado*, which traditionally used the meat from the head of bluefin tuna, but is as good made with yellowfin or even albacore tuna fillet.

1 kg tuna fillet
80 ml extra virgin olive oil
10 small white onions,
   thinly sliced
1 fresh bay leaf
6 whole black peppercorns
sea salt
4 garlic cloves, sliced
200 ml fino sherry
2 teaspoons sweet Spanish
   paprika
1 tablespoon sherry vinegar
small handful of oregano
   leaves, roughly chopped

1 With a sharp knife, remove any dark bloodline and skin from the tuna. Cut the tuna into 3 cm cubes.

2 Pour the olive oil into a *rondeau* (see page 383) or heavy-based deep frying pan and place over medium heat. Add the onion and bay leaf, peppercorns and a pinch of sea salt. Stir, then cook for 8 minutes, stirring occasionally. Add the garlic and cook for 8–10 minutes more, stirring occasionally, until the onion is soft but not browned.

3 Pour in the sherry and scrape the base of the pan to deglaze. Bring back to a simmer and cook for a further 2 minutes, then add 550 ml of water. Return to a simmer and cook for 5 minutes before adding the paprika, sherry vinegar and oregano. Season well with salt and simmer for another 8 minutes.

4 Add the tuna, nestling it into the sauce, and simmer over low– medium heat for 30 minutes. Resist the temptation to stir, as you don't want to break up the tuna – instead, gently shake the pan from time to time.

5 Spoon a few pieces of tuna into shallow bowls and serve with plenty of onion sauce.

REVUELTO DE HINOJO MARINO Y ERIZOS

EGGS WITH SAMPHIRE AND SEA URCHIN

SERVES 4–6

Chef Miguel López cooks where the real people live. San Fernando is a gritty town to the south of Cádiz where tower blocks punctuate the ancient fishing villages on the shores of the *esteros*, the saltmarshes that have sustained life here for thousands of years. His nearest neighbour is the family of Camarón de la Isla, the late gypsy superstar who grew up in the humble fisherman's cottage. Across the road is a labyrinthine series of ponds created before Roman times, where salt was harvested in summer and, in the wetter months, fish were fattened on the tiny shrimp and algae that spawned in the ponds filled with sweet rainwater. Miguel champions the saltwater weeds that thrive on the banks between the waterways, and the eels and fish that grow fat and sweet in this amazing man-made ecosystem.

The *revuelto* is a classic Spanish egg dish. Wetter and more elaborate than scrambled eggs, it could be a breakfast dish, a snack or a light meal. Miguel López picks samphire and combines it with sea urchin in one of the most delicious *revueltos* I have ever tasted. With such a simple dish, it's important to use the best free-range eggs you can find. And be judicious with sea urchin, as it can easily overpower: only use fresh (not frozen) sea urchin or, if unavailable, try salmon roe. Samphire grows naturally on the seashore and along some inland waterways, and can be found in some markets. If you have trouble finding it, substitute asparagus.

70 g (small bunch) samphire, washed and dried
12 large eggs
sea salt
50 g fresh sea urchin roe
1 tablespoon extra virgin olive oil

1 Remove and discard any woody stems from the samphire. Break the eggs into a bowl, add a pinch of salt and whisk well. Gently mix through the samphire and sea urchin roe.

2 Pour the olive oil into a large non-stick frying pan and place over medium heat. When the oil is hot, pour in the egg mixture and allow it to just set, about 30–45 seconds. Using a spatula, begin moving the set egg from the outside of the pan towards the centre, working your way around the edges of the pan. Bringing set egg into the centre allows raw egg to make contact with the base of the hot pan. Do this for 5 minutes or until the egg is just set, but there is still a little liquid left (the residual heat will finish cooking the egg).

3 Remove from the heat and serve straight away.

ARROZ CALDOSO A LA MARINERA

FISHERMAN'S RICE

SERVES 4-6

We were running late for the lunch service at La Venta la Feria. We had heard so much about the famous *guisos marineros* ('fishermen's dishes') of the region around Puerto de Santa María that we had to try them. When we arrived the restaurant was in full swing, with families sitting at large tables sharing vast dishes of steaming rice. Not paella, but wet and soupy *arroz*. 'I am sorry,' said the waiter, 'we are not cooking the *guisos* until tomorrow.' Like most of the other tables, we ordered *arroz caldoso a la marinera*. It was absolutely stunning.

650 g clams
sea salt
1 medium-sized calamari
   (about 450 g), cleaned – ask
   your fishmonger to do this,
   reserving the tentacles
3 ripe tomatoes
60 ml extra virgin olive oil
3 white salad onions,
   finely diced
3 garlic cloves, roughly chopped
3 fresh bay leaves
½ large red capsicum (pepper),
   roughly chopped
1.3 litres fish stock
   (see page 380)
pinch of saffron threads
250 g Calasparra rice
12 raw prawns, peeled
   and deveined

1 Wash the clams under cold running water and place in a bowl. Cover with cold water and a good pinch of salt. Leave to stand for 30 minutes then, using your hands, lift the clams into another bowl. Cover with fresh water and add a pinch of salt. Repeat three times – this encourages the clams to purge themselves of sand.

2 Rinse the calamari. Cut the body and wings into 1–2 cm squares and the tentacles into 2–3 cm lengths.

3 Cut the tomatoes in half and grate the cut side against a cheese grater over a bowl to pulp the flesh. Discard the skin.

4 Pour half the olive oil into a *perol* (see page 380) or wide heavy-based saucepan and place over medium–high heat. When the oil is hot, add the calamari, season with salt and cook for 2–3 minutes each side until lightly browned and the flesh has firmed. Remove and set aside.

5 In the same pan, make a *sofrito* by adding the remaining olive oil and placing over low–medium heat. When the oil is hot, add the onion with a pinch of salt and cook for 15 minutes, stirring occasionally, until soft but not browned. If the onion begins to colour, reduce the heat. Stir in the garlic and bay leaves and cook for 2 minutes. Add the capsicum and cook for 15 minutes or until soft. Add the tomato pulp and continue cooking for 15 minutes, stirring occasionally, until the *sofrito* has reduced to a jam-like consistency.

6 Heat the stock in a saucepan, then pour into the pan with the *sofrito*. Turn the heat up to medium–high and bring to the boil. Add the calamari and bring back to a simmer, then reduce the heat to medium and cook for 10 minutes, stirring occasionally.

7 Meanwhile, in a small heavy-based frying pan, toast the saffron for a minute or so over medium heat until you just start to smell the aroma. Add a couple of tablespoons of the hot stock to the saffron,

swirl it around, then tip the contents of the frying pan back into the pan with the *sofrito*.

8 Sprinkle in the rice, season with salt and stir, then bring to a simmer and cook for 10 minutes. Add the clams and prawns, bring back to a simmer and cook for 5–6 minutes or until the seafood is cooked and the rice is done but not overcooked – it should still be slightly firm to the tooth.

9 Bring the pan to the table and serve directly into shallow bowls.

A hearty rice dish (see page 136)
at a traditional roadside inn

SALT

A great pyramid of salt rises from the flat marshlands that flank the Gulf of Cádiz. His eyes squinting in the white glare, salt worker Manuel Ruiz slowly spreads out the drying salt with a wooden rake, its leading edge making a harsh scraping sound as it combs through the fat crystals. Not much has changed here on the San Vicente salt pans since they were built by the Romans. In spring, seawater is let into the shallow pans. Over summer, the heat evaporates the water, leaving crystals of salt. Some is harvested from the surface as *sal de hielo*, delicate crystals sold to gourmets. Manuel breaks off from his raking to fill a bag for a man who's going back to his farm to salt-down pig legs to make jamón. He says what is left over will be used to preserve olives.

Salt sits at the heart of Spanish cuisine – not just as a seasoning, but as a preservative that transforms tuna into *mojama*, pork loin into *lomo*, little fish into *anchoas* and, of course, ham into jamón. The Spanish are super-skilled in the judicious use of salt to transform meat, fish, fruit, vegetables and milk into delicious preserved products that are shipped around Spain and across the globe. Manuel goes back to his raking. During the season, he will make over a thousand tonnes of sea salt. 'Ha,' he laughs, 'just like the Romans – but I have a tractor!'

CORVINA A LA ROTEÑA

FISH IN TOMATO BRAISE

SERVES 4

Not only does each region and province have its own speciality, some towns are renowned for their particular way of preserving fish. Rota, to the north of Cádiz city, has been an ocean port since Phoenician times. After the discovery of the Americas, when explorers returned from the New World to Spain with tomatoes and capsicums, the cooks in Rota developed a delicious sauce of braised tomatoes and green capsicums with the added punch and sweetness of onions. It is most commonly used to cook *corvina*, a fish similar to sea bass. As we don't have sea bass in Australia, I use barramundi, which has a similar texture. This recipe was given to me by the chef at a popular restaurant in Sanlúcar de Barrameda called Taberna El Loli.

6 large ripe tomatoes

140 ml olive oil

1 large brown onion, diced

sea salt

2 garlic cloves, finely chopped

2 fresh bay leaves

2 green bull horn capsicums (peppers) or 1 green regular capsicum (pepper), diced

150 ml fino sherry

40 ml brandy

freshly ground black pepper

2 whole baby barramundi (about 400–500 g each)

100 g plain flour

1 Cut the tomatoes in half and grate the cut side against a cheese grater over a bowl to pulp the flesh. Discard the skin.

2 First make a *sofrito*. Pour half of the olive oil into a large heavy-based frying pan and place over low–medium heat. When the oil is hot, add the diced onion with a pinch of salt and cook for 15 minutes, stirring occasionally, until soft but not coloured. Stir in the garlic and bay leaves and cook for 2 minutes. Add the capsicum and cook for 15 minutes or until soft. Add the tomato pulp and continue cooking for 15 minutes, stirring occasionally, until the *sofrito* has reduced to a jam-like consistency.

3 Add the fino sherry and brandy to the *sofrito*, then bring back to a simmer. Add 250 ml of water and return to a simmer again, then season with salt and pepper and simmer for 10 minutes.

4 Meanwhile, prepare the fish by cutting off the fins and tails using kitchen scissors and cutting off their heads using a sharp knife. Cut each fish widthways into pieces 2–3 cm wide and season with salt. Place the flour in a shallow bowl and season with salt and pepper. Coat the fish well in the seasoned flour, lightly shaking off any excess.

5 Pour the remaining olive oil into another frying pan and place over medium–high heat. Add the fish in batches of three or four pieces at a time and cook on each side for a minute or so until lightly browned. Transfer the fried fish to the simmering sauce, cover and cook for a further 8–10 minutes over medium heat until the fish is cooked through.

6 Place several pieces of fish on each plate and cover with sauce.

ARROZ con BACALAO y ALCACHOFAS

RICE WITH SALT COD AND ARTICHOKES

SERVES 4

Restaurante El Ventorrillo del Chato is an old coach inn on the sandy spine of the isthmus that connects the city of Cádiz to the mainland. Antique furniture and arcane equine bridlery adorns the walls, and there is a certain laddishness about the place. Perhaps it is the restrained cheek of the suited waiters or the name itself (*el chato* is *Gaditano* slang for 'flat nose', as the original owner had a great big honker), but the same robustness and vitality can be found in the good, honest yet finessed *Gaditano* cooking here. In this dish, the chef marries two strong flavours – artichokes and salt cod – with rice cooked in a rich *sofrito*. Try this early in the season, when smaller artichokes are available, or use preserved artichokes instead. And remember you'll need to start desalinating the salt cod a couple of days in advance.

300 g salt cod fillet
pinch of saffron threads
60 ml extra virgin olive oil
3 white onions, finely diced
sea salt
3 garlic cloves, chopped
3 fresh bay leaves
½ large red capsicum (pepper),
  roughly diced
3 ripe tomatoes, cut in half,
  grated, skins discarded
220 g Calasparra rice
6 spears asparagus, cut in half

BRAISED ARTICHOKES

juice of 1 lemon
4 large artichokes
2 small white onions, diced
3 garlic cloves, diced
large handful of flat-leaf
  parsley leaves,
  roughly chopped
sea salt and freshly ground
  black pepper

1 Wash the excess salt off the salt cod, then place in a large bowl. Cover with water and leave to soak for 36 hours, changing the water three times. Drain, then cut the fillet into four thick slices.

2 To prepare the artichokes, half-fill a bowl with water and add the lemon juice. Use a paring knife to peel and trim the outer layers of the artichokes, leaving only the heart and several centimetres of peeled stem. Place in the acidulated water to stop them from discolouring.

3 Drain the artichokes and place in a large saucepan with the onion, garlic and parsley. Cover with cold water and season with salt and pepper, then bring to a simmer over medium heat. Reduce the heat to low and simmer gently for 20 minutes or until the artichokes are soft. Remove the artichokes and set aside, then strain the stock and reserve for cooking the rice.

4 In a small heavy-based frying pan, toast the saffron for a minute or so over medium heat until you just start to smell the aroma. Add a couple of tablespoons of the artichoke stock to the saffron, swirl it around, then tip the contents of the frying pan back into the pan with the artichoke stock.

5 Make a *sofrito* by pouring half of the olive oil into a 34 cm paella pan or large, deep frying pan and placing over low–medium heat. When the oil is hot, add the onion with a pinch of salt and cook for 15 minutes, stirring occasionally, until soft but not browned. Stir in the garlic and bay leaves and cook for 2 minutes. Add the capsicum

and cook for 15 minutes or until soft. Add the tomato pulp and continue cooking for 15 minutes, stirring occasionally, until the *sofrito* has reduced to a jam-like consistency.

6 Add the rice, asparagus and salt to the *sofrito* and mix in well. Place the paella pan on a large gas burner or the flat grillplate of a barbecue (the heat needs to cover the entire base of the pan, so the rice cooks evenly). Add 850 ml of the artichoke stock, stir once and bring to a simmer. From now on, resist the temptation to stir.

7 Arrange the artichokes evenly over the rice and cook for 10 minutes; during this time, the rice will expand a little. Place the salt cod slices in between the artichokes and cook for another 6–7 minutes or until the rice is done but not overcooked – it should still be slightly firm to the tooth.

8 Increase the heat to high for 2 minutes, so a crust forms on the bottom. This is called the *socarrat* and is highly prized.

9 Remove the pan from the heat, cover with a clean tea towel and leave to sit for 5–7 minutes; this allows the last of the liquid to be absorbed and the flavours to develop. Serve straight from the pan.

Lunch of cod and artichokes in rice (see page 144)
in the characterful Restaurante del Chato

PESCAÍTO FRITO

DEEP-FRIED MACKEREL

SERVES 4-6

The first thing I do when I arrive back in Andalusia is head to the nearest *freiduría* and buy a paper cone of deep-fried fish. A *freiduría* is Spain's equivalent of a fish and chip shop, serving all manner of semolina-dusted fish and seafood throughout the day and well into the night. Some of the fish – *cazón* (dogfish) in particular – is marinated in a fragrant blend of herbs and sharp vinegar that gives the fish a clean, fresh tang. This version was inspired by Restaurante Miguel in San Fernando, just outside Cádiz.

4 blue mackerel or other
  small fish, such as sand
  whiting (about 150–200 g
  each), cleaned
2 tablespoons dried oregano
1 tablespoon ground cumin
3 garlic cloves, finely chopped
100 ml white wine vinegar
1 litre olive oil, for deep-frying
150 g fine semolina
sea salt and freshly ground
  black pepper
1 teaspoon fine salt
lemon wedges, to serve
  (optional)

1 Remove the head from the fish and discard. Rinse the fish well, inside and out, then cut into slices, starting with an 8–10 cm length at the tail end, then 2 cm thick slices for the rest of the body.

2 Place the fish pieces in a glass or ceramic bowl and add the oregano, cumin, garlic and vinegar. Leave to marinate for 1 hour.

3 Pour the olive oil into a heavy-based saucepan or wok. Heat the oil to 170°C or until a cube of bread dropped into the oil browns in 15 seconds.

4 Place the semolina in a large bowl and season with sea salt and pepper. Season the fish well with the fine salt, mixing well with your hands. Take the fish from the bowl, but don't drain. Dredge the fish in the semolina.

5 Working in batches of four or five pieces of fish at a time, deep-fry for about 7–8 minutes until crisp and brown. Drain on a plate lined with paper towel and season with sea salt.

6 Repeat with the remaining pieces of fish, allowing the oil to come back to the correct heat before you cook each batch.

7 Serve with lemon wedges, if using.

CHICHARRONES

CRISP PORK JOWL

SERVES 6

The food at Casa Manteca is wonderful, but there is not a chef to be seen. This local drinking hole in the historic heart of Cádiz feels like part sports bar and part corner grocer. Behind the bar are shelves stacked with the finest preserved food from around Spain. You want mussels? The bartender will open a tin to order. You want *mojama*? A loin of cured tuna will be thinly sliced as you watch. Jamón, cheese, razor clams, and my favourite – *chicharrones* – are all served onto plates by the bar staff. *Chicharrones* are Spain's answer to pork crackling: slowly fried pieces of pork skin, fat and flesh that are deliciously salty and the perfect balance of juicy and crispy.

1 kg pork jowl (pre-order
   from your butcher)
   or pork belly
60 g rock salt
12 whole black peppercorns
2 teaspoons dried oregano
3 fresh bay leaves
8 garlic cloves, skin on
250 ml extra virgin olive oil
sea salt

1 Using a very sharp knife, cut the pork jowl into 2 cm cubes. Place in a glass or ceramic bowl with the rock salt and peppercorns. Mix well, then cover and refrigerate for 12 hours to cure.

2 Rinse the salt off the pork under cold running water, then leave to drain in a colander.

3 Place the pork in a *perol* (see page 380) or flat-bottomed wok and add the oregano, bay leaves and garlic, along with 250 ml of water. Place over medium heat, cover and simmer, stirring occasionally, for 30 minutes or until the water has evaporated.

4 Add the olive oil, stir well, then cover and cook over low–medium heat for 1½ hours, stirring occasionally so the meat doesn't stick. Be careful, as the *chicharrones* will spit during cooking – when they're done, they should be browned and crisp.

5 Using a slotted spoon, remove the *chicharrones* from the oil and drain on a plate lined with paper towel. Season well with sea salt, then transfer to a serving plate. Eat while still warm or at room temperature.

SHERRY

At an age when retirement is well behind most people, Doña Pilar Plá Pechovierto is still a powerhouse in the world of sherry. Widowed forty years ago, at a time when Spanish women were still supposed to stay at home cooking and cleaning, she took over the family business, El Maestro Sierra, and turned it into a world-renowned producer admired for its boutique sherries. She very quickly had to learn the intricacies of the *solera* system of aging sherry, in which new sherry is added to the top barrels of the stack, while each year a little of the most mature sherry is racked to the lower barrels, from where it is bottled. She offers us a glass of oloroso. Nutty and complex, it probably contains a little of the company's very first vintage from 180 years ago. Despite the heat outside, the air inside the bodega is cool and moist. She grabs my arm, 'This is a temple to climate,' she says. 'The wind from El Puerto de Santa María cools the barrels and we spray them with water pumped from the well below us.'

Later we taste Doña Pilar's other sherries with her daughter María del Carmen Borrego Plá. We have to move as one of the workers starts to rack a barrel near us, siphoning off sherry by sucking on a hose. He stops when the sherry hits his mouth. 'We may be old-fashioned here,' says Doña Pilar, with a smile forming on her lips, 'but we are happy.'

FINO
SOLERA

OLOROSO
1/120

GALLETAS DE ALMENDRAS Y LIMÓN

ANNIE'S ALMOND AND LEMON BISCUITS

MAKES ABOUT 20

Annie Manson is a Scot with a love of sherry – which is not that surprising, as some great whiskys are aged in old sherry casks. She lives in Vejer de la Frontera, a white hilltop town just inland from the coast. On a clear day you can see to Cabo de Trafalgar. On a very clear day you can see past Gibraltar toward the Rif mountain range in Morocco. Her love of the Andalusians and their food is palpable, and the way she cooks is very Spanish. But one of her best dishes is a biscuit that combines the freshest of Spanish ingredients with the best of Scottish baking skills – a biscuit she serves with a small glass of thick, sweet Pedro Ximénez sherry.

300 g blanched almonds
225 g white sugar
finely grated zest of 2 lemons
½ teaspoon almond essence
2 egg whites
20 whole blanched almonds,
to decorate

1 Preheat the oven to 170°C/150°C fan.

2 Line two baking trays with baking paper.

3 Using a food processor, grind the almonds to the consistency of breadcrumbs. Add the sugar, lemon zest and almond essence, pulse a couple of times to mix, then place in a large bowl.

4 In a clean bowl, whisk the egg whites to soft peaks. Using a large metal spoon, fold a third of the egg white into the almond mixture to loosen the mixture, then gently fold in the remaining egg white.

5 Place tablespoonfuls of the mixture evenly onto the prepared baking trays, leaving enough room between the biscuits so they can spread a little. Gently flatten them, then place an almond on top of each biscuit, pressing down lightly.

6 Bake for 20 minutes until golden, then allow to cool a wire cake rack. The biscuits will be soft when they come out of the oven, but will harden up as they cool. Any not eaten straight away can be kept for up to 6 days in an airtight container.

Annie B's Spanish Kitchen 🍷✕

www.anniebspain.com

Annie Manson is a Scot whose understanding of the way of life in Cádiz is palpable, and she shares her enthusiasm for the province and its culture in the best way possible, taking clients to visit markets and producers then returning with the goods to cook authentic versions of local dishes. Her hands-on cooking classes are held in her beautiful house, a restored Andalusian patio home in Vejer de la Frontera, with views overlooking the local church, the Mediterranean and Morocco in the distance.

El Ventorrillo del Chato 🍷✕

Avenida Vía Augusta Julia S/N, Cádiz; tel 956 25 00 25
www.ventorrilloelchato.com

Originally a coaching inn on the ribbon-thin sandy isthmus that connects Cádiz to the mainland (Via Augusta was the old road to Rome), this formal restaurant is furnished with antiques and serves old-fashioned but exceptionally tasty food. Start with the tuna tartare, then move on to the chickpeas cooked in cod stock, beautifully fragrant tripe, paella and *babetas*, or pasta braised in stock (see page 128).

Taberna Casa Manteca 🍷✕

Calle del Corralón de los Carros 66, Cádiz; tel 956 21 36 03

Even though they don't cook a thing in this little corner bar, this is where you'll find some of the best bar food in Spain. Everything served here is among the finest tinned, salted, fermented and otherwise preserved food in the nation delivered in a fun atmosphere by the owner Tomás Ruiz, son of a famous bullfighter.

Bar Pájaro Pinto 🍷✕

Plaza Tío de la Tiza 12, Cádiz; tel 956 21 20 82

Cádiz is dotted with little squares like this plaza, and most of them have a bar or two for snacking and drinking. Come here for the *zanahorias aliñás* (carrots marinated in spices), and the *chipirones* (baby cuttlefish) cooked on the grillplate.

Bar El Veedor 🍷✕

Calle Vea Murguía 10, Cádiz; tel 956 21 29 64

Traditionally, imported goods were called *ultramarinos* and were sold in bar-like shops, where there were two sections: one for imported goods, and the other for liquor. This old bar still has the two sections, and is an authentic place to have a glass of sherry and perhaps some cheese or jamón.

Parador de Cádiz 🍷 ✕ ⌂

**Avenida Duque de Nájera 9, Cádiz;
tel 956 22 69 05**
www.parador.es

Also known as the Hotel Atlántico, this
ultra-modern parador perched at the end of
the peninsula has stunning views across the
Atlantic and over the plains to the sierras.

Bodega el Maestro Sierra 🍷 ✕

**Plaza Silos 5, Jerez de la Frontera;
tel 956 34 24 33**
www.maestrosierra.com

Nothing much has changed since the 1960s
at this very picturesque bodega, where
sherries have been made since 1830 – its
oloroso is particularly outstanding. Open
for cellar-door sales.

La Moderna 🍷 ✕

Calle Larga 67, Jerez de la Frontera

Back in its day it might have been modern,
but La Moderna is now an old-school
bar serving old blokes some really good
albóndigas (meatballs) and *riñones al vinagre
de Jerez* (kidneys with sherry vinegar).

Bar Juanito 🍷 ✕

**Calle de Pescadería Vieja 8, Jerez de la
Frontera; tel 956 34 12 18**
www.bar-juanito.com

A stalwart of the city since 1943, this is as
good a place as any to drink sherry and
sample some local dishes. The bar is backed
by a mosaic mural depicting an old bodega.
Try the *albóndigas* (meatballs) or *costillas en
adobo* (pork ribs marinated with herbs and
cooked in lard and sherry vinegar). The
classic dish here, however, is *alcachofas*,
slow-cooked artichokes (see page 126).

Tabanco San Pablo 🍷 ✕

Calle San Pablo 12, Jerez de la Frontera; tel 956 33 84 36 www.tabancosanpablo.es

Tabancos are taverns that originally sold sherry. Then they were licensed to give customers
a little to taste, and therefore some food needed to be served. Look out for *tabancos* throughout
the Jerez district as fun places, often with original nineteenth-century décor, for a drink and
a snack. This one attracts a young crowd sipping glasses of fino and sharing bowls of olives.

El Guitarrón de San Pedro 🍷 ✕

**Calle Bizcocheros 16, Jerez de la
Frontera; tel 649 65 69 18**

Sit down, have a beer or a sherry and enjoy
the locals who drop by for a flamenco guitar
jam. The tortillas here weigh in at a massive
5 kilos and are very juicy and delicious. They
also pride themselves on their sheep's milk
cheese cured in wheat bran, El Bosqueño.

Hotel Asta Regia

**San Agustín 9, Jerez de la Frontera;
tel 956 32 79 11
www.hotelastaregiajerez.com**

This newly built, affordable and comfortable
hotel is located on a pleasant plaza in the
global capital of sherry, just a short walk
from historic bars and taverns.

Hotel Chancillería

**Calle Chancillería 21, Jerez de la
Frontera; tel 956 30 10 38
www.hotelchancilleria.com**

A charming hotel overlooking the old town,
complete with a restaurant that combines
traditional flavours with modernist
techniques.

Taberna El Loli

**Calle Pozo Amarguillo 16, Sanlúcar de
Barrameda; tel 956 36 96 73**

This little place in the old town is known
for its *corvina a la Roteña*, fish in the style
of Rota, a town 10 kilometres away that's
famous for a rich onion sauce made with
capsicums.

Hospedería Duques de Medina Sidonia

**Plaza Condes de Niebla, 1, Sanlúcar de
Barrameda; tel 956 36 01 61
www.fcmedinasidonia.com**

Here's a chance to stay in a twelfth-century
palace in the beautiful sherry-producing
town of Sanlúcar de Barrameda. Still
owned by Doña Isabel Álvarez de Toledo,
the 21st Duchess of Medina Sidonia, there
are just nine rooms available as overnight
accommodation.

Casa Balbino

Plaza del Cabildo 14, Sanlúcar de Barrameda; tel 956 36 05 13 www. casabalbino.com

At this busy bar in the central square, over forty different seafood dishes are served, including
their famous *tortillas de camarones* (fried shrimp cakes, pictured above). Find a small table,
order at the bar and when you've eaten your fill, the barmen will tot up the bill in chalk
directly on the marble bar.

Aponiente

**Calle Puerto Escondido 6, El Puerto de
Santa María; tel 956 85 18 70
www.aponiente.com**

In 2013 chef Ángel León was named the
top chef in Spain by the Royal Spanish
Academy of Gastronomy. His food is at
the vanguard of modern Spanish cooking,
and is truly delicious. One of his most
famous dishes is rich and creamy rice
cooked with algae and smoked fish in bitter
orange pickle. Pictured is his head chef,
Juan Luís Fernández.

Venta la Feria

**Carretera de Sanlúcar km 2, El Puerto de
Santa María; tel 956 85 95 02
www.ventalaferia.com**

A *venta* is the Spanish equivalent of an
English inn. Over the years, this particular
venta, on the road between Sanlúcar de
Barrameda and Cádiz, has specialised in
rice dishes. Here you'll find some great
examples of rich rice dishes and *guisos
marineros*, or fishermen's stews, made with
fish from the bay. Don't let the mock-inn
décor put you off – this is the real deal.

Cádiz El Chico 🍷✕

**Plaza España 8, Grazalema;
tel 956 13 20 27**

In the Sierra de Grazalema Natural Park you'll find Grazalema, a maze of cobbled streets that twist and turn. Near the town's square is this little oak-panelled restaurant that specialises in roasted meats such as venison and lamb. Come here for lunch, as the menu is limited in the evenings. While you're here, take a look at the old water-driven mill on the edge of town – it's powered by the Río Guadalete, the river that eventually flows into the Atlantic at El Puerto de Santa María.

Hotel Fuerte Grazalema 🍷✕🏠

Baldío de los Alamillos Carretera A-372, km 53, Grazalema; tel 902 34 34 10 www.fuertehoteles.com

This modern hotel situated in the Sierra de Grazalema Natural Park may feel slightly institutional, but it's affordable and has an excellent location, with the village of Grazalema only 5 kilometres away, and Ronda within a half-hour's drive.

Restaurante Casa Miguel 🍷✕🏠

Calle San Onofre 49, San Fernando; tel 956 89 16 76

South of the old city of Cádiz, in a lively and slightly gritty maritime suburb, chef Miguel López cooks fish freshly harvested from the ancient salt pans across the road. His restaurant's plain façade and working fishermen's bar hides the most amiable courtyard and dining room, and his respectful and simple preparation of the local seafood harvest is recognised as being among the best in Spain. Try the *anguila frita*, fried eel (pictured above); *pescaíto frito*, fried fish (see page 149); *arroz con algas*, rice with seaweed; and *revuelto de hinojo marino y erizos*, eggs with samphire and sea urchin (see page 134).

Sal Virgen de la Salina de San Vincente 🛍

Carretera de la Carraca 48, San Fernando; tel 627 91 20 91 www.salvirgen.es

A chance to see how salt has been made in the *esteros* wetlands surrounding Cádiz for thousands of years, plus salt sales of the very fine *sal de hielo*.

Casa Varo 🍷✕

Calle Nuestra Señora de la Oliva 9, Vejer de la Frontera; tel 956 44 77 34
www.casavaro.com

In a small square by the Convento de las Monjas Concepcionistas is this restaurant that treads the line between modernism and tradition, serving fresh versions of classic dishes – perhaps croquettes of sea urchin, cuttlefish cooked in its own ink and 'meatballs' of tuna in onion sauce.

Bar Navarro 🍷✕

Calle Juan Bueno, 8, Vejer de la Frontera; tel 956 45 02 74

In this cute little bar in the old part of town, you'll find some good jamón and a few rustic dishes cooked by Pepi Navarro (see page 104).

Casa La Siesta 🍷✕🏠

Los Parralejos S/N, Vejer de la Frontera; tel 699 61 94 30
www.casalasiesta.com

This country house hotel in the hills behind Vejer de la Frontera makes a luxurious base for exploring the region.

La Casa del Califa 🍷✕🏠

Plaza de España 16, Vejer de la Frontera; tel 956 44 77 30
www.lacasadelcalifa.com

Right in the heart of the Arab-built white village of Vejer de la Frontera, this Michelin-recommended hotel has comfortable rooms and a restaurant specialising in the food of North Africa and the Middle East.

El Campero 🍷✕

Avda de la Constitución, local 5C, Barbate; tel 956 43 23 00
www.restauranteelcampero.es

This is the restaurant you come to in Spain to experience nose-to-tail eating of tuna, all 24 different cuts of it: try *marmo*, cut from the back of the neck, or the rich cured *ventresca* or belly, the 'wagyu of the sea'. The location is in a modern part of this ancient town, but the retro-nautical theme and excellent service encourages lingering over a long lunch.

Herpac 🛍️✕

Polígono Industrial El Olivar S/N, Barbate; tel 956 43 13 76
www.herpac.com

This factory on the edge of the fishing town of Barbate produces a large range of salted and preserved tuna and other fish, and there's an outlet at the front of the factory where you can buy good-quality *mojama* and various cuts of tuna preserved in jars and cans.

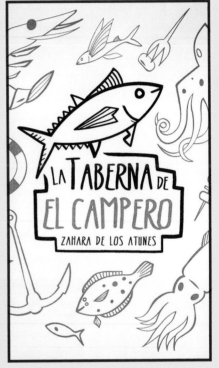

La Taberna de El Campero 🍷✕🏠

Calle María Luisa 6, Zahara de los Atunes; tel 956 43 90 36

The younger sibling of the more refined El Campero in Barbate, this is a much simpler bar serving seafood in nearby Zahara de los Atunes, just along the coast.

La Sacristía 🍷✕🏠

Calle San Donato 8, Tarifa; tel 956 68 17 59
www.lasacristia.net

This charming guesthouse in a seventeenth-century townhouse is situated in the southernmost town in Europe, just across the Strait of Gibraltar from Morocco – it makes a perfect place to while away a few days at the beach.

Great white apartments rise from the sand in an almost unbroken line from somewhere near Gibraltar to the coast of Granada. Málaga's Mediterranean shores, once a string of villages, have been consumed by the Costa del Sol, Europe's seaside playground. Here fishing cottages have become fish and chip shops for the English, and the olive groves have been uprooted for golf courses. This is also one of the most dynamic provinces in Spain, where a youthful energy and sunny disposition prevails.

The capital city of Málaga is the fourth most-wealthy city in the country, and has been attracting people from overseas since the Phoenicians established a port here in 700 BC. The Romans and the Arabs followed, leaving behind a rich legacy. Málaga's skyline is dominated by an eleventh-century Moorish citadel, itself built over a first-century Roman theatre. Happily, the latest invasion, mass tourism, hasn't trampled over the architectural heritage, but simply built around it. What's more, the influx of tourist euros has enabled chefs to offer experimental cuisine, with the likes of Málaga chefs Dani García and José Carlos García serving some of the most exciting modernist food in Spain. The concentration of visitors also supports two excellent museums: one housing the Carmen Thyssen collection, and another dedicated to local painter Pablo Picasso.

To the west lies Marbella, perhaps one of the best-known tourist towns on the planet, but its shores are also host to one of the busiest fishing ports on the Mediterranean. And at its heart is an old town that is very much intact, its narrow laneways and sheltered town square shaded by orange trees.

Behind the bustling coastal strip of the Costa del Sol lies a classic Andalusian landscape, with ancient cities, small towns nestled into steep mountains, and plains planted with olive groves and vineyards. Ronda, for example, straddles a dramatic hundred-metre-deep gorge, the two halves of the city joined by the soaring arches of the Puente Árabe, way above the clear green waters of the Guadalevín River. Inland, in places like Ronda and Antequera, relics of the province's traditional cuisine hold sway, such as *migas*, moist blood sausage and breadcrumbs (see page 344), and *porras*, simple cold soups thickened with bread (see page 179) – hearty dishes with a punch of flavour that belies the simplicity of their making.

It is the fish, however, that draws me back to Málaga. Here the cooks' appreciation for simple and fast ways of turning the small fish, prawns and shellfish of the Mediterranean into the most delicious dishes keeps me on the streets well into the night, searching for yet another way of eating prawns and calamari.

The Guadalevin cascades for 100 metres
as it flows by the historic city of Ronda

ACEITUNAS ALIÑADAS

MARINATED OLIVES

Up in the Sierra de las Nieves, behind the resort town of Marbella, Paqui Martín prepares a great big bowl of preserved olives in the kitchen of her old farmhouse. With its squat profile and terracotta roof tiles, hers is typical of those built in the 1700s. In the surrounding hills orange trees and scores of olive trees thrive, and the air is perfumed by wild fennel and thyme. She says that her olives are already naturally fragrant as they ripen among these herbs, but she loves to make them even more aromatic by marinating them in garlic, red peppers, fennel, thyme and garlic. The Spanish call the marinating process *aliñar*, and there are as many different versions as there are Spaniards. Enjoy these with an aperitif before a meal, or with a glass of sherry as a snack.

2 kg raw olives

about 200 g fine salt

1 garlic bulb, broken into cloves and crushed, but not peeled

200 ml white wine vinegar

2 tablespoons dried thyme

2 green bull horn capsicums (peppers) or 1 regular green capsicum (pepper), diced

1 large red capsicum (pepper), diced

1 litre olive oil

1 First remove the bitterness from the olives by slitting each one lengthways four or five times with a small sharp knife. Place in a glass or ceramic bowl, cover with cold water and leave to soak for 15 days, changing the water daily.

2 Make a brine by mixing the salt with 2 litres of water. Pour enough brine into the bowl to cover the olives. Add the garlic, vinegar, thyme and capsicums. Stir well, then cover and leave to cure for 5 days.

3 Drain, then place the olives, herbs, garlic and capsicum into sterilised glass jars (see page 383) and cover with the olive oil. Seal and store in a dark place for up 6 months.

CONCHAS FINAS

SCALLOPS WITH LEMON

SERVES 4–6

Málaga's Mercado de la Merced is like a concrete jewel box – brutal on the outside, but with a wealth of Andalusian food culture inside. Stallholder José Antonio Romero taps the bench on which his clams sit. Obediently, they close their gaping shells. He grew up in and around the market, never straying far from his dad's seafood stall. So perhaps it is no surprise that he followed in his father's footsteps – and is still affectionately known as *El niño de las almejas*, or 'Clam boy'. He holds out a large fat clam. 'The best way to eat these,' he says, 'is straight from the shell.' To prove a point, he takes a clam, cuts the adductor muscle and squeezes over some lemon. He hands it to me – it is delicious, with the salty tang of the sea and a lingering sweetness. When you can get your hands on really fresh shellfish such as oysters, mussels, clams and scallops, eating them straight from the shell, washed down with a flinty white wine, is one of life's little joys.

If you can find live scallops in the shell, so much the better: simply insert a small sharp knife between the top and bottom shells and run the blade under the white adductor muscle; leave the red roe intact.

12 fresh scallops, on the half shell
sea salt and freshly ground black pepper (optional)
juice of 1 lemon
extra virgin olive oil

1 Sprinkle each scallop with a pinch of salt and a turn of pepper (if using). Follow with a squeeze of lemon juice and a drizzle of extra virgin olive oil.

2 Turn each scallop over in its shell, then eat straightaway.

AJOBLANCO DE PIÑONES

CHILLED PINE NUT GAZPACHO

SERVES 4-6

I like to think of gazpachos as loosely related cold soups that have pounded bread and garlic at the root of their family tree. Added to this could be nuts, often vegetables or perhaps fruit – one of chef Dani García's signature dishes in the past has been cherry gazpacho with anchovy. *Ajoblanco* is a deliciously refreshing pick-me-up and is usually made with almonds, but this version uses pine nuts, which are native to the Mediterranean coast. Keep a jug of this in the fridge on a hot summer's day when family and friends are around.

100 g two-day-old bread,
    without crusts
200 g pine nuts
½ garlic clove
100 ml mild-flavoured
    extra virgin olive oil,
    plus extra to serve
1½ tablespoons sherry vinegar
1 tablespoon sea salt

1 Break the bread into pieces about the size of a walnut. Place in a shallow bowl, cover with cold water and leave to stand for 5 minutes.

2 Use your hands to firmly squeeze out the bread, then place in a blender. Add the pine nuts, garlic, olive oil, sherry vinegar and salt and blend thoroughly to form a very smooth paste. Add 1.5 litres of cold water and blend again until smooth and velvety.

3 Chill in the fridge for 2–3 hours before serving. Garnish with a few drops of extra virgin olive oil.

PORRAS ANTEQUERANAS DE TOMATE, AJO Y NARANJA

TOMATO, GARLIC AND ORANGE CHILLED SOUPS

SERVES 4–6

Small bowls of these three soups are served as a tasty starter in traditionalist chef Charo Carmona's restaurant Coso San Francisco, in the old town of Antequera, about 50 kilometres north of Málaga. They are all offshoots of gazpacho – itself a product of *la cocina pobre*, 'the cuisine of the poor'. By adding whatever you have around to moist bread, you can create variations that are not only delicious but sustaining.

sea salt

extra virgin olive oil, for drizzling

CHILLED TOMATO SOUP

200 g two-day-old bread,
 without crusts

4 ripe tomatoes

1 green bull horn capsicum
 (pepper) or ½ regular green
 capsicum (pepper), diced

2 small garlic cloves, peeled

100 ml mild-flavoured extra
 virgin olive oil, such
 as hojiblanca

1 tablespoon sherry vinegar

CHILLED ORANGE SOUP

300 g two-day-old bread,
 without crusts

450 ml freshly squeezed orange
 juice (from 3–4 oranges)

1 garlic clove, peeled

60 ml mild-flavoured extra virgin
 olive oil, such as hojiblanca

CHILLED GARLIC SOUP

250 g two-day-old bread,
 without crusts

4 garlic cloves, peeled

40 ml sherry vinegar

100 ml mild-flavoured extra virgin
 olive oil, such as hojiblanca

1 For the chilled tomato soup, break the bread into pieces about the size of a walnut. Place in a shallow bowl, cover with cold water and leave to stand for 5 minutes. Meanwhile, peel and chop the tomatoes, then place in a blender with the capsicum and garlic and blend until smooth. Use your hands to firmly squeeze out the bread, then add it to the blender, along with the olive oil and vinegar. Blend to a very smooth puree, then season with salt and blend again. Transfer to a bowl and refrigerate for an hour or so until thoroughly chilled.

2 For the chilled orange soup, break the bread into pieces about the size of a walnut. Place in a shallow bowl and cover with the orange juice, mixing well with your hands, then leave to stand for 5 minutes. Transfer the bread and orange juice to a blender, along with the garlic, and blend until very smooth. With the blender running at its slowest speed, gradually drizzle in the olive oil. Puree until very smooth, then season with salt and blend again. Transfer to a bowl and refrigerate for an hour or so until thoroughly chilled.

3 For the chilled garlic soup, break the bread into pieces about the size of a walnut. Place in a shallow bowl, cover with cold water and leave to stand for 15 minutes. Lift the bread out of the water and let it drain, but don't squeeze it. Place in a blender with the garlic and vinegar and blend to a smooth puree. With the blender running at its slowest speed, gradually drizzle in the olive oil. Puree until emulsified, then season with salt and blend again on high speed. Transfer to a bowl and refrigerate for an hour or so until thoroughly chilled.

4 To serve, pour each soup into small serving bowls and drizzle with a little extra virgin olive oil.

PIMIENTOS Y TOMATES RELLENOS

STUFFED TOMATOES AND CAPSICUMS

SERVES 6

The truth of the matter is that the photographer for this book, Alan Benson, followed his nose while the rest of us were eating lunch. Somehow he garnered an invitation into the kitchen of Coso San Francisco, where a young chef was frying off one of my favourite dishes – stuffed tomatoes and capsicums. This is a simple dish you'll find cooked in homes across Andalusia. You need small capsicums for this dish – look for them in good greengrocers or Middle Eastern food shops.

9 medium-sized tomatoes

9 small green capsicums
   (peppers)

1 litre olive oil, for deep-frying

2 eggs

100 g plain flour

sea salt and freshly ground
   black pepper

STUFFING

2 tablespoons extra virgin
   olive oil

1 brown onion, finely diced

sea salt

2 garlic cloves, finely chopped

1 small green capsicum
   (pepper), finely diced

150 g two-day-old bread,
   without crusts, cut into
   large cubes

300 ml milk

550 g pork mince

550 g veal mince

1 egg, lightly beaten

70 g jamón, finely diced

½ teaspoon freshly grated
   nutmeg

2 tablespoons chopped
   flat-leaf parsley

1 For the stuffing, pour the olive oil into a heavy-based frying pan and place over medium heat. Add the onion and a pinch of salt and cook for 10 minutes, stirring occasionally, until soft and translucent. Add the garlic and green capsicum and cook for 10 minutes or until the capsicum is soft. Set aside to cool. Place the bread in a bowl, cover with the milk and stand for 10 minutes. Use your hands to squeeze out the bread (discard the milk), then transfer to a large bowl. Add the mince and work well with your hands until the mixture becomes a little sticky. Add the egg, together with the cooked onion and capsicum, jamón, nutmeg, parsley and 1 tablespoon of salt. Mix thoroughly, then cover and set aside.

2 Slice off the top 5 mm of each tomato. Using a teaspoon, hollow out the tomato by scraping out the cores and seeds. Cut about 5 mm off the stalk end of each capsicum, then use a small sharp knife to cut out the seeds and membranes. Using a teaspoon, stuff the tomatoes and capsicums firmly with the mince mixture – the stuffing should be mounded just over the rim. Smooth with the back of a spoon.

3 Pour the olive oil into a *perol* (see page 380) or flat-bottomed wok and heat to 160°C or until a cube of bread dropped into the oil browns in 20 seconds. Crack the eggs into a bowl and beat lightly. Place the flour in a shallow bowl and season with salt and pepper.

4 Fry the capsicums first. Take each capsicum and dip the open end into the seasoned flour and then into the beaten egg. Using tongs, gently lower the capsicums into the hot oil, open end first, and cook for a minute or so until the stuffing browns a little. Carefully turn the capsicums and leave to cook on one side for 8–10 minutes, then turn and cook for a further 8–10 minutes or until cooked through. Drain on paper towel. Cook the tomatoes in the same way.

5 Sprinkle the capsicums and tomatoes with sea salt and serve warm.

HUEVOS RELLENOS

EGGS STUFFED WITH TUNA

SERVES 6

This is classic old-school Spanish cooking straight from the kitchen of El Estrecho in Marbella. *Estrecho* means 'straits' or 'narrows' in English, and sure enough, you'll find this restaurant down a very narrow laneway. The chef here is Reyes Cantarero, who learned to cook classic *Malageuño* dishes from her mother, who in turn learned from her mother-in-law. These stuffed eggs make a great addition to a salad buffet or as a little dish to have with a glass of wine or sherry, just like they do in Marbella. Tomato *frito* is a Spanish condiment that's available from Spanish food stores; if you can't find it, just leave it out. As you can see from the photograph, Spaniards have a heavy hand with the mayo – but feel free to use less than the amount given here, if you prefer.

13 eggs, hard-boiled

2 × 110 g cans tuna in oil, drained

100 g piquillo peppers (see page 380), drained

400 g garlic mayonnaise (see page 380)

sea salt

80 ml tomato *frito* (optional)

1 tablespoon finely chopped flat-leaf parsley

1 tomato, sliced

1 Peel the eggs. Carefully slice each egg in half lengthways so as not to break the whites. Remove and reserve the yolks, leaving the whites with a cavity to stuff.

2 Place the drained tuna, peppers, 80 g of the mayonnaise and 12 of the hard-boiled egg yolks in a food processor. Season with a pinch of salt and blend to a rough puree. Transfer to a piping bag fitted with a 1 cm plain nozzle and generously fill each egg half. Place the stuffed egg halves on a plate and leave in the fridge to chill for an hour.

3 Place an egg half on top of another egg half and press gently to form an entire egg shape again. Repeat with the remaining egg halves.

4 Spread 80 g of the mayonnaise over a large serving plate, then arrange the stuffed eggs on top. Cover with the remaining mayonnaise and return to the fridge for a couple of hours before serving. Grate the remaining egg yolk over the top, then garnish with tomato *frito* (if using), chopped parsley and sliced tomato.

ESPINACAS CON GARBANZOS Y PIÑONES

SPICED SPINACH WITH CHICKPEAS AND PINE NUTS

SERVES 4–6

Andalusians love spice. Not spicy as in chilli-hot, but spicy as in rich blends of exotic seeds, nuts and bark. One of the most potent relics of the Moorish culinary tradition in Spain are the spice stalls in the markets, which are reminiscent of Arabic souks. Here spice traders sell readymade mixes of spices, perhaps for snails, tripe, *potaje* soup or *berza* stew (see page 194). This fragrant recipe for spinach and pine nuts comes from Paqui del Pino, a trader who sells 120 different spices at the Antequera Market.

180 g dried chickpeas

30 g pine nuts

80 ml olive oil

1 garlic bulb, broken into cloves, but not peeled

2–3 slices two-day-old bread

sea salt

1½ tablespoons ground cumin

2 teaspoons sweet Spanish paprika

700 g spinach leaves, well-washed and drained

1 tablespoon sherry vinegar

1 Soak the chickpeas overnight, then drain and rinse under cold running water.

2 Bring a large saucepan of water to the boil. Add the chickpeas and simmer for 1½ hours or until tender, then drain.

3 Meanwhile, toast the pine nuts in a heavy-based frying pan over medium heat for 2–3 minutes or until aromatic and lightly browned. Transfer to a plate and set aside.

4 Pour the olive oil into the frying pan and place over medium heat. Add the garlic cloves and cook for 2–3 minutes or until their skins have browned a little. Add the bread and cook for 4–5 minutes on each side or until crisp and brown, seasoning both sides with salt. Drain the bread and garlic on paper towel.

5 When the fried bread and garlic are cool enough to handle, squeeze the garlic out of its skins into a mortar. Break the fried bread into small pieces with your hands, then add to the mortar a little a time, pounding with the pestle as you go to make a rustic paste. Add the cumin, paprika and a quarter of the cooked chickpeas. Season with a pinch of salt and grind with the pestle to make a rough paste – Andalusians call this *majada*. (Alternatively, place the ingredients in a food processor and blend to a rough paste.)

6 Pour 1.5 litres of water into a large saucepan and add 2 teaspoons of salt. Bring to the over high heat, then drop in the spinach and, once the leaves have wilted down, cover and cook for 3–4 minutes, stirring once or twice. Spoon in the *majada* and mix well, then add the pine nuts and remaining chickpeas. Bring back to a simmer, then reduce the heat to medium and continue cooking for 5–6 minutes, stirring occasionally.

7 Season with sherry vinegar and salt to taste, then serve.

GAZPACHUELO

WARM SEAFOOD AND POTATO SOUP

SERVES 4-6

We went to see one of Málaga's great traditional chefs to learn to make this classic seafood soup. He introduced himself as Pepe Oreja. 'This was a dish that was made when there was a death in the village,' said the retired chef. 'You would make too much and send a pot over to the grieving family,' he explained, as he carefully thickened the soup with garlic mayonnaise. 'It is rich but humble and very comforting.' Before we left, I asked him why he was called Pepe Oreja (*oreja* means 'ear'). 'Are you kidding?' he asked, with a laugh. He turned to reveal that one ear was twice the size of the other. Funnily enough, I had been too busy listening to what he was saying to notice his ears until that moment.

3 kg mussels, scrubbed and beards removed
3 fresh bay leaves
175 ml dry white wine
3 medium-sized potatoes, peeled and cut into 1 cm cubes
12 raw prawns, peeled and deveined
400 g garlic mayonnaise (see page 380)

1 Place a large heavy-based saucepan over high heat. When the pan is hot, add the mussels, bay leaves and wine all at the same time. Cover and cook for 6–7 minutes, stirring once or twice, until most of the mussels have opened. Remove the open mussels from the pan, then cook any stubborn ones a little longer (some have tougher adductor muscles than others) until they open and remove them as well.

2 Leave the juices in the pan, add 1 litre of water and bring to a simmer, then add the potato and simmer gently for 15 minutes. Add the prawns and cook for a further 5 minutes, then take the pan off the heat.

3 Remove the mussel meat from the shells, then return the mussel meat and any juices to the pan. Leave the soup to cool for 10 minutes.

4 Put the garlic mayonnaise into a bowl and whisk in 125 ml of the warm stock from the soup pan to temper the mayonnaise. Add the tempered mayonnaise to the soup and gently whisk through. (The mayonnaise may split if the soup is too hot; if this happens, sieve the soup to remove the potato, prawns and mussels, then blitz the liquid with a stick blender to emulsify before returning everything to the soup.)

5 Ladle into bowls and serve warm; do not reheat.

LOS BARS

BARS

The bar at Málaga's Antigua Casa de Guardia is not much to look at. A dark concrete box with great barrels lining one wall, it's old and dark and the barmen are rough. One laughingly calls himself El Gorila. A wealthy middle-aged couple enter off the street and order some drinks. 'We live in Madrid now,' the husband says. 'But when we come home to see our families, this is the first place we come to after getting off the train,' adds his wife. They explain that the bodega was founded in the 1840s when the road out the front flanked the docks, before the bay was filled in. It has since survived European wars and the Spanish Civil War, when many of the city's buildings were burned down. Up in the hills, a winery linked to the bar provides the wines poured from the old oak barrels. Sitting somewhere between sherry and table wines, the wines of Málaga have their own robust charm and match perfectly with simple bar fare of olives stuffed with tiny mussels. The place is packed, with people of all ages crammed in. Some come for the old-fashioned atmosphere; some to catch up with friends; other to make the most of the strong, cheap drink.

A short cab ride away, in another long, thin bar, the crowd is, as they say, going off. El Pimpi Florida is a 1980s time warp, from its stainless-steel bar to the smoked-glass gantry it reeks of what passed for cool in the late twentieth century. It's late at night in the middle of the week, but the beer is flowing and the plates of shellfish are charging out of the kitchen. From the sound system comes the glorious sound of Spanish '80s pop – you may not know the words, but you know the sentiment. Some women are dancing with their arms in the air, and one lithe young woman scrambles onto her boyfriend's shoulders, her thighs wrapped tight around his neck. It is now too busy to get in through the front door, so newcomers enter via the kitchen, where some stay and start chatting to the cooks as they sauté clams and mussels. Some girls return with drinks to keep the party going in the kitchen, while the Euro-beats play on in the bar on the other side of the door.

Locals mingle, eat and drink well into the
night at the infamous bar El Pimpi Florida

GAMBAS con HABICHUELAS

PRAWNS WITH WHITE BEANS

SERVES 4

While the humble prawn is often elevated on the gastronomic altar of the hotplate (see page 354) or rapidly baptised in boiling salty water (see page 72), just as often it is used to flavour less costly ingredients. Across the south of Spain, prawns appear in rice and pasta dishes, where their rich, tangy flavour and hint of iodine enriches more filling, starchy ingredients. This is a really lovely dish of prawns cooked in a rich tomato sauce with creamy white beans, a good dish for a brisk day and perfect with a full-bodied white wine. This recipe was inspired by the version cooked by Chef Reyes Cantarero at El Estrecho in Marbella.

300 g dried cannellini beans

1 fresh bay leaf

2 tomatoes

1 white onion, peeled

1 garlic bulb

2 flat-leaf parsley sprigs,
   plus extra chopped
   parsley, to serve

2 dried choricero or ñora
   peppers (see page 379)

80 ml olive oil

1 kg raw prawns, peeled
   and deveined

sea salt

1 Soak the beans for at least 3 hours or overnight, then drain and rinse under cold running water.

2 Place the beans in a large saucepan, along with the bay leaf, tomatoes, onion and garlic (all still whole). Add the parsley sprigs and dried peppers, then pour in 40 ml of the olive oil and cover with 2.6 litres of cold water. Bring to the boil over high heat, then reduce the heat to medium and simmer for 80–90 minutes or until the beans are soft and cooked.

3 Take the pan off the heat, fish out the parsley sprigs and discard. Transfer the now-soft peppers, tomatoes, onions and garlic to a plate. When cool enough to handle, peel and core the tomatoes and place in a blender. Quarter the onion and add to the blender. Cut the peppers in half and remove the seeds, then place skin-side down on a board and scrape the flesh from the skin. Add the flesh of the pepper to the blender. Cut the top off the garlic bulb and squeeze the pulpy flesh out of the skins into the blender. Add a ladleful of the bean-cooking liquid and blend to a smooth paste.

4 Scrape the paste into the pan, then stir well over high heat. Bring to a simmer, then reduce the heat to medium and season with salt to taste.

5 Pour the remaining olive oil into a large frying pan and place over high heat. When the oil is hot, add the prawns and cook for a minute or so on each side or until cooked, seasoning both sides with salt. Add the prawns to the pan with the beans and gently stir through, then cook for a further 1–2 minutes.

6 Serve in shallow bowls, sprinkled with a little chopped parsley.

BERZA

FLAMENCO STEW

SERVES 6

They serve this hearty stew on Friday nights at the Museo de Arte Flamenco Juan Breva in Málaga, prepared by the local women for those who come to see the evening performance. Outside the auditorium is a list of the rules regarding how to behave during a flamenco performance: a strict etiquette applies as to when to applaud, when to *olé* and when to remain in respectful silence. Happily, there are no such hard-and-fast rules for making *berza*, and it is often cooked with a variety of vegetables, but pumpkin usually plays the starring role.

400 g dried chickpeas
1 garlic bulb
600 g pork ribs, cut into
   4 pieces
500 g pork belly
300 g raw chorizo sausages
150 g *morcilla* sausages
600 g pumpkin (squash),
   peeled and cut into
   2 cm cubes
2 large waxy potatoes, peeled
   and cut into rough 2 cm
   pieces using the 'click'
   method (see page 379)
250 g flat runner beans,
   cut into 3 cm length
1 tablespoon chopped mint
sea salt

1 Soak the chickpeas overnight, then drain and rinse under cold running water.

2 Using a fork, prick the garlic bulb all over. Place the chickpeas, garlic, pork ribs and pork belly in a large heavy-based saucepan and cover with 4 litres of water. Bring to the boil over high heat, then reduce the heat to medium and simmer for 2 hours or until pork is tender and the chickpeas are soft. As the *berza* cooks, skim off any impurities that rise to the surface.

3 Add the chorizo, *morcilla*, pumpkin, potato, runner beans and mint to the *berza*. Bring back to the boil, then reduce the heat and simmer for 45 minutes.

4 Take out the pork ribs, pork belly, chorizo and *morcilla*. When they are cool enough to handle, cut the ribs into smaller pieces and the belly into six cubes. Cut the sausages into thick slices. Return all the meats to the pan and simmer for a minute, just to heat through.

5 Season the *berza* with salt to taste, then ladle into deep bowls, making sure there is plenty of meat, chickpeas and vegetables in each one.

LOS CHIRINGUITOS

BEACH SHACKS

The sun beats down on Abdella Tif Tallim as he tends to his sardines cooking next to a fire on one of the more rustic beaches in Marbella. Born on the coast of Morocco, he shares the Spaniards' love of seafood and cooks the *espetos* perfectly. This method of skewering fish and grilling them over the embers of a fire is found all around the Mediterranean. Abdella uses bamboo skewers soaked in water to impale the fish. 'In the old days they used green canes from the *cañaverales* (wetlands) to cook the fish. They would split the canes and slide the fish in,' he explains. Every now and then, he nudges the coals and turns the fish.

Once cooked, the sardines are sent inside to a small shack-like bar on the water's edge where they are joined by plates of flash-fried fish and prawns and served with glasses of chilled wine and ice-cold beer. Known as a *chiringuito*, this is one of thousands of casual beachside bars that line the Mediterranean coast of Spain. Some are simple shacks of dubious structural integrity, while others are more salubrious open-air bars that are incredibly popular in summer. These are places that take nothing seriously ... except for good fish and cold drinks.

ESPETOS

CHARCOAL-GRILLED SARDINES

SERVES 4-6

Andalusians are mad about their sardines and have myriad opinions as to which are best, and the best way to prepare them. Personally, I love *espetos*. You take whole sardines straight from the sea (with their guts left in) and thread them onto canes soaked in water, then you stick the canes into the sand in front of a fire on the beach. The flavour is sensational. Here I offer a more accessible method of cooking the sardines on a charcoal grill or barbecue – but if you do find yourself with canes and a fire, cook the fish about 30 cm from the fire for a few minutes on each side or until done. I can recommend the large and fleshy frozen Portuguese sardines available from specialist Spanish stores and some fishmongers.

1 kg large sardines, uncleaned

50 g coarse sea salt

2 lemons, cut into thirds

1 Rinse, but do not gut or scale the sardines. Place in a bowl and sprinkle with the salt. Set to one side.

2 Preheat a charcoal grill or barbecue to very hot.

3 Place the sardines evenly over your grill. Don't overload the grill, as you want them to cook quickly and form a crust. Resist the temptation to fiddle with your sardines. Let them cook for 5 minutes until the skin turns dark brown and firm, then turn and cook for a further 5 minutes.

4 Transfer to a plate and, when just cool enough to handle, peel away and discard the skin.

5 The way to eat these sardines is like playing a harmonica, using your hands and your mouth. The lemon is to clean your hands, not to season the sardines.

CALAMARES RELLENOS

STUFFED CALAMARI BRAISED IN WINE AND PAPRIKA

SERVES 4

Calamari and pork have a flavour affinity and appear together in dishes across the Iberian peninsula. This version is from Coso San Francisco in Antequera, where it is usually garnished with straw potatoes, as in the photo. As these are not traditionally served with this dish, I've taken the liberty of leaving them out below. Remember to ask for calamari by name as it is more tender than its tougher cousin that is simply known as squid.

4 small calamari (about
 250 g each), cleaned
 (see page 20), or ask your
 fishmonger to do this
100 ml extra virgin olive oil
1½ brown onions, finely diced
sea salt
40 g jamón, finely diced
100 g two-day-old bread,
 without crusts, cut into
 large cubes
150 ml milk
300 g pork mince
½ teaspoon freshly grated
 nutmeg
1 egg, beaten
1 tablespoon chopped
 flat-leaf parsley
4 ripe tomatoes
2 garlic cloves, finely chopped
1 teaspoon sweet Spanish
 paprika
100 ml dry white wine

1 Rinse the calamari well, then roughly chop the tentacles and wings, but keep the bodies whole.

2 Pour 40 ml of the olive oil into a heavy-based frying pan and place over medium heat. Add a third of the diced onion with a pinch of salt and cook for 10 minutes, stirring occasionally, until the onion is soft and translucent. Add the jamón and chopped calamari tentacles and wings. Season with salt and cook for 5 minutes or until the calamari is cooked. Remove from the heat and set aside.

3 Place the bread in a bowl, pour over the milk and leave to stand for 5 minutes. Use your hands to firmly squeeze out the bread (discard the milk), then transfer to a large bowl. Add the pork mince, cooked calamari mixture, nutmeg, egg, parsley and a pinch of salt, and mix well with your hands.

4 Using a teaspoon, stuff each calamari body with the pork mixture, making sure it is firmly packed in, then secure the opening with a toothpick. Place the stuffed calamari on a plate and cover with plastic film, then refrigerate for 1 hour to firm up the stuffing while you make the sauce.

5 Preheat the oven to 190°C/170°C fan. Cut the tomatoes in half and grate the cut side against a cheese grater over a bowl to pulp the flesh. Discard the skin.

6 Place a large heavy-based flameproof casserole over medium–high heat. When it is hot, add the remaining olive oil and the stuffed calamari and cook for 4–5 minutes, turning occasionally, until lightly browned. Remove and set aside. Add the remaining diced onion and a pinch of salt, reduce the heat to medium and cook, stirring occasionally, for 10 minutes or until the onion is soft and translucent. Stir in the garlic and cook for a minute, then add the tomato pulp and paprika and cook for 10 minutes, stirring occasionally. Pour in the

white wine, scraping the base of the casserole to deglaze, then return
the stuffed calamari to the sauce. Add enough water to cover the lower
third of the calamari with liquid. Bring the sauce to a simmer, then
cover the casserole with a lid and cook in the oven for 40 minutes.

7 Remove the casserole from the oven and carefully lift out the
calamari. Allow to cool a little, then slice each calamari into three
pieces crossways. To serve, place a stuffed calamari on each plate
and ladle over some of the sauce from the casserole.

The fishing port at Marbella is one
of the busiest on the Mediterranean

HUESOS DE PESCADO FRITOS

DEEP-FRIED FISH BONES

SERVES 4-6

La Traíña is a restaurant on an avenue not far from Marbella's fishing port. It is named after the family fishing boat, itself named after the colloquial contraction of 'spider web' and here referring to a boat's net. Naturally, the restaurant specialises in fish – fresh fish cooked in the classic *Marbellero* style. One of the greatest surprises was a plate of deep-fried grouper bones. When fish are filleted, there's always some flesh and skin left clinging to the skeletons – and, rather than wasting these morsels, the bones had been deep-fried, making the skin crisp and the flesh sweet and sticky. The family generously shared their tip for successful frying: use fresh clean oil, ideally a 30:70 blend of olive and sunflower oils.

1 kg fish skeletons (such
    as snapper or grouper),
    including collars
300 ml olive oil, for deep-frying
700 ml sunflower oil, for
    deep-frying
300 g plain flour
sea salt
lemon wedges, to serve

1 Prepare the skeletons by taking a pair of sturdy kitchen scissors and cutting across the ribs to remove all the spines at the top and the bottom of the fish. Use a large knife to cut between every second vertebrae – you should end up with 2–3 cm lengths of backbone with ribs attached.

2 Pour the deep-frying oils oil into a heavy-based saucepan or flat-bottomed wok and heat to 170°C or until a cube of bread dropped into the oil browns in 15 seconds.

3 Place the flour in a shallow bowl and season well with salt. Wash the fish bones in cold water and, while still wet, season generously with salt and dredge in the flour, coating them thickly.

4 Gently lower four pieces at a time into the hot oil and fry for 10–12 minutes, or until well browned and quite crisp. Repeat with the remaining pieces.

5 Drain on paper towel, season again with salt, then serve with lemon wedges.

LOMO EN ORZA

PRESERVED PORK LOIN

SERVES 6

When we think about the Spanish way of preserving pork, we tend to think about jamón and chorizo, but Spaniards also preserve pork under fat, just as the French do for confit duck. In Spain it is called *confitado*, and is made by gently poaching pork with garlic and herbs in its own fat. It sounds decadent, but the result is delicious and makes a hearty starter. Some Andalusians still prepare this dish in traditional terracotta pots, used since Roman times and known as *orza* – hence the name *lomo en orza*. This recipe comes from Charo Carmona, the chef at Coso San Francisco in Antequera, who serves it as part of her traditional menu.

850 g pork loin
60 g coarse sea salt
1.5 kg lard
5 garlic bulbs, halved
  horizontally
1 tablespoon black peppercorns
8 fresh bay leaves
fried potatoes (see page 294),
  to serve

1 Trim the pork loin of the silver outer membrane. Place the loin in a bowl and sprinkle over the salt, making sure it is well covered. Cover with plastic film and refrigerate for 12 hours, preferably overnight.

2 Melt the lard in a heavy-based saucepan over medium heat. Wash the salt off the pork loin and pat dry, then add to the pan, along with the garlic, peppercorns and bay leaves – the pork should be completely covered by the lard. Reduce the heat to low and simmer gently for 2 hours; the garlic should be lightly browned, but not too dark. Add 150 ml of water and cook for a further 30 minutes or until the water has evaporated.

3 Remove from the heat and transfer the pork and garlic into a glass jar or ceramic *orza* and pour over the melted lard. Leave to cool to room temperature, then store in the fridge. The preserved pork will keep for up to 1 month, as long as it is completely covered in the lard.

4 To serve, transfer the pork, garlic and lard to a heavy-based saucepan and heat gently for 20 minutes or until warmed through. Remove the pork, cut into slices and serve with pieces of garlic and fried potatoes.

CALLOS con GARBANZOS

TRIPE WITH CHICKPEAS

SERVES 6

'There is a weekly rhythm to the menu in Spanish bars,' says Ildefonso Guerrero, owner of El Estrecho in Marbella. 'As Monday is market day, the chef puts on a hearty stew to feed the country folk who come in to town to sell their animals and produce from their gardens. This will be served again on the Tuesday. Come Wednesday, we have a dish called *ropa vieja* or 'old cloth', which is based on Monday's stew.' The tripe stew at El Estrecho is the best I have tasted. Rich, sticky and gently spiced, but with the refreshing tang of mint, it is perfect to warm a crowd on a cold day.

400 g dried chickpeas
60 ml olive oil
1 large brown onion,
    finely diced
sea salt
2 garlic cloves, finely chopped
1 red bird's eye chilli,
    finely chopped
4 tomatoes, peeled and
    roughly chopped
1 garlic bulb
1.2 kg blanched honeycomb
    tripe, rinsed and cut into
    1.5 cm pieces
300 g raw chorizo sausages
12 black peppercorns
1 tablespoon sweet
    Spanish paprika
1½ teaspoons ground cumin
2 cinnamon quills
8 cloves
3 fresh bay leaves
2 tablespoons chopped mint
2 tablespoons chopped
    flat-leaf parsley
200 g *morcilla* sausages
freshly ground black pepper

1 Soak the chickpeas overnight, then drain and rinse under cold running water.

2 Pour 60 ml of the olive oil into a large heavy-based saucepan and place over medium heat. Add the onion and a pinch of salt and cook, stirring occasionally, for 10 minutes or until soft and translucent. Add the chopped garlic and chilli and cook for another 2 minutes, then add the tomato and continue cooking for 10 minutes, stirring occasionally. Take the garlic bulb and pierce it several times with a fork, then add it to the pan, along with 4 litres of cold water. Add the tripe, chorizo, peppercorns, paprika, cumin, cinnamon, cloves, bay leaves, mint, parsley and a teaspoon of salt. Bring to the boil over high heat, skimming away any impurities that rise to the surface.

3 Add the chickpeas and bring back to the boil, then reduce the heat and simmer for 4½ hours or until the tripe is cooked and soft; the cooking time for tripe varies a great deal.

4 Add the *morcilla* and simmer for 5–8 minutes or until cooked. Remove the *morcilla* and chorizo, cut into 2 cm thick slices and return to the pan. Cook for a few minutes more, then season with salt and pepper to taste.

5 Ladle into bowls and serve.

MOLLETES

SPANISH BREAD ROLLS

MAKES 12

Spanish bakers are proud of their traditions, and sometimes will go to extreme lengths to protect their culinary legacy. One baker we visited even claimed their family had invented these practical and tasty flat buns, served across Spain for breakfast, but the truth of the matter is that *molletes* have been baked in this part of the world for centuries. These are easy to make, albeit with a wet and sticky dough, and are a perfect foil for savoury fillings. Try them rubbed with the cut side of a juicy tomato half and filled with slices of jamón, with *sobrasada* (a soft cured pork sausage available from Spanish delis) and streaky bacon cooked until crisp, or with pan-fried *morcilla* and padrón peppers.

1 kg bread flour, plus extra
   for dusting
20 g sea salt
30 g fresh yeast or
   15 g dried yeast
700 ml warm water
60 ml olive oil

1 Whisk together the flour and salt in a large bowl. Dissolve the yeast in the warm water in a smaller bowl, then add the olive oil. Pour into the flour and use a wooden spoon or clean hands to mix to a rough dough. Turn out the dough onto a lightly floured bench – it will be quite wet. Knead by stretching out the dough with the palm of one hand while holding down the edge of the dough with the fingers of the other hand. Continue to knead for 10 minutes or so until the dough is elastic. Cover with plastic film and leave to rest for 10 minutes.

2 Cut the dough into 12 even pieces, roughly the size of a ping pong ball. Pat out each piece of dough on the palm of one hand, using the fingers of the other hand to shape it into a disc roughly 1 cm thick. Place on a well-floured baking tray and cover loosely with a clean plastic bag. Leave the rolls to prove in a warm place for 1 hour or until doubled in size.

3 Meanwhile, preheat the oven to 220°C/200°C fan.

4 Bake the rolls for 7 minutes or until they are lightly browned on top and sound hollow when rapped on the base with your knuckles. Allow to cool before slicing and filling.

TEJERINGOS

FAT CHURROS

SERVES 6–8

The orange trees shade the old town square. The heady fragrance of their blossoms fills the air, mingling with the aromas of coffee, chocolate and frying dough. La Plaza de los Naranjos, in the centre of Marbella's old town, has retained its fishing village charm. Next to the thirteenth-century chapel is Churrería Ramón, serving thick crisp *tejeringos*, which are like *churros*, but with a crunchier crust and a chewy, light interior. A special machine extrudes them in a tight coil, but as this is difficult to achieve by hand with such a dense dough, here I suggest piping them out in short lengths.

300 g bread flour
½ teaspoon bicarbonate of soda
½ teaspoon fine salt
7 g sachet dried yeast
1 litre olive oil, for deep-frying

1 Mix the flour, bicarbonate of soda, salt and yeast in a bowl with a whisk.

2 Pour 1 litre of water into a heavy-based saucepan and bring to a simmer over high heat, then reduce the heat to low. Sprinkle in a quarter of the flour mixture at a time, using a wooden spoon to mix each addition in well. Once all the flour mixture has been added, keep stirring for 3 minutes or so until you have a smooth, pasty dough.

3 Remove from the heat and leave the dough to stand in a warm place, covered with a clean cloth, for 30 minutes.

4 Pour the olive oil into a heavy-based saucepan or flat-bottomed wok and heat to 170°C or until a cube of bread dropped into the oil browns in 15 seconds.

5 Scrape the dough into a piping bag fitted with a 1.5 cm plain nozzle. Working in batches, pipe 15 cm lengths of the dough directly into the hot oil and deep-fry for 5–6 minutes, then turn and fry the other side for 5–6 minutes or until brown and crisp. Remove with a slotted spoon and drain on paper towel.

6 Eat while hot, tearing off pieces to dip into milky coffee or thick Spanish-style hot chocolate.

The charming old town at the heart of Marbella
is filled with the scent of orange blossom

LOS CUSODOS

THE CUSTODIANS

Author and food historian Fernando Rueda was living in the Catalan capital of Barcelona when the pangs of nostalgia for Málaga hit him. He returned to Antequera and had a bowl of *maimones*, a basic bread and garlic soup. 'It reminded me of my mother,' he said. 'I started weeping. The taste triggered memories of my childhood. It awakened the museum of flavours in my brain.' From there, he set out on a quest to document the province's traditional recipes. He would arrive in a town and ask to see the oldest women and from them, one by one, he gathered the recipes of Málaga. 'This is essential,' he says, clutching his fist. If you lose your recipes, you lose your identity. For many years, people didn't cook traditional dishes because they were the dishes from the lean years. We were embarrassed by our history.'

Thankfully, that has now changed. Fernando has found a kindred spirit in chef Charo Carmona from Coso San Francisco in Antequera: 'I cook relics,' she says with a laugh. 'Our recipes are part of our cultural inheritance. They hold evidence of the Romans, Moors, Jews, New World Conquests and famines,' she says. 'We,' she continues, referring to chefs like her with a passion for the past, 'are the custodians of traditional dishes, because as people cook them less at home, we cook them for everyone.'

Fernando goes further: 'These dishes are like religious images. You can be illiterate, yet when you look at a religious statue, you still understand the symbols. Traditional food is the same, because it tells the story of where it has come from. The same is not true of modernist food, which is why we neither understand it nor love it, and why it won't be passed on.'

MOVIDA'S GUIDE TO MÁLAGA

Mercado Central de Atarazanas 🍴🛍️

Calle Atarazanas S/N, Málaga

The main door to this market is an old Arab gate to the city. Here you'll find some really good quality seafood and a range of very interesting stallholders. Drop by Manuel Villamuela (Stalls 257–9), a butcher with a very good understanding of local meat cookery and impeccable English. Also worth a look on your travels are the Mercado de la Merced (Calle Merced S/N, Málaga) and Mercado de Abastos Antequera (Plaza San Francisco S/N, Antequera).

Mesón Lo Güeno 🍷🍴

Marín García 9, Málaga; tel 605 99 06 88
www.logueno.es

In the heart of town, just a few streets off the main promenade of Calle Larios, is this little bar, where basic tapas are served from an L-shaped counter: *boquerones* (pickled anchovies), snails, kidneys in sherry sauce, salt cod in tomato sauce and creamy white beans with tomato and clams. The extended à la carte menu is available at the bar, at the high tables in the laneway or in the wood-lined dining room across the lane.

Restaurante José Carlos García 🍷🍴

Plaza de la Capilla, Puerto de Málaga; tel 952 00 35 88
www.restaurantejcg.com

One of the kings of *Nueva Cocina Andaluza* ('the new cuisine of Andalusia'), JCG, as he is known, takes the basics of Andalusian food and extrapolates them into a 20-course degustation in his ultra-modern portside dining room with just six tables. Dishes may include ultra-fine slivers of raw prawn with pine nuts and *ajoblanco* ice-cream, or a fillet of gently cooked hake with gel beads of *puchero* (fish and potato stew).

Antigua Casa de Guardia 🍷 ✕

Alameda Principal 18, Málaga;
tel 952 21 46 80
www.antiguacasadeguardia.net

This is a dark, unadorned place with oak barrels on one wall, and a long, low wooden bar on which your order is marked in chalk. Order old-fashioned Málaga wines Pedro Ximénez, Moscatel or Pajarete by the glass or bring your own bottle to be filled. Have a fat olive stuffed with a pickled mussel or the local speciality of *conchas finas*, a large mussel served raw in its shell.

El Pimpi 🍷 ✕

Calle Granada 62, Málaga;
tel 952 22 89 90
www.elpimpi.com

This old-school bar and restaurant is famous for being famous – and so attracts the famous, whose photos hang on the whitewashed walls, their signatures scrawled on old barrels. There is a pleasant covered patio and several other dining rooms where you can try the croquettes made with *puchero* (see pages 120), eggplant served with cane-sugar syrup (see page 235) and the *rosquillas*, bagel-like rolls filled with hot sardines.

El Pimpi Florida 🍷 ✕

Carretera de Almería 13, Málaga;
tel 952 29 26 25

This bar is so much fun. It's in Cuatro Esquinas de El Palo, a suburb of Málaga. Not only will you be served really good seafood, but you'll inevitably get drawn into shouting along to '80s Spanish pop and '60s mariachi music. Not to be confused with the famed El Pimpi.

Museo de Arte Flamenco 'Peña Juan Breva' 🍷 ✕

Calle Ramon Franquelo 4, Málaga;
tel 952 22 13 80
www.museoflamencojuanbreva.com

Three Fridays a month they have some of the best flamenco music and dancing in the country here, and for the cost of admission they will feed you some *berza*, a rich stew (see page 194). During the day, it is home to displays of flamenco memorabilia collected over two centuries and spread across three floors, including costumes, photos, paintings and sculptures of famous singers, dancers and musicians.

Molina Lario 🏠

Calle Molina Lario 20–22, Málaga;
tel 952 06 20 02
www.hotelmolinalario.com

This completely new four-star luxury hotel has retained a nineteenth-century exterior. Set in the fashionable heart of town, it has views of the cathedral.

Room Mate Larios 🏠

Calle Marqués de Larios, 2, Málaga;
tel 952 22 22 00
www.larios.room-matehotels.com

The Calle Marqués de Larios is a pedestrian mall where the *Malgueños* come to promenade on streets paved with marble. The polished, chic aesthetic continues inside the hotel, with a chequered motif throughout and a terrace with views across the city.

Castillo de Santa Catalina 🏠

Calle Ramos Carrión 38, Málaga;
tel 952 21 27 00
www.castillodesantacatalina.com

Your own four-star hilltop seventeenth-century castle, set in beautiful gardens with views across the Mediterranean yet just a short taxi ride from town.

La Chancla 🏠

Paseo Marítimo del Pedregal 64, Málaga;
tel 952 20 69 00
www.lachanclahotel.com

Cheap and cheerful beachside hotel with un-ironic 1980s décor in what was once a fishing village. This is where Spaniards come to party.

Churrería Ramón ✕

Calle Valdés 1, Marbella

Light-as-air *churros* (known here as *tejeringos*) are fried to order in this open-air shop in the old town square of Plaza de los Naranjos. In spring this white-walled square, with its bars and shops and fifteenth-century chapel, is filled with the aroma of orange blossom.

El Estrecho 🍷 ✕

**Calle San Lázaro 12, Marbella;
tel 952 77 00 04
www.barelestrecho.es**

Estrecho means 'narrow', and it is an apt description for the tiny laneway where you'll find this smart restaurant that has been serving delicious and authentic Málaga classics since 1954. Try *huevos rellenos*, eggs stuffed with tuna and smothered in mayonnaise (see page 182) or *carne mechada*, slices of pork in a pepper, clove and bay vinegar dressing with onions. Especially delicious is the *alubias a la marenga*, a fisherman's bean and prawn stew with saffron.

La Traíña 🍷 ✕

**Avenida Severo Ochoa 49, Marbella;
tel 952 82 12 17**

Fishing boats bring in squirmingly fresh fish daily, to supply this *Love Boat* kitsch seafood restaurant run by Luis Morón. Go straight for the *huesos fritos*, sweet, sticky and meaty bones of a grouper-like fish that have been deep-fried until crisp and delicious (see page 204).

Los Hermanos Haro 🍷 ✕

Avenida Duque de Ahumada S/N, Marbella

You come to this *chiringuito* shack for the *espetos*, beer and beach. *Espetos* aficionados maintain that the only time of year to eat these is from May to September, when the Mediterranean sardines are being caught.

Coso San Francisco 🍷 ✕ 🏠

**Calle Calzada 29, Antequera;
tel 952 84 00 14**

In the heart of Antequera, a town in the hills behind Málaga, is this charming and welcoming boutique hotel, with a traditional restaurant set in the courtyard of an old house and an open fire in winter. Chef Charo Carmona is a champion of the traditional dishes of region, such as *maimones*, a simple garlic and bread soup, or the luscious *lomo en orza*, pork loin confit (see page 207), cooked in lard laced with much garlic.

Pedro Romero 🍷 ✕

**Calle Virgen de la Paz 18, Ronda;
tel 952 87 11 10
www.rpedroromero.com**

Hemingway dined in a few places in Spain in his time, and this was one of them. You get the feeling that some of the waiters here may even have served him. It's all white tablecloths, cheesy moustaches and celebrity bullfighter photos in the five dining rooms, where you'll find some excellent versions of traditional dishes, including good soft *migas con morcilla*, rabbit *estafado* with potatoes, and partridge with beans and carrots *en escabeche*.

Traga Tapas 🍷 ✕

Calle Nueva 4, Ronda; tel 952 87 72 09

Near the Plaza de Toros in the spectacular town of Ronda is this funny little tapas bar serving fast fun food, such as very good croquettes, white anchovies with lemon and even some very nice little pig trotters – a perfect place for a snack before walking down the spectacular gorge straddled by the eighteenth-century bridge.

La Fuente de la Higuera ✕ 🏠

**Partido de los Frontones S/N, Ronda;
tel 952 16 56 08
www.hotellafuente.com**

A quiet rural retreat a short drive from Ronda, this old mill has a swimming pool by the lawn and is surrounded by oak forest.

Casa Guajar 🏠

**Monda, Sierra de las Nieves
tel 952 45 97 66**

A lovely little renovated farmhouse in an olive grove near the Parque Natural Sierra de las Nieves, owned by the charming Paqui Martín.

The view from Casa Guajar

It's mid-morning, and the narrow streets and alleys of Córdoba are filled with the aroma of onions and garlic frying in olive oil. Rich and enticing, there is no other smell like it. Every time that perfume hits my nose I am taken back to those years I spent living here, spending time in the hills with my family on weekends, catching the bus to and from the crowded market, and the long hours I spent cooking in restaurants as I was starting my career as a chef. That sweet smell of a *sofrito*, the start of a thousand variations on the Cordoban kitchen classics, lets me know I am home.

That distinctive aroma hangs in the still air of the historic centre of town much longer than it does in the newer parts of the city. Built by the Moors, the old town of Córdoba is more like the labyrinth of interconnecting laneways you might find in a North African medina than the heart of a European city, and is just as tricky to navigate. The breezes struggle to find their way through the maze too, and it can be stifling in summer, which may be the reason there are so many wonderfully refreshing, yet sustaining cold soups here, such as *gazpacho, ajoblanco* and the famous *salmorejo cordobés*, a savoury puree of tomato, bread and garlic dressed with a little chopped egg and jamón (see page 232).

For a large part of the Middle Ages, Córdoba was the cultural hub of Europe, a place where Muslims, Christians and Jews came together to learn the classics and study maths and sciences. A sacred site long before the Romans invaded and declared the city their capital of Hispania in 206 BC, the sprawling cathedral doesn't point skywards like the great Gothic edifices of more northern cities but, being a former mosque, channels you inwards to its cool forest of columns supporting ochre-hued arches and a dark stone heaven.

My mother's family live in a small hilltop village in the countryside to the south of the capital. I love this landscape of undulating fields sown with cereals, plains planted with ancient olive trees, and wide valleys carved by rivers streaming down from the mountains. Dominating this bucolic scene are the towns and villages, their sites originally chosen to be easily defended from marauding forces, and often crowned with a crumbling fort or castle straddling a rocky outcrop. Today, in less turbulent times, their lively squares host weekday markets, while bodegas and olive oil processing plants spread out over the flats on the outskirts of town.

Summers get very hot in Córdoba, and there are few better ways to seek respite from the heat of the afternoon than in the cool embrace of an old stone-lined bodega, where you can while away the hours with the *Cordobeses*, a people of refined yet laidback manner and unstinting hospitality.

DESAYUNO DE ACEITUNERO

OLIVE PICKER'S BREAKFAST

SERVES 4-6

The table was laid for breakfast. Not an everyday breakfast, but a breakfast suitable for an olive picker. Thick slices of ripe orange were drizzled with honey gathered from bees that had feasted on *azahar*, the orange blossoms. Next to them were slices of *bacalao* scantly coated with the local Luque olive oil. Served with ice-cold pulpy orange juice and plenty of coffee, this is a refreshing way to start the day.

600 g skinless salt cod fillet
6 oranges
3 tablespoons light-flavoured honey
extra virgin olive oil, for drizzling
300 g jamón serrano, cut into bite-sized pieces
loaf of crusty bread

1 Wash the excess salt off the salt cod, then place in a large bowl. Cover with water and leave to soak for 36 hours, changing the water three times. Drain, then cut the fillet into four thick slices.

2 Peel the oranges and cut into thick slices, removing any pips. Lay the orange slices on a serving plate and drizzle with honey.

3 Drain the cod, cut into 3 mm thick slices and arrange on a separate plate. Drizzle with olive oil.

4 Arrange the jamón on another plate, then cut the bread and serve on a bread board.

5 Serve with coffee and freshly squeezed orange juice.

BACA
16,75

Bacalao Sin Hueso Con H
10'00 Euros Kilo 8'00 Kilo
Euros

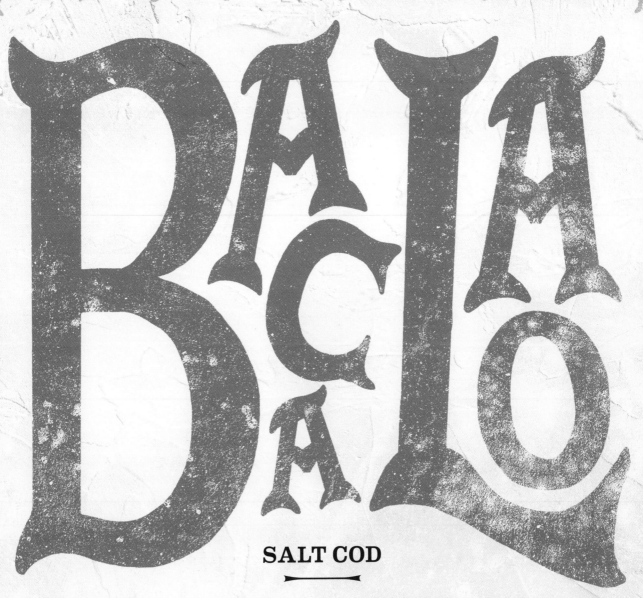

BACALAO

SALT COD

▶

On the edge of Castro del Río, a landlocked town to the south of the city of Córdoba, sits a huge processing plant for salt cod. Cod has been harvested from the northern Atlantic, dried and salted, and then traded across Europe since the Middle Ages. With the Catholic Church declaring as many fast days as days when meat could be eaten, salt cod became a household staple across Spain. It was transportable, durable and tasty.

The factory manager of Albacor takes us into a dimly lit coolroom. Reaching from floor to ceiling is a wall of creamy-white salted cod fillets, salt crystals glistening in the dim light.

He explains that across Spain people appreciate their cod differently: 'On the coast they like it less salted, but in the interior they like it more salty. In the days of carrier mules it was a long journey from the port to the mountains, and well-salted cod was guaranteed to last.' He picks up a perfectly salted loin of fine-fleshed cod. 'The irony is that it used to be the food of the poor. Now people aren't obliged to eat it, but they desire it – and because of its superb flavour, it has become the food of the rich! That said, Easter is still the busiest time of the year for us, as everyone wants to eat *bacalao* over the religious festival, in keeping with tradition.'

SALMOREJO

CHILLED BREAD AND TOMATO SOUP

SERVES 4-6

Once the food of the poor, this classic blend of bread, tomato, garlic and olive oil makes the perfect chilled soup to revive and refresh. Purists would have it that the only time to make *salmorejo* is at the end of summer, when the tomatoes have reached their peak of ripeness. Then there are those who claim the secret lies in the selection of a subtle and fruity extra virgin olive oil, such as picual or hojiblanca. Whatever the case, this simple dish is all the better when made using the best ingredients you can find: thin-skinned and ripe heirloom tomatoes, fresh and robust extra virgin olive oil, free-range eggs, and good-quality jamón serrano. This version comes from the Cofradía del Salmorejo Cordobés, an organisation dedicated to promoting authentic Cordoban traditions.

1 kg ripe tomatoes

200 g two-day-old bread, without crusts

1 garlic clove, chopped

125 ml extra virgin olive oil, plus extra for drizzling

1 teaspoon sea salt

4 hard-boiled eggs, sliced lengthways

80 g jamón serrano, finely chopped

1 Wash the tomatoes, remove the stems and cores and roughly chop the flesh. Place in a blender and blend to a smooth puree. Strain the puree through a fine-mesh sieve set over a bowl to remove the seeds and skin. Return the puree to the blender.

2 Break the bread into small pieces into the blender, then add the garlic and olive oil and season with salt. Blend to a smooth puree. Transfer to a bowl, cover with plastic film and refrigerate until chilled, about 2–3 hours.

3 Pour the chilled soup into bowls, decorate with the egg slices and jamón, and drizzle with olive oil.

BERENJENAS con MIEL

FRIED EGGPLANT WITH HONEY

SERVES 4-6

The Moors were said to have a legendary sweet tooth, finishing many of their dishes with honey (although these days this dish is often served with *miel de caña*, Spanish sugarcane syrup). Andalusian honey is outstanding, with beehives often placed in orange groves in the hills, where the bees forage on orange blossoms and wildflowers, producing a light honey with floral notes. Honey also contains amino acids that, combined with the savoury elements in meat and vegetable dishes, create a pleasing sensation in the mouth – this makes a great snack to serve with drinks.

3 large eggplants (aubergines)
1.2 litres milk
250 g plain flour
sea salt and freshly ground
    black pepper
1 litre sunflower or vegetable
    oil, for deep-frying
200 ml mild-flavoured honey

1 Slice the tops off the eggplants, then cut them lengthways into 5–7 mm thick slices. Place the eggplant slices in a large bowl and cover with the milk. Place a small weight on top, such as a plate, to keep the eggplant submerged. Leave to soak for 1 hour.

2 Pour the oil into a heavy-based saucepan or wok and heat to 170°C or until a cube of bread dropped into the oil browns in 15 seconds.

3 Place the flour in a shallow bowl and season with salt and pepper. Working in batches of four or five slices at a time, remove the eggplant from the milk, shaking off any excess, then dip in the flour to coat well.

4 Deep-fry the eggplant in batches for 5–6 minutes on each side until nicely crisped and brown. Remove and drain on paper towel, then season with salt.

5 Place on a serving plate, drizzle with honey while still hot and serve straight away.

PISTO CORDOBÉS

EGGPLANT, CAPSICUM AND TOMATO BRAISE

SERVES 4-6

Just behind the magnificent twelfth-century Church of San Miguel in Córdoba is a small square that at night is laid out with tables and chairs. A three-storey whitewashed building, trimmed with ochre around the door and window frames, is home to Taberna San Miguel, also known as Casa El Pisto. Once the haunt of the city's famous and infamous bullfighters, artists and scoundrels, today the house speciality is *pisto cordobés*, a vegetable and tomato braise finished with a soft-cooked egg.

3 eggplants (aubergines)

1 green bull horn capsicum
(pepper) or ½ green regular
capsicum (pepper)

1 red bull horn capsicum
(pepper) or ½ red regular
capsicum (pepper)

80 ml extra virgin olive oil

1 large brown onion, diced

3 fresh bay leaves

fine salt

3 garlic cloves, finely chopped

10 tomatoes, peeled and
roughly chopped

4 zucchini (courgettes),
cut into 1 cm cubes

GARNISH

80 ml extra virgin olive oil

1 garlic clove, chopped

3 tablespoons fresh
breadcrumbs

4-6 eggs (1 per person)

sea salt

1 tablespoon chopped chives

1 Cut the tops off the eggplants and peel away most of the black skin, then cut the flesh into 2 cm cubes. Remove the stalks and seeds from the capsicums, then cut the flesh into 1 cm cubes.

2 Pour half of the olive oil into a *rondeau* (see page 381) or large deep saucepan and place over low-medium heat. Add the onion, bay leaves and a pinch of salt and cook for 15 minutes, stirring occasionally, until the onion is soft and translucent. Stir in the garlic and cook for a further 2 minutes, then add the eggplant and capsicum, turn the heat up to high and cook for 3-4 minutes, stirring gently but constantly. Add the tomato and zucchini, then season with salt. Reduce the heat to low, cover and cook for 1 hour or so until the vegetables are well-braised, soft, thick and saucy. Check the seasoning.

3 For the garnish, pour 1 tablespoon of the olive oil into a small frying pan and place over medium heat. Add the garlic and breadcrumbs and cook, stirring, for 2-3 minutes or until crisp and brown. Using a slotted spoon, lift out the garlic and breadcrumbs and drain on paper towel. Discard the oil and wipe out the pan with paper towel. Add the remaining olive oil to the pan and place over medium heat. Fry two or three eggs at a time until the whites are cooked but the yolks are still runny.

4 To serve, spoon the *pisto* onto warmed plates and place an egg on top of each one. Sprinkle over the fried garlic and breadcrumbs, then scatter over a pinch of salt and some chopped chives.

LA HISTORIA DE PX.

THE PEDRO XIMÉNEZ STORY

▸

Antonio Sánchez Romero stands beside a table in the dispatch area of Bodega Toro Albalá. It is mid-morning, and he and a few friends are sampling his fino as a forklift stacks pallets into a waiting truck. With his Johnny Depp sunglasses and Hunter S. Thompson fatigues, Sánchez exudes an air of dangerous excitement. His cellars were once Aguilar de la Frontera's electricity substation, now a high temple of mould-covered concrete stacked with blackened barrels lit by a few swinging bulbs. He pours a sample of the oloroso from a barrel filled in 1950. Dark and nutty, it has the body of much younger wine. 'Some way to go yet,' he says, smiling.

At the very back of the cellar are the barrels marked PX or Pedro Ximénez. 'The story goes that the grape variety was named after an English soldier called Peter Simmons,' Sánchez says dismissively, 'who supposedly brought the grapes from the Canary Islands. Others suggest that it was a Moorish grape variety, while some think it has evolved to suit our climate here.' PX grapes are harvested then laid out on mats to dry under the sun for a week or so until the sugar content of their juice reaches about 300 g per litre. The dried grapes are pressed to yield a sweet, thick must, which is fermented to create a sweet, viscous wine that darkens over time. Sánchez smiles as he offers a barrel sample. The wine is dark in the gloom, thick like syrup, rich like chocolate, and full of fruit and old oak. Layer after layer of the different PX wines have been brought together to rest in this one barrel, a barrel that has been quietly aging since 1893. Sánchez puts this in context: 'The grandsons of the men who made this wine would be frail old men now . . . if alive at all. But at 120 years old, this PX is doing rather nicely, don't you think?'

SETAS con OLOROSO

MUSHROOMS IN OLOROSO

SERVES 4-6

I was served this dish in a dining room just made for long lunches. Restaurante Las Camachas is located in the town of Montilla, which is famous for its oloroso and Pedro Ximénez. Deep in the heart of this labyrinthine dining establishment is a room lined with sherry barrels. After the waiter has taken your order, he asks what you would like to drink. Fino? Amontillado? He then takes his *venencia*, a small cup on a bamboo stick, dips it into a barrel and fills your glass. Meanwhile in the kitchen, the chef throws a handful of mushrooms into a scorching-hot pan with butter, bacon and garlic, then deglazes the pan with oloroso. The end-result is sweet and nutty, smoky and earthy. Our waiter suggests we try it with the same oloroso in which it was cooked.

500 g large oyster mushrooms
3 rashers streaky bacon
70 g butter
2 garlic cloves, quartered
sea salt and freshly ground
    black pepper
70 ml oloroso sherry
1 tablespoon chopped
    flat-leaf parsley

1 Tear some of the larger mushrooms in half with your hands. Cut the bacon into strips roughly 2 cm by 1 cm.

2 Melt the butter in a large frying pan over medium heat. Add the bacon and garlic and cook for 5 minutes or until they start to brown.

3 Increase the heat to medium–high, then add the mushrooms. Season with salt and pepper and cook for 5–6 minutes or until the mushrooms are lightly browned.

4 Pour in the sherry, scraping the base of the pan to deglaze, then turn up the heat to high and let the sherry reduce to form a scant sauce with the butter. Stir in the parsley, then serve straight away.

RABO DE TORO

OXTAIL BRAISE

SERVES 6

One of the stories surrounding the origin of this dish is that it was made with the tails of the *toros bravos*, the bulls killed in the bullfights. When a bull is killed in a fight, it is dragged out of the ring by horses and sent to the market or butchers, so this is plausible. There are, however, references to oxtail stew in Roman texts. All that aside, this is a simple to make, hearty meal for a family, and is irresistible in winter, when the smell of slow-cooking meat, herbs and sherry fills the kitchen. This version is from Restaurante Las Camachas in Montilla, and is perfect with potatoes – perhaps *Patatas a lo pobre*, Poor man's potatoes (see page 323). It's worth cooking a double batch of this braise so you can use half to make the delicious *Arroz de rabo de toro*, Oxtail rice (see page 246).

2.2 kg oxtail (ask your butcher to cut the oxtail into slices through the joints)
2 tablespoons plain flour
100 ml olive oil
sea salt
4 ripe tomatoes
2 brown onions, diced
1 garlic bulb, cut in half horizontally
3 fresh bay leaves
5 carrots, diced
1 green bull horn capsicum (pepper) or ½ green regular capsicum (pepper), diced
250 ml fino sherry
2 dried choricero or ñora peppers (see page 379)
12 whole black peppercorns
4 cloves
1 teaspoon sweet Spanish paprika
1 tablespoon chopped thyme

1 Trim any excess fat from the oxtail. Place the flour in a large bowl, add the oxtail and coat with flour, shaking off any excess.

2 Pour 40 ml of the olive oil into a large frying pan and place over medium–high heat. Working in batches, fry the oxtail for 3 minutes on each side until well browned, seasoning on both sides with salt. Remove and set aside on a plate or baking tray.

3 Cut the tomatoes in half and grate the cut side against a cheese grater over a bowl to pulp the flesh. Discard the skin.

4 Pour the remaining olive oil into a large flameproof casserole and place over high heat. Add the onion, garlic (cut-side down), bay leaves and a pinch of salt. Cook, stirring occasionally, for 10 minutes or until the onion and garlic are nicely browned. Add the carrot and capsicum, reduce the heat to medium and cook for 10 minutes, stirring occasionally. Add the tomato pulp and cook for another 5 minutes, then stir in the sherry and bring to a simmer.

5 Preheat the oven to 180°C/160°C fan.

6 Add the oxtail, dried peppers, peppercorns, cloves, paprika and thyme to the casserole. Pour in 1.3 litres of water, mix well and bring to a simmer. Season with salt and cover the casserole with a cartouche (a circle of baking paper cut to size and laid directly onto the surface of the braise), then a lid. Place in the oven and cook for 3–4 hours or until the meat is soft and, with a little pressure from your fingers, comes away from the bone. Some oxtail takes longer to cook than others, so start checking it after 3 hours.

7 Remove the garlic bulb and dried peppers and discard. Skim away a little of the fat from the surface with a ladle before serving.

The geometric designs of the Moors
dominate Cordoban decoration and decor

ARROZ DE RABO DE TORO

OXTAIL RICE

SERVES 6

Bodegas Campos describes itself as 'a museum to the art of eating'. This sprawling institution began as a bodega for wines from Montilla-Moriles in 1908. When it expanded in the 1960s, it started selling wine by the glass and serving snacks, then in the 1980s the focus shifted to food, and eventually the restaurant opened. Here the food is simple, honest Cordoban cuisine. What I love is that not only do they serve really good *Rabo de toro*, or Oxtail braise (see page 242), but they also transform the leftovers into croquettes and this delicious rich, dark rice dish.

1 quantity Oxtail braise
  (see page 242)
60 ml extra virgin olive oil
1 large brown onion,
  finely diced
1 tablespoon chopped thyme
sea salt
3 garlic cloves, finely chopped
½ red capsicum (pepper),
  finely diced
6 asparagus spears, peeled and
  cut into 4 cm lengths
120 ml oloroso sherry
freshly ground black pepper
250 g Calasparra rice
100 g frozen peas, defrosted

1 While the oxtail is still hot, remove it from the casserole and set aside until cool enough to handle. Using a ladle, skim away as much of the fat from the surface of the sauce as you can. Strain the sauce through a fine-mesh sieve into a heatproof measuring jug, extracting as much flavour as possible from the vegetables by lightly pushing them through the sieve, then add enough water to the strained sauce to make 1.3 litres in total. Pour into a large saucepan and bring to a simmer, then remove from the heat.

2 When the oxtail is cool enough to handle, use your fingers to remove all the meat from the bones.

3 Pour the olive oil into a *perol* (see page 380) or wide heavy-based saucepan and place over medium heat. When the oil is hot, add the onion, thyme and a pinch of salt and cook for 12–15 minutes, stirring occasionally, until the onion is soft and translucent. Stir in the garlic and cook for 1–2 minutes. Add the capsicum and asparagus and cook for 12–15 minutes, stirring occasionally, until the capsicum and asparagus are soft.

4 Pour in the sherry, scraping the base of the pan to deglaze. Add the strained oxtail sauce and meat, season with salt and pepper and bring back to a simmer. Stir in the rice, then simmer for 16–17 minutes, stirring occasionally, until the rice is cooked but still has a little bit of bite to the tooth. Add the peas and stir to warm through.

5 Spoon into warm bowls and serve hot.

COCINAR CON FUEGO

COOKING WITH FIRE

Every time I return to Córdoba, I make a beeline for El Churrasco. A labyrinth of rooms furnished with antiques, tiles and exposed wooden beams, the atmosphere in this long-established restaurant is one of ageless continuity. I set myself up at the bar and order a loin of pork, then watch it being grilled over charcoal while enjoying a glass of sherry. The chefs cook on vast ranges made with plates of inch-thick steel that have warped and buckled over decades of continuous exposure to the eternal beds of glowing, red-hot coals.

The word *churrasco* itself is believed to have come from the Iberian word *sukarra*, merging the concepts of *su* ('fire') and *karra* ('flame'). And the Spanish love cooking with fire. Any chance they get, they will gather sticks and chop wood to make a fire for cooking. On the coast, this may be small sardines; inland, dried olive branches and vine trimmings add their distinctive flavour and aroma to rice dishes cooked over their embers. Into wood-fired ovens go legs of lamb and whole suckling piglets. The flavour of cooking over real flames from the dying coals of a wood fire or the glowing chunks of charcoal is irreplaceable. The heat is intense, and as the fat and meat juices drop onto the fire below, they vaporise, creating plumes of aromatic smoke that add layers of delicious flavour, along with the lingering tang left by the woodsmoke itself.

The chefs at El Churrasco cook over charcoal made from holm oak, the aroma of which fills every corner of the intimate dining room, converted cellar and patio that make up this amazing restaurant. Despite the comfort of these dining areas, there is something mesmerising about standing at the bar and watching the chefs cook with fire.

CHURRASCO

GRILLED PORK TENDERLOIN

SERVES 4–6

While the word *churrasco* means different ways of grilling meat in different parts of the world, in Córdoba *churrasco* can only mean one thing. Take a tenderloin of pork, grill it over a bed of coals and serve it with two sauces: one made with silky piquillo peppers, and the other vivid with green herbs. In the old Jewish quarter, there is a restaurant called El Churrasco, and their recipe is now replicated across the city. If you don't have access to a charcoal grill, cook the pork on the flat grillplate of a barbecue or on a stovetop chargrill pan.

2 pork tenderloins, about 300 g each
40 ml extra virgin olive oil
1 tablespoon sea salt

SALSA DE PIQUILLO

1 × 500 g tin piquillo peppers, drained
1 teaspoon hot Spanish paprika
1 garlic clove, peeled
1 tablespoon sweet smoked Spanish paprika
1 tablespoon ground cumin
125 ml extra virgin olive oil
sea salt

SALSA VERDE

2 tablespoons fennel seeds
large handful of oregano leaves
4 garlic cloves, peeled
handful of flat-leaf parsley leaves
200 ml extra virgin olive oil
sea salt
juice of 1 lemon

1 Using a sharp knife, make about 7–8 incisions, each about 1 cm deep, along the length of the pork tenderloins; this helps them to cook quickly and evenly. Place the tenderloins on a large plate, rub with the olive oil and sea salt, then cover with plastic film and set aside.

2 To make the salsa de piquillo, place all the ingredients in a blender and blend until smooth. Season to taste with salt, then pour into a small serving bowl.

3 To make the salsa verde, toast the fennel seeds in a small frying pan over medium high heat for 1–2 minutes, until just browned and the aroma of fennel fills the kitchen. Place in a blender or small food processor, along with all the other ingredients, and blend just enough to make a rustic sauce. Pour into another small serving bowl.

4 Heat a barbecue (ideally wood or charcoal) until very hot. Grill each of the four sides of the tenderloins for 3–4 minutes or until cooked but still just a little pink in the middle. Remove from the heat and allow to rest in a warm place, covered loosely with foil, for 5 minutes.

5 To serve, cut the tenderloins into 2 cm thick slices and serve with the two salsas.

RIÑONES A LA PLANCHA

GRILLED KIDNEYS

SERVES 4-6

I am not generally a lover of kidneys, but these are sensational. Salty and tangy, they crisp as they sizzle on *la plancha* (the grillplate). The Spanish love lamb kidneys cooked until they have a delicious crunchy crust. As they prefer eating their lambs young, the kidneys lack the renal tang those sold here sometimes have. To get around this, we soak the kidneys overnight in milk before cooking them. This recipe comes from El Churrasco restaurant in Córdoba's old Jewish quarter, where the grillplates are heated over charcoal, giving a hint of smoke to the kidneys. In the past I have cooked these on a hot grillplate over an old-fashioned wood barbecue and they were excellent. They are delicious as a snack with a glass of fino sherry.

400 g lamb's kidneys
300 ml milk
80 ml olive oil
sea salt and freshly ground
    black pepper

1 Using a sharp knife, clean the kidneys by slicing them in half lengthways and using the point of the knife to trim away the white core and sinew. Place in a bowl, pour over the milk and cover with plastic film, then refrigerate for at least 3 hours, preferably overnight.

2 Drain the kidneys and discard the milk. Pat the kidneys dry between layers of paper towel. Cut the kidneys lengthways again, so each kidney is now in four slices.

3 Heat the flat grillplate of a barbecue until it is extremely hot; it should be as hot as you can get it. Cook the kidneys in two batches. Drizzle half the olive oil onto the grillplate and spread it out well, using a very fat wad of paper towel. Once the oil starts to smoke, carefully place the first batch of kidneys on the grill. Season well with sea salt and cook for about 5 minutes or until crisp and brown. Turn over, season again, and cook for another 4–5 minutes. The idea is to crisp and caramelise the kidneys really well and cook them all the way through.

4 Remove and place on a serving plate. Season again with salt and a little pepper.

5 Clean the grillplate with paper towel to remove any crusty bits before cooking the second batch of kidneys as above.

6 Serve straight away.

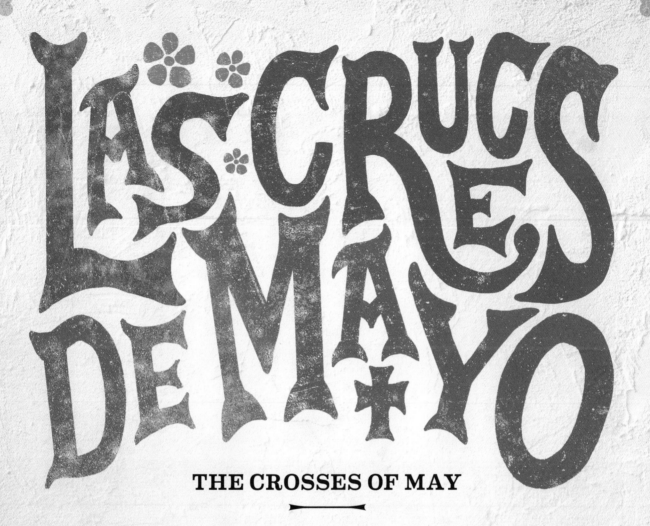

LAS CRUCES DE MAYO

THE CROSSES OF MAY

The big red cross stands in the middle of the little square in an inner-city neighbourhood of Córdoba, surrounded by blooming plants in pots and draped with garlands of flowers. The band is playing a *Sevillana* – all flamenco guitars and syncopated handclaps. Young women are dancing a flamenco, their arms raised dramatically above their heads, their hands tracing delicate arcs through the air. A string of lights above a makeshift bar spills warm yellow light into the square, where a father pours glasses of chilled fino while his son clings to his trousers.

This is *Las Cruces de Mayo* – 'The Crosses of May' – ostensibly a religious festival commemorating St Helen's fourth-century pilgrimage to Jerusalem to find the true cross. But with all the drinking, dancing and flirting, you could be

forgiven in thinking it was a paean to Bacchus. This is just one celebration in an ongoing calendar of festivals that roll through the Andalusian year: from saint's days to festivals celebrating the return of migratory tuna, from those marking the planting and harvesting of crops to historical events, there is bound to be a festival happening in some part of Andalusia on any given day. And it's a safe bet that feasting, singing and dancing will be involved.

Las Cruces de Mayo is quite beautiful, with women and children decorating their crosses with blossoms in secret, away from the prying eyes of the competition; all are vying for the 1000 euros in prize money for the best decorated cross and surrounds. What I really love, though, is that the pop-up bars are generally run by the local Catholic brotherhoods.

LECHE FRITA

FRIED MILK WITH BRANDY

SERVES 4-6

Spain is not a nation of desserts. Those desserts that are part of the national repertoire are simple and delicious, and just as likely to be made at home as in a restaurant. *Leche frita* is basically milk custard flavoured with citrus peel and cinnamon that is allowed to set until quite solid and then cut into pieces, fried and served with a coating of cinnamon sugar. The waiters at Las Camachas restaurant in Montilla finish with a theatrical flambé of brandy to set their dish apart from that served at home.

1 orange
1 lemon
1 litre milk
40 g butter
220 g caster sugar
3 cinnamon quills
8 egg yolks
100 g cornflour
4 eggs
150 g plain flour
1 litre olive oil, for deep-frying
80 ml brandy

CINNAMON SUGAR

90 g caster sugar
1 tablespoon ground cinnamon

1 Wash the orange and lemon in very hot water to remove any wax coating. Use a vegetable peeler to remove the zest in wide strips, leaving behind the bitter white pith.

2 Place the milk, butter, sugar, cinnamon sticks and citrus zests in a heavy-based saucepan over medium heat. Bring to a simmer, then remove from the heat and leave to infuse for a few minutes. Strain into a bowl, discarding the cinnamon and citrus zests.

3 In a medium-sized heatproof bowl, whisk the egg yolks and cornflour to a smooth paste. Pour a quarter of the warm infused milk into the egg yolk mixture and whisk thoroughly to prevent any lumps forming. Add the remaining milk and whisk well, then pour into a clean saucepan. Place the pan over medium heat and stir the custard constantly with a whisk until smooth, then use a wooden spoon to get into the corners of the pan. Cook, stirring constantly, for 20–22 minutes until you have a thick, smooth custard; the flavour of the cornflour should be completely cooked out.

4 Lightly oil the base and sides of a 23 cm × 14 cm baking dish. Pour in the custard and, using a spatula, smooth the surface. Set aside to cool to room temperature, then chill in the refrigerator for several hours or until quite firm.

5 When you are ready to fry the custard, remove from the refrigerator and cut into 2.5 cm cubes. Break the eggs into a bowl and beat with a fork. Place the flour in a shallow bowl.

6 Pour the olive oil into a heavy-based saucepan or wok and heat to 170°C or until a cube of bread dropped into the oil browns in 15 seconds. Working in batches so as not to crowd the pan, dust the custard cubes in the flour then dip in the beaten egg to coat on all sides. Carefully lower into the hot oil and fry for 6-7 minutes, turning occasionally, until the outside of the custard cubes is nice and brown and the

inside is soft and warm. Using a slotted spoon, carefully lift out the *leche frita* and drain on paper towel. Repeat with the rest of the custard cubes.

7 Meanwhile, make the cinnamon sugar by mixing the cinnamon with the sugar in a bowl.

8 Dust the *leche frita* with a little cinnamon sugar and place on serving plates. Heat the brandy in a small saucepan until it is just simmering. Remove the pan from the heat and ignite the brandy with a long match or a lighter, being careful to keep your fingers away from the flame. Pour the flaming brandy over the *leche frita* and serve while still alight.

PICOS

SPANISH VANILLA SLICE

MAKES 12

In true Andalusian style, these little pastries are filled with a crème pâtissière that is rich with egg yolks. This gives the filling a silky texture that contrasts with the crisp crunch of the pastry. Eat these with coffee and perhaps a small glass of brandy, just as the townsfolk of Aguilar de la Frontera do at Pastelería Bernardino Solano, where this version was photographed.

500 g rough puff pastry
   (see page 380) or readymade
   puff pastry, thawed if frozen
1 egg yolk, lightly beaten

FILLING
12 egg yolks
½ teaspoon vanilla extract
200 g caster sugar
80 g cornflour
1 litre milk

1 Preheat the oven to 210°C/190°C fan and line a baking tray with baking paper.

2 Place the chilled pastry on a well-floured bench and roll into a rectangle about 36 cm × 24 cm and about 5 mm thick. Trim the edges of the rectangle evenly to neaten, then cut into six 12 cm squares. Cut each square in half on the diagonal, then brush off any excess flour.

3 Beat the egg yolk with 1 teaspoon of cold water to make a glaze. Brush the pastry triangles with the glaze, then place on the prepared baking tray and lightly prick with a fork.

4 Bake for 14–15 minutes or until crisp and brown. Leave to cool on the tray for 5 minutes, then carefully transfer to a wire rack.

5 Meanwhile, to make the filling, place the egg yolks in a bowl and whisk in the vanilla extract and sugar. When the sugar has dissolved, gently fold in the cornflour.

6 Pour the milk into a saucepan and place over medium heat until it just breaks into a simmer. Take off the heat then leave to cool for a minute or so.

7 Add a ladleful of the hot milk to the egg yolk mixture and whisk well to prevent any lumps forming. Slowly pour in the rest of the milk, stirring constantly, until smooth. Pour the custard into a clean saucepan and place over low–medium heat. Cook, stirring constantly with a wooden spoon and working it into the corners of the pan, for about 12–15 minutes or until you have thick custard; the flavour of the cornflour should be completely cooked out. Leave to cool.

8 To assemble the *picos*, take a pastry triangle and, starting at the right angle and using a bread knife, cut it almost in half horizontally, keeping the long side connected like a book. This takes a little patience and a steady hand. Use a dessertspoon to fill the pastry triangle with the vanilla custard, smoothing the edge with a wet palette knife. Repeat with the remaining pastries and serve immediately.

TOCINO DE CIELO

FAT FROM HEAVEN

In Spain, fat is good, for it means flavour. And *tocino* means pig fat, so you can imagine that pig fat that is *de cielo* ('from heaven') is doubly special. The name of this dish also plays into the religion-related superstitions of reconquest Spain, when pork and Christ were inextricably linked – Moors and Jews who converted to Christianity would hang pork products by their front door to prove the point. The irony then is that this dish is Moorish in origin, the creation of a people inordinately fond of sugar. Incredibly sweet and indecently rich, a small piece of *tocino de cielo* makes a delicious full stop to any meal.

350 g white sugar
350 g caster sugar
18 egg yolks
2 whole eggs

1 Have ready a 30 cm × 20 cm heatproof glass or ceramic baking dish.

2 Place the white sugar in a medium-sized heavy-based saucepan and cook over high heat, without stirring, for about 5–8 minutes or until the sugar starts to become liquid and darker around the sides. Using a wooden spoon, stir the sugar until it has all melted and caramelised, then pour the hot caramel into the dish, tilting to spread it evenly. Leave to cool on the bench.

3 Preheat the oven to 200°C/180°C fan.

4 For the custard, make a syrup by placing the caster sugar in a heavy-based saucepan with 180 ml of water. Bring to the boil over high heat, stirring to dissolve the sugar, then reduce the heat to medium and simmer for 12–15 minutes or until the syrup is thick and a little viscous.

5 Meanwhile, place the egg yolks and eggs in a stainless steel bowl and mix with a wooden spoon.

6 Remove the syrup from the heat and leave to cool for 30 seconds or so, then gradually add the hot syrup to the beaten egg, a little at time, stirring to mix it in well. Pour the custard into the baking dish on top of the set caramel. Place the dish in a deep roasting tin and pour enough cold water into the tin to come halfway up the sides of the dish. Bake in the oven on the middle shelf for 40 minutes or until set but still a little wobbly in the centre.

7 Carefully remove from the oven and lift the baking dish out of the water. Allow the *tocino de cielo* to cool to room temperature, then cover with plastic film and refrigerate for 2–3 hours or until cold.

8 Run a flat-bladed knife around the edge of the dish and invert the *tocino de cielo* onto a large serving tray or platter. Cut the custard into small pieces and serve after dinner or with coffee. (Any leftovers will keep in an airtight container in the fridge for up to a week).

MOVIDA'S GUIDE TO CÓRDOBA

Restaurante El Churrasco ♟ ✕

Calle del Romero 16, Córdoba;
tel 957 29 08 19
www.elchurrasco.com

This barbecue and grill restaurant
is a Córdoba institution. A cluster of
interconnecting rooms lead upstairs, around
corners, onto a patio shaded by an ancient
fig tree and down into a sacristy-like cellar.
The aroma of woodsmoke from the wood-
fired grills is pervasive, and the food is
made for sharing – the steaks are great,
or try the house speciality of wood-grilled
pork loin with two sauces.

Bodega Guzmán ♟ ✕

Calle de los Judíos 7, Córdoba;
tel 957 29 09 60

With its tiled walls and benches, old
bullfighting paraphernalia and walls lined
with barrels from which the barmen
pour your fino, this old bodega offers cool
respite from the summer heat. The food
is typical bar food: jamón, pickled olives
and meatballs. Try the tuna with roast
capsicum – both are from tins, and
together they are delicious.

Taberna El Gallo ♟ ✕

Calle María Cristina 6, Córdoba;
tel 957 47 17 80

You'll find this time-worn bar behind a set
of carved green wooden doors. Inside, it
seems as if not much has changed since the
1960s, especially the décor and fluorescent
lighting. But that's not why you're here:
what you want is cold beer and hot prawns
deep-fried in the lightest, crispest batter.

Choco by Kisko García ♟ ✕

Calle Compositor Serrano Lucena 14,
Córdoba; tel 957 26 48 63
www.restaurantechoco.es

A short taxi ride out of the old town, among
the flats where the real people live, is this
immaculate modern Spanish dining room.
Here Kisko García serves up polished gems

cut from the rough diamonds of the local
cuisine. These could include a delicious
corn puree (*mazamorra*) streaked with
mackerel, or perhaps a handmade cracker
topped with succulent marinated white
anchovies (*boquerones*) on a bed of the rich
paste of roasted tomato, bread and garlic
known as *salmorejo*.

Taberna San Miguel Casa El Pisto ♟ ✕

Plaza San Miguel 1, Córdoba;
tel 957 47 83 28
www.casaelpisto.com

Taking up one corner of a small square on
the edge of Córdoba's old town, this tavern
and bar serves very good *pisto* (see page 236),

as its name suggests. But you should also consider the slow-cooked pig's trotters (*manitas de cerdo*) or pork ribs, with the meat falling off the bone, balanced by a salad of lettuce hearts.

Bodegas Campos 🍷✕

Calle Lineros 32, Córdoba;
tel 957 49 75 00
www.bodegascampos.com

Originally a bodega selling wines from the Montilla–Moriles region in 1908, this has since morphed into a tavern and restaurant offering old-school Cordoban cooking with a few modern touches. Between courses of excellent *salmorejo*, chilled bread and tomato soup (see page 179) and *arroz de rabo de toro*, creamy rice with oxtail (see page 246), take a wander through the cool dark dining rooms or across the patio, where plants clamber up the columns and old bullfighting posters are pasted on the walls.

Mercado Victoria 🍷✕

Paseo de la Victoria, Córdoba;
tel 608 72 12 40
www.mercadovictoria.com

Like Madrid's famous San Miguel tapas market, Mercado Victoria is made up of scores of concessions selling different tapas: perhaps one specialising in olives, another in jamón or little cups of *salmorejo* and sherry. It's housed in the old Caseta del Círculo de la Amistad, a restored nineteenth-century iron and glass edifice in a park, and is a fun place to sample some tapas and mingle with locals.

Las Casas de la Judería 🍷✕🏠

Calle Tomás Conde 10, Córdoba;
tel 957 20 20 95
www.casasypalacios.com

Four-star accommodation in a historic building just 200 metres from the Mezquita and close to the Alcázar de los Reyes Cristianos. With a swimming pool and shady courtyard, this offers a touch of luxury.

Hotel Macià Alfaros 🍷✕🏠

Calle Alfaros 18, Cordoba; tel 957 49 19 20
www.maciahoteles.com

Clean, affordable and busy hotel on the edge of the busy tourist centre. A short walk to Roman ruins and market.

Casa de los Azulejos 🍷✕🏠

Calle Fernando Colón 5, Córdoba;
tel 957 47 00 00
www.casadelosazulejos.com

A short stroll from Córdoba's Plaza de la Corredera is this comfortable and characterful guesthouse decorated with ornate metalwork and tiles from Seville, as was the fashion in the 1930s.

Restaurante Las Camachas 🍷✕

Avenida Europa 3, Montilla;
tel 957 65 00 04
www.restaurantelascamachas.com

Ask for fino straight from the barrel – it matches amazingly well with myriad dishes served here, including partridge pate and mushrooms cooked on the grill with oloroso. In the heart of Córdoba's Montilla–Moriles winemaking region, this is old-school Andalusian dining.

Bodega Toro Albalá 🍷

Avenida Antonio Sánchez 1, Aguilar de la Frontera; tel 957 660 046
www.toroalbala.com

Set in a former electricity substation, this bodega produces excellent aged oloroso and Pedro Ximénez (see page 239) under the guidance of characterful owner Antonio Sánchez Romero. His personal museum houses thousands of objects, ranging from prehistory, through the classical period (including the skeleton of a Roman slave), to the modern era; it is breathtaking in its audacity and awesome in its scope.

Pastelería Bernadino Solano 🛍✕

Calle Moralejo 50, Aguilar de la Frontera;
tel 957 66 02 61
www.pasteleriasolano.com

In the charming hilltop town of Aguilar de la Frontera, you'll find this everyday pastry shop where the locals buy their sweet treats. It is the home of renowned coffee meringues and equally delicious iced almond sponges.

Albacor 🛍✕

Calle San Marcos 22, Castro del Río
www.albacor.es

If you like salt cod, you'll love Albacor. About 35 kilometres south-east of Córdoba, this is the factory outlet for some rather excellent, high-end salt cod products.

Spring storms had dusted the Sierra de Segura with snow. When we stopped in a small village, it was eerily still. There were no footprints, and the only sound was the bleating of sheep. A crow sat on the cross on top of the roofless church, its bare stone walls now stripped of their whitewash and plaster. Long abandoned, this ghost village is testament to a time when Spaniards lived in the isolated extremities of their nation. Now it provides shelter for sheep, tended by a farmer who lives in a modern house in the protected valley below.

The road dropped through a pass and wound around, eventually revealing a city nestled into the side of a hill, on which was built a magnificent Arab fortress. With the simple yet beautiful lines of the Castle of Santa Catalina melding into the abrupt rocky outcrop, this seemed to be another country entirely. This was my first visit to Jaén, a landlocked province that had somehow escaped my attention until now.

Strategically sited on the route between Andalusia and Castile, the city of Jaén was an important key to the Moors' Iberian empire (the name itself comes from the Arab *khayyān*, or 'crossroads of the caravans'), and it still contains the best-preserved Arab baths in Spain. Many Spaniards come to pay homage at the stunning Renaissance cathedral built to house the Veil of Verónica.

The countryside surrounding Jaén is dominated by olive trees. Although owned by different families and cooperatives, this is the largest olive plantation on the planet, with some of the trees planted at the end of the eighteenth century, while others are less than a generation old. In late autumn the roads are filled with tractors and trucks carting olives to the mills, and when the pressing starts, the sweet aroma of fresh olive oil hangs in the air for weeks at a time. Any land not dedicated to olives or small farms is largely given over to wilderness. Great swathes of the province have been designated as natural parks, attracting hikers, horse riders, canoeists and anglers. The reserves are also open to hunters, who target the herds of wild boar and deer that roam the forests; as a result, game dishes are a speciality of the region.

For me, however, the city of Úbeda was the greatest surprise. A settlement since before Roman times, the Moorish city was completely destroyed during the late Middle Ages, then rebuilt during the Renaissance, following the same street layout, with palaces lining the central Plaza de Vázquez de Molina. The cobbled streets wind around convents and homes that lean over the streets, narrowing the sky to a sliver and making it difficult to walk two abreast. Glance past the buildings in any direction, though, and Úbeda is revealed as a speck of a city engulfed by olive groves.

AJO LABRAO

POUNDED EGG AND GARLIC MAYO

SERVES 4–6

This delicious mayonnaise is served on toasted bread as a starter at one of Jaén province's most famous yet remote restaurants, La Finca Mercedes, perched high in the hills near Cazorla. For many Spaniards, a true garlic mayo or *alioli* is never made with egg yolk, but is simply a salt and garlic puree emulsified with very fine extra virgin olive oil, added drop-by-drop. The process can be quite tense, as a single drop added too hastily can cause it to split. *Ajo labrao* uses hard-boiled egg yolk to help the olive oil emulsify, making it both more foolproof and richer-tasting. Any leftovers will keep for up to four days in the fridge, and can be used in the same way you'd use any mayo.

2 garlic cloves
1 teaspoon sea salt
4 hard-boiled egg yolks
150 ml extra virgin olive oil
4–6 slices sourdough bread
200 g caperberries (optional)

1 Place the garlic and salt in a mortar and use the pestle to grind to a fine paste. Add the egg yolks and gently pound to a smooth paste.

2 Start adding the olive oil a few drops at a time, making sure each addition is emulsified into the egg yolk and garlic mixture before adding any more. Slowly increase the amount of oil being added each time, making sure it is being thoroughly incorporated. Finish the *ajo labrao* by giving it a quick whisk.

3 Cut the bread in half and toast under a grill for a minute each side until browned. (You could do this in a toaster, but the heat from a grill is drier and makes crunchier toast.)

4 Smear the *ajo labrao* onto the toast and serve with caperberries, if you like.

The Jaénese landscape is dominated by
olive groves, and punctuated by white villages

ACEITE

OLIVE OIL

Looking down at the valley floor is like looking at an ochre canvas dabbed with a matrix of pale green spots, and the pattern extends over the ridge and into the next valley. Olive trees stretch to every horizon. Spain is the world's largest olive oil producer, and Jaén is considered the Spanish capital of olive oil, with over half a million hectares of olive groves. Most are recent plantings, but some date back centuries.

'This one is about 180 years old,' says José Antonio Jiménez, who owns a boutique olive oil factory and associated farms with his brother and another family. He recounts how, in the old days, the farmers would take three healthy cuttings, dig a hole and plant the three cuttings together. 'Look at this – this is how they grow,' he says, patting the fat gnarled trunk of one of these olive trees, which share a root system. He explains that the oil from these older trees may be less aromatic, but it is much more stable and stays fresher longer. Back in his factory, he shows us the hydraulic presses and mats once used to crush the olives, but now supplanted by a state-of-the-art olive mill. 'We love old trees, but we love new technology!' José exclaims. While the old presses have a romance about them and a story to tell, the new machinery produces better, fresher-tasting oil.

In this province, they are so proud of their olive oil that waiters will often suggest different oils to match different dishes, in the same way a sommelier does with wine. 'We don't just produce the most,' says José proudly, 'we produce the best.'

RIN RÁN

PÂTÉ OF POTATO, SALT COD AND PEPPERS

SERVES 4-6

Traditionally *rin rán* was made during winter, when the last of the greens had withered, and the best bet for a nourishing meal was to visit the cellar and gather an armful of potatoes and onions, then cook them with dried fish and any other vegetables to hand. With the pungency of raw onion, the deep flavour of salt cod and the richness of olive oil, this is particularly good slathered over chunks of crusty bread. This recipe is based on a version from La Finca Mercedes restaurant.

300 g salt cod fillet

1 kg potatoes, peeled and
  cut into 2–3 cm cubes

5 dried choricero or ñora
  peppers (see page 379)

3 ripe tomatoes

sea salt

1½ tablespoons cumin seeds

pinch of saffron threads

4 garlic cloves, peeled

100 ml olive oil

12 green olives, pitted and
  roughly chopped

1 white onion, finely diced

2 tablespoons sweet
  Spanish paprika

extra virgin olive oil,
  for drizzling

caperberries, to serve

1 Wash the excess salt off the salt cod, then place in a large bowl. Cover with water and leave to soak for 36 hours, changing the water three times. Drain, then shred the fish by hand.

2 Place the potato, dried peppers, tomatoes and a pinch of salt in a heavy-based saucepan, cover with cold water and bring to the boil over medium heat. Simmer for 15 minutes, then add the salt cod and simmer for 6–8 minutes or until the cod is cooked through and potato is soft.

3 Using a slotted spoon, remove the potato, dried peppers, tomatoes and cod from the pan and place on separate plates, reserving the stock in the pan. Once the peppers are cool enough to handle, use a small knife to scrape the flesh away from the skin, then discard the skin. Peel the tomatoes.

4 Heat a small heavy-based frying pan over medium heat, add the cumin seeds and toast for 1–2 minutes, stirring occasionally, until lightly browned and fragrant. Transfer the seeds to a pestle and mortar and set aside. Add the saffron to the pan and lightly toast until aromatic, then remove from the heat and add 2 tablespoons of the hot stock from the saucepan.

5 Pound the cumin seeds to a fine powder using the pestle and mortar. Add the garlic and grind to a paste, then add the saffron liquid and the flesh from the peppers and tomatoes and slowly work into a paste with the pestle. (Alternatively, place the ingredients in a food processor and pulse to form a rustic paste.)

6 In a separate bowl, mash the potato and cod with a potato masher and add the paste. Mix in the olive oil, olives, onion and paprika, along with 100 ml of the reserved stock, to make a rustic-looking mash. Season with salt to taste.

7 Serve in large scoops, drizzled with extra virgin olive oil and garnished with caperberries.

ANDRAJOS

RUSTIC VEGETABLE AND HANDMADE PASTA STEW

SERVES 6

A humble dish that's most popular in the countryside, *andrajos* translates as 'rags', a reference to the way the handmade pasta is presented, like torn strips of clothing. In the colder months of winter, this is often made with hare or salt cod, but during Holy Week the flesh is forsaken for vegetables – and it's this version we offer here, based on a recipe from La Finca Mercedes.

sea salt

about 175 g plain flour, plus extra for dusting

60 ml extra virgin olive oil, plus extra for drizzling

1 garlic bulb, broken into cloves, skin on

2 dried choricero or ñora peppers (see page 379)

1 teaspoon black peppercorns

2 ripe tomatoes

1 onion, diced

2 green bull horn capsicums (peppers) or 1 small green regular capsicum (pepper) diced

3 medium–large potatoes, peeled and roughly cut into 2 cm cubes using the 'click' method (see page 379)

300 g runner beans, topped and tailed, then cut into 3–4 cm lengths

½ teaspoon hot Spanish paprika

1 tablespoon sweet Spanish paprika

2 red capsicums (peppers)

600 g broad beans in pods, shelled

2 tablespoons chopped mint

1 To make the pasta, pour 150 ml of cold water into a bowl and add 1 teaspoon of salt, then, using your fingertips, mix in the flour a little at a time until you have a firm dough (you may need to add a little extra flour if the dough is too sticky). Scrape down your fingers, then gather the dough into a ball. Transfer to a lightly floured bench and knead for 2–3 minutes until smooth. Shape the dough into a ball, then wrap in plastic film and return to the bowl. Leave to rest in a cool place for 30 minutes.

2 On a well-floured bench, roll out the dough to a thickness of about 2 mm – you should end up with a sheet of pasta about 55 cm by 35 cm. Dust the top with flour, then cut into rough ribbons about 4 cm wide and 6–7 cm long. Lay the pasta on a tray or board in a single layer, then dust with a little more flour and cover with a dry tea towel.

3 Pour the olive oil into a *rondeau* (see page 383) or large deep saucepan and place over medium heat. When the oil is hot, add the garlic and peppers and cook for a minute or so until the peppers begin to brown. Remove the peppers and continue cooking the garlic, stirring occasionally, for 6–7 minutes or until soft.

4 Remove the garlic and, when cool enough to handle, squeeze the garlic flesh from the skins into a mortar. Add the peppers, peppercorns and a pinch of salt to the mortar and pound to a paste with the pestle. Cut the tomatoes in half and grate the cut side against a cheese grater over a bowl to pulp the flesh. Discard the skin.

5 In the same pan, cook the onion with a pinch of salt over medium heat, stirring occasionally, for 10 minutes or until soft. Add the green capsicum and continue cooking, stirring occasionally, for 10 minutes or until soft. Add the tomato pulp and cook for another 10 minutes to make a *sofrito* with a jam-like consistency. Add the paste from the mortar and cook for 2 minutes, stirring occasionally. Add the potato to the pan and cook for a few minutes, turning them in the sauce, then add the runner beans and cook for 2 minutes.

6 Add 1.5 litres of water to the pan and increase the heat to high. Just as the sauce comes to the boil, reduce the heat to medium and add the hot and sweet paprika. Simmer for 35 minutes or until the potato is cooked through.

7 Meanwhile, roast the red capsicums. Preheat the oven to 200°C/180°C fan. Place the red capsicums on a baking tray, drizzle with olive oil and sprinkle with a little salt, then roast in the oven for 30 minutes or until the flesh is soft and the skin has blackened. Transfer to a small bowl and cover with plastic film. When cool enough to handle, peel away the skin and remove the seeds and stem. Tear the flesh into 2–3 cm strips.

8 Add the pasta and broad beans to the pan, gently mix through the sauce, then cover with a lid and reduce the heat to low. Simmer very gently for 12 minutes, stirring occasionally, or until the pasta and beans are cooked.

9 Stir in the mint and red capsicum strips, then ladle into bowls. Drizzle with extra virgin olive oil and serve immediately.

EL RECOLECTOR

THE FORAGER

The drop to the river below is brutally sheer. The siren-like lure of gravity draws my gaze beyond the castle wall on which I sit to the river, cascading some 300 metres below. Foraging has never been this dangerous. With local businessman and lover of wild food Iñigo Caño Arbaiza, we've spent the morning clambering around the grounds of a thirteenth-century tower, looking for spiny wild asparagus called *espárragos de piedra*. Despite their thorny bushes, Iñigo refuses to wear gloves: '*Gato con guantes no caza*' he says ('A cat with gloves cannot hunt'). We find lots of wild asparagus bushes, but not too many spears.

After several hours, and with a few cuts and sore legs, we return to central Jaén for a coffee in the plaza, proud of our scant handful of bounty. There we find scores of old men proffering fat bunches of wild asparagus. Whole baskets full of them. 'I love foraging,' says Iñigo. 'Every season the forests and the countryside throw up different species of mushrooms. You watch the weather, the sun and the rain, because wild foods are very specific about when they appear.' He takes a sip of his coffee. 'And then you have to be quick, as there are the professional foragers who head to our wild areas and pick all the mushrooms and other wild foods for restaurants and sell them for profit. For most of us, though, it just offers the chance to go into our beautiful countryside and return with a sense of pride – and something to feed the family.'

ESPÁRRAGOS Y HUEVOS

WILD ASPARAGUS AND EGGS

SERVES 4-6

There is a wild asparagus that grows in Spain that is simply garden-variety asparagus gone feral. Then there is *espárragos de piedra*, a kind of asparagus that grows from a spiky maze of bramble-like vines, the spears of which have an intense flavour and aroma. I was shown this dish by amateur forager Iñigo Caño Arbaiza, who used a technique I had never seen before but which, he tells me, is common in the countryside. He slow-cooked the wild asparagus in water and olive oil, then emulsified it with more olive oil and runny fried eggs to create a rustic dip. The result is incredibly delicious, and is something you might make for a special breakfast or to share at an informal gathering when a few friends are cooking together. I can assure you it goes really well with crusty bread and a glass of red wine.

3 bunches thin asparagus, ideally wild
300 ml mild-flavoured extra virgin olive oil
sea salt
4 eggs
crusty bread, to serve

1 Wash and drain the asparagus, then remove any tough parts from the bases of the stems by bending the spears – they will break where the woody stem gives way to the tender part of the spear. Cut the spears into 2–3 cm lengths.

2 Place the asparagus in a heavy-based frying pan with 1 tablespoon of the olive oil, a pinch of salt and 500 ml of water. Bring to the boil over high heat, then reduce the heat to medium and simmer for 6 minutes or until the asparagus is soft (tougher wild asparagus will take longer to cook). Drain.

3 Return the drained asparagus to the same pan and add another tablespoon of the olive oil. Sauté the asparagus over medium–high heat for 4 minutes, then season with salt and add another 200 ml of the olive oil. Take the asparagus off the heat but leave in the pan to keep warm while you cook the eggs.

4 Fill a large ceramic serving bowl with hot water to warm.

5 Pour the remaining 60 ml of the olive oil into a large frying pan and place over medium heat. When the oil is hot, break the eggs into the pan and fry for 1–2 minutes or until the whites are cooked but the yolks are still very runny.

6 Pour the water from the bowl and wipe it dry. Tip in the contents of the asparagus pan. Using an egg flip, add the eggs to the bowl.

7 Using a knife and fork, cut the eggs into small pieces; as you do this, you will also cut some of the asparagus, and this is fine. Keep cutting and mixing with your knife and fork until the egg is in tiny pieces and has emulsified with the oil. When it is ready, the mixture should be creamy, with the oil and egg combined. Serve immediately with bread.

PIPIRRANA JIENENSE

VEGETABLE SALAD

SERVES 4

There are as many different versions of *pipirrana* as there are Andalusian cooks – but essentially, this is a light, fresh salad of tomato, cucumber, capsicum and onion, flavoured with garlic and perhaps dressed with wine vinegar and olive oil. Some versions are spiced up with ground cumin seeds, and in Cádiz it is sometimes served with preserved mackerel. But in Jaén it is made with a mayonnaise-like sauce to create a wet salad that you eat with a spoon. Ideally made the day before and chilled overnight to allow the flavours to meld, this is a sensational dish for a hot day.

3 hard-boiled eggs
1 garlic clove, peeled
sea salt
1 green bull horn capsicum (pepper) or ½ green regular capsicum (pepper), finely chopped
100 ml olive oil
1 kg ripe tomatoes, peeled and cut into rough cubes
2 tablespoons chopped oregano
1 × 120 g tin good-quality tuna in oil
250 ml chilled water
1 tablespoon aged red wine vinegar
freshly ground black pepper

1 Remove the yolks from the eggs, then finely chop the whites.

2 Place the garlic in a mortar with a teaspoon of salt and use the pestle to grind to a smooth paste. Add half of the green capsicum, and continue pounding until you have a rough paste, then add the egg yolks and gently pound to a smooth paste.

3 Start adding the olive oil a few drops at a time, making sure each addition is emulsified into the egg yolk, capsicum and garlic mixture before adding any more. Slowly increase the amount of oil being added each time, making sure it is being thoroughly incorporated. Finish the dressing by giving it a quick whisk.

4 Place the tomato in a large bowl with the chopped egg white, remaining capsicum and oregano. Pour the oil from the tuna into the bowl, then break up the tuna with your hands and add it to the bowl as well.

5 Add the dressing and stir to mix through, then pour in the chilled water and vinegar. Mix well and season to taste with salt and pepper. Cover with plastic film and refrigerate – overnight, if possible.

6 Spoon the chilled salad into bowls and serve.

Late spring snow blankets a deserted village in the Sierras

HABAS con BACALAO y ACEITE

BROAD BEANS AND SALT COD

SERVES 4

Thick tapestry-like drapes covered the doorway of Taberna Casa Gorrión, an old tavern not far from Jaén's cathedral. There was still snow on the peaks of the sierras, and the drapes were shielding those inside from the icy wind blowing down from the mountains. The parts of the tavern walls not covered in oil paintings of old men and still lifes of food and drink were stained by over a century's worth of tobacco smoke. We ordered this classic local spring dish of broad beans and salt cod. It's really more of a concept than a recipe, but the combination is just so phenomenal that I had to include it here.

200 g salt cod fillet
1 baguette
extra virgin olive oil,
   for drizzling
800 g broad beans in pods

1 Wash the excess salt off the salt cod, then place in a large bowl. Cover with water and leave to soak for 36 hours, changing the water three times. Drain, remove any skin and bone from the cod, then cut into 1 cm thick slices.

2 Slice the baguette. Place the fish on the bread and drizzle well with olive oil.

3 To eat, pod the broad beans and enjoy them, perhaps with a glass of beer or wine, then eat some bread and cod. Simple.

MORCILLA BLANCA

WHITE SAUSAGE

MAKES 2 KG

You know a city takes their smallgoods seriously when the *charcutería* section of the market takes up more than a quarter of the entire floor space. Jaén's Mercado de San Francisco is a temple to meat, with numerous stalls dedicated solely to jamón or preserved sausages in all their incarnations. The *Jienenses* are particularly fond of *morcilla blanca*. While its darker cousin, *morcilla*, is made with blood, *morcilla blanca* is made from fatty pork blended with peppery spices and given a pleasing golden tinge by turmeric or saffron. If you have a mincer (or a friendly butcher to mince the meat for you) and a food processor or electric mixer with a sausage attachment, *morcilla blanca* is surprisingly easy to make – and will keep in the refrigerator for a week or, wrapped carefully in plastic film, can be frozen for up to three months. Sliced and served as part of a charcuterie platter, it's a true crowd pleaser.

3 metres 36 mm wide pork
    sausage casings
1 kg onions, finely diced
250 g short-grain rice
1 garlic bulb
500 g pork jowl or belly,
    skinned
1 tablespoon freshly ground
    white pepper
1 teaspoon hot Spanish paprika
½ teaspoon freshly grated
    nutmeg
½ teaspoon ground cloves
½ teaspoon turmeric or
    ground saffron
1 tablespoon fine salt
7 egg whites

1 Wash the sausage casings well, inside and out, then soak in cold water for 3 hours.

2 Place the onion in a saucepan and just cover with water, then bring to the boil over high heat. Reduce the heat to medium and simmer for 10 minutes or until the onion is cooked but still has a firm bite. Drain well. Lay a clean tea towel over a baking tray or large plate and spread the onion over the tea towel, then cover with another tea towel. Pat to dry, then place in the fridge to chill.

3 Place the rice and 500 ml of water in a heavy-based saucepan. Bring to the boil over high heat, then reduce the heat to medium and simmer for 12 minutes or until the rice is almost cooked but still slightly firm in the centre. Drain well, then spread out on a baking tray or large plate. Cover with a clean tea towel and chill in the fridge for 2 hours.

4 Meanwhile, preheat the oven to 190°C/170°C fan. Place the garlic on a baking tray and roast for 30 minutes or until soft. Leave until cool enough to handle, then squeeze the flesh from the skins and crush before chopping finely.

5 Cut the pork into 2 cm × 1 cm pieces, then pass through the fine die of a mincer. (If you don't have a mincer, ask your butcher to do this for you.) Place the minced pork in a large bowl and add the onion, rice, garlic, pepper, paprika, nutmeg, cloves, turmeric or saffron, salt and egg whites. Mix well with very clean hands for several minutes until the mixture is smooth and starts to feel sticky, then cover with plastic film and refrigerate for 2 hours.

6 Knot one end of the sausage casing, then slide the open end onto the nozzle of the sausage attachment of your food processor or mixer. Start filling the sausage casing with the meat mixture, taking care to make it neither too loose nor too tight, to form a 20 cm long sausage. Leave about 5 cm of unfilled casing then tie off with kitchen string and cut. Repeat until you have used all the meat mixture – you should have five or six sausages.

7 Bring a stockpot or very large saucepan of water to the boil over high heat, then reduce the heat until the water is just simmering. Carefully slip a heatproof plate into the pan, to prevent the sausages from sitting directly on the base of the hot pan, then slide the sausages into the simmering water and cook very gently for 20 minutes or until firm to the touch.

8 Carefully remove the sausages and cool on a baking tray or large plate, covered with tea towels.

9 The sausages are now ready to eat. Slice and serve as a snack with drinks.

LA COCINERA Y SU CAZADOR

THE CHEF AND HER HUNTER

José Ramón is a hunter. He is also the husband of Mercedes Castillo, chef at La Finca Mercedes in La Iruela, a village near Cazorla, and together they make a formidable team. Their food is famous in a province itself famous for its game. As well as bringing home his quarry for her to cook, he works front of house in the restaurant. There is a reassuring stillness about him. 'You need still hands to be a good shot,' José explains. 'A good shot is a clean shot – dead in an instant. Fear makes meat tough.'

People come to Jaén province to fish and hunt. Huge tracts of land have been preserved as wilderness, and pockets of settlement in the natural parks are nestled into forests and valleys that make for fruitful hunting and fishing. For older Spaniards, years of starvation are still within living memory, a time knowing how to kill was a matter of survival. Even today, the hunting season is eagerly anticipated, with birds in feather and small game in fur taking pride of place in the markets.

Knowing how to cook the bounty of the hunt has been turned into a culinary artform, with those capable of rendering classic game dishes garnering much respect. 'The secret to good game is a good death,' says Mercedes. 'You also need to know where the meat is tender and where the gristle is, and a good knife to trim the meat. Then you need to know how to cook it – and what to drink with it!'

SOLOMILLO DE JABALÍ

MARINATED LOIN OF WILD BOAR

SERVES 4

This recipe was given to me by Mercedes, the chef at La Finca Mercedes, near Cazorla. If you can't get hold of wild boar, try this with pork or venison. During the marinating time, the acid from the wine and apples helps to break down the muscle fibres in the meat, and the resulting sauce is quite delicious.

800 g wild boar loin

2 granny smith apples, peeled, cored and cut into 1 cm dice

1 tablespoon dried oregano

600 ml red wine

4 garlic cloves, roughly chopped

1 tablespoon smoked sweet Spanish paprika

80 ml extra virgin olive oil

1 brown onion, finely diced

sea salt and freshly ground black pepper

1 litre olive oil, for deep-frying

2 potatoes, peeled and cut into 1 cm thick slices

4 green bull horn capsicums (peppers) or 2 green regular capsicums (peppers)

1 Use a very sharp knife to trim away any sinew and 'silver' outer membrane from the wild boar. Cut the loin crossways into 3 cm thick medallions. Place the boar medallions in a bowl with the apple, oregano, wine, garlic and paprika. Mix well, then cover with plastic film and leave to marinate in the refrigerator for 12–24 hours.

2 Remove the boar from the marinade and place on a large plate. Strain the marinade into a bowl and reserve the apple, garlic and oregano in the sieve, as well as the strained marinade.

3 Pour half of the extra virgin olive oil into a heavy-based saucepan and place over medium–high heat. When the oil is hot, add the onion and cook for 10 minutes, stirring occasionally, until soft and translucent. Reduce the heat to medium and add the reserved apple, garlic and oregano, then cover and cook for 10 minutes, stirring occasionally, until the apple is very soft. Add the marinade and bring to the boil over high heat, then reduce the heat to medium and cook for 10 minutes or until the sauce has reduced by half.

4 Meanwhile, pour the remaining extra virgin olive oil into a large frying pan and place over high heat. When the oil is hot, add the boar medallions and cook on one side for 2–3 minutes or until browned, then season with salt and pepper and turn over. Season the other side and cook for 2–3 minutes or until browned on the outside but still rare in the centre. Transfer the boar to the sauce, return to medium heat and baste the medallions in the sauce for 3 minutes. Remove from the heat and allow to rest.

5 Pour the olive oil for deep-frying into a heavy-based saucepan or wok and heat to 170°C or until a cube of bread dropped into the oil browns in 15 seconds.

6 Add half of the potato slices to the oil and deep-fry, stirring occasionally, for 10–12 minutes or until cooked through. Remove, drain on paper towel and season with salt. Repeat with the remaining potato slices.

7 Deep-fry the whole green capsicums in the same oil for 3 minutes, turning occasionally. Remove, drain on paper towel and season with salt.

8 Place two or three boar medallions on each plate and spoon over some sauce, then serve with fried potato and capsicum to the side.

BATATAS AL COÑAC

SWEET POTATOES BRAISED WITH
BRANDY, HONEY AND SPICES

SERVES 6

Mum used to cook these for me when I was a kid, but I had forgotten all about them until I saw them on a menu in a restaurant in Úbeda. Braising fruit in honey or sugar is an ancient way of preserving them, and is still popular in more remote regions of Andalusia. When sweet potatoes arrived from the New World, they were candied along with the fruit. Although not traditional, I sometimes like to add prunes, dates and dried figs to the sweet potatoes as they are cooking. These are delicious with cream or ice cream.

3 medium sweet potatoes,
    peeled and cut into 2 cm
    thick rounds
90 g unsalted butter
200 ml mild-flavoured honey
230 g caster sugar
2 cinnamon quills
zest of 1 orange, in long strips
6 cloves
80 ml dry white wine
140 ml brandy

1 Preheat the oven to 170°C/150°C fan.

2 Place the sweet potato in a flameproof casserole, along with the butter, honey, sugar, cinnamon, orange zest, cloves, wine and 80 ml of the brandy. Stir well, then bring to a simmer over low–medium heat. Place a cartouche (circle of baking paper) on the surface of the liquid, to keep the sweet potato submerged, then cover with the lid. Bake in the oven for 2 hours or until the liquid is reduced and syrupy but not too thick.

3 Remove from the oven and increase the temperature to 200°C/180°C fan. Remove the lid and cartouche, then place the casserole over high heat for 4–5 minutes or until the syrup has reduced to a thick glaze, using a spoon to gently baste the sweet potato and turn the rounds through the syrup. The sweet potato may break up a little, but try to keep it as intact as possible. Return to the oven and bake, uncovered, for a further 15 minutes or until the sweet potato is dark ruby in colour.

4 Remove from the oven and gently stir through the remaining brandy. Transfer to a deep ceramic dish and leave to cool to room temperature, then refrigerate. Serve chilled.

MAGDALENAS

MADELEINES

MAKES 10

Spaniards have madeleines for breakfast, dipping these little sponge cakes into their *café con leche*. This recipe was inspired by those I bought at the Monasterio de la Purísima Concepción in Úbeda. Once upon a time nuns baked pastries in return for alms, but these days the transaction is a retail one, with fixed weights and prices. When buying pastries from a convent, the money is offered on *el torno*, a wooden cylinder worn smooth by countless hands, then the nuns place the pastries and change on the cylinder and spin it back around to you. In this way the nuns' sanctity is preserved, and you'll rarely catch more than a glimpse of a wimple through cracks in the old woodwork.

3 eggs
125 g caster sugar
100 ml mild-flavoured
    extra virgin olive oil
50 ml milk
finely grated zest of 1 lemon
200 g self-raising flour
1 tablespoon white sugar

1 Preheat the oven to 210°C/190°C fan and place 10 paper patty pan cases in a muffin tray.

2 Break the eggs into a bowl and beat with an electric hand-held beater or freestanding mixer until they have doubled in volume. With the motor running, gradually add the caster sugar and beat until the sugar is dissolved and the mixture is pale and creamy. Gradually pour in the olive oil while still beating. When well combined, beat in the milk and lemon zest. Sift in the flour and gently fold it in with a metal spoon. Leave the batter to stand for 5 minutes.

3 Half-fill the patty pan cases with the batter, then top up evenly and sprinkle with a little white sugar.

4 Bake the madeleines for 15 minutes or until browned on top and a skewer inserted in the centre comes out clean.

5 Allow the madeleines to cool in the tray for 5 minutes before transferring them, still in their cases, to a wire rack to cool. They can then be stored in an airtight container for up to 3 days.

6 Serve for breakfast with *café con leche*.

PASTELES DE GLORIA

GLORIOUS MARZIPAN PASTRIES

MAKES 18

I noticed a small woman struggling with bags laden with bread as she walked up the narrow cobbled street towards the Monasterio de la Purísima Concepción. Leaning against the heavy wooden door, she carried the loaves over the threshold and offered them as a donation to the nuns inside. Skilled bakers themselves, they concentrate on making sweets, including the doughnut-shaped biscuits known as *roscos de huevo*, crumbly biscuits called *polvorones de anís* or *polvorones de almendras* (made with almonds), and these delicious treats. The small woman liked them too. Placing a ten-euro note on the wooden *torno*, she called out to the sister on the other side, 'May I have a box of the *glorias*, sister? And keep the change.'

100 g caster sugar
6 egg yolks (from 55 g eggs)
1 egg yolk, beaten with
   1 tablespoon water

MARZIPAN

280 g blanched almonds
300 g icing sugar
2 egg whites (from 55 g eggs)
½ teaspoon lemon juice
½ teaspoon almond essence

1 Cover a large plate with baking paper.

2 Place the sugar and 50 ml water in a small heavy-based saucepan and bring to the boil over medium heat, stirring to dissolve the sugar. Reduce the heat to low–medium and simmer until the syrup has reduced to a thick consistency and reached what is known as 'soft ball' stage (112–115°C on a sugar thermometer). To test this without a thermometer, drop ¼ teaspoon of the syrup into a cup of cold water – if you can easily form the syrup into a ball under water, it has reached soft ball stage.

3 Meanwhile, gently whisk the egg yolks in a heatproof bowl until smooth. While the syrup is still hot, pour it very slowly into the egg yolks, stirring constantly and vigorously with a wooden spoon. Tip the mixture back into the same saucepan and cook over low heat, stirring constantly, for 10 minutes or until it has a similar consistency to thick polenta. Use a spatula to get into the corners of the pan, alternating with a small whisk to smooth out any lumps.

4 Pour the egg-yolk mixture onto the prepared plate, smoothing it out with the spatula, then place in the refrigerator for an hour to set.

5 Meanwhile, to make the marzipan, place the almonds in a food processor and pulse to the consistency of fine breadcrumbs. Transfer to a bowl with the icing sugar and mix together, then add the egg whites, lemon juice and almond essence. With clean hands, mix well to form a stiff paste. Shape into a 20 cm long log and wrap in plastic film, then refrigerate for an hour to set.

6 Preheat the oven to 170°C/150°C fan and line a baking tray with baking paper.

7 Roll the egg-yolk mixture into 18 × 1 cm spheres between your palms.

8 Cut the marzipan log into three. Roll out each piece into a square about 2–3 mm thick, then cut into 6 cm squares. Place an egg-yolk sphere in the middle of each square and bring the corners of the square together to enclose the sphere, pressing gently to seal. Turn over so the seal is on the bottom, then uses your fingers to shape each one into a square with a domed top.

9 Place the pastries on the prepared baking tray, then brush with the eggwash. Bake for 18 minutes or until the tops are slightly browned. Remove from the oven and leave on the tray to cool to room temperature.

10 Serve after dinner with a glass of oloroso sherry or dessert wine.

TENEMOS
BOTELLAS DE
AGUA

THE NUNS

Three nuns are sitting on chairs behind a heavy iron grille. They quietly finger their rosaries as they introduce themselves: María José, Clara and Teresa, of the *Clarisas Descalzas* order. Many of Andalusia's best pastries are made by nuns – and we have visited many convents, hoping to learn why their pastries taste better than those from pastry shops, but so far our efforts had proved fruitless.

When I pose the question to them, they pause for a moment, then quietly discuss it among themselves. Overcoming an initial reluctance and slight awkwardness in conversation – something we put down to their practice of living and working in silence – Sister María José insists that the recipes the sisters use are no different to those used by others: 'They came with the girls from their mothers' kitchens when

they entered the convent.' Sister Teresa adds: 'The best ingredients are like law to us – the olive oil must be the best extra virgin.' Then it is Sister Clara's turn to speak: 'We work in silence. We are not here to make sweets. We are here to work with God.' At this, Teresa becomes quite gregarious and animated: 'When we are mixing the ingredients and rolling the pastries, we are at one with God. Our job is to love God and to love his people. The pastries we make are so good because we make them with love for God.'

The nuns go on to describe how they make their sweet treats without actually passing on a recipe. And with that we take our leave, somehow purchasing far more biscuits and pastries than it is humanly possible to eat in a week.

ROSCOS DE VINO

SWEET WINE AND FENNEL BISCUITS

MAKES 20

It took several visits to different convents to track down this recipe. Of course, I could have gone to a baker or chef and asked them for the recipe, but the best *roscos* are made by nuns. When I went to convents and asked the question, I was met with lots of silent shaking of heads and exceptionally polite refusals – until we came across a nun who had once worked with our researcher/driver's girlfriend and were granted an audience with the sisters of the Monasterio de la Concepción Franciscana in Jaén. Although they wouldn't give me their closely guarded recipe, they did pass on a few tips for making these lovely rich little biscuits.

60 g blanched almonds

1 teaspoon fennel seeds

500 g plain flour, plus extra for dusting

125 g caster sugar

pinch of ground cinnamon

130 ml mild-flavoured extra virgin olive oil

130 ml Pedro Ximénez sherry

50 ml anís or other sweet anise liqueur

1 litre olive oil, for deep-frying

150 g icing sugar

1 Place the almonds and fennel seeds in a heavy-based frying pan and toast over medium heat, tossing them occasionally and watching closely to make sure they don't burn, for 5 minutes or until lightly browned and the aroma of fennel fills the kitchen. Remove from the heat and leave to cool a little, then transfer to a food processor and pulse to the consistency of fine breadcrumbs.

2 Mix the ground almonds and fennel, flour, caster sugar and cinnamon in a bowl with a whisk. In another bowl, mix the extra virgin olive oil, Pedro Ximénez and anise liqueur. Pour the wet ingredients over the dry ingredients and mix with a wooden spoon until the dough comes together, then work with your hands until a smooth dough is formed.

3 Weigh out the dough into 20 × 50 g pieces, then roll each piece between your palms into a ball. On a lightly floured bench, roll each ball into a 13 cm long log. Brush the end of each log with a little cold water, then join the ends together to form a ring and press to seal. Spread the biscuits out on a tray or large plate lined with baking paper.

4 Pour the olive oil into a heavy-based saucepan or wok and heat to 180–190°C or until a cube of bread dropped into the oil browns in 10–15 seconds.

5 Using a metal slotted spoon, carefully lower five biscuits at a time into the hot oil. Deep-fry for 30 seconds or until browned, then turn over and cook for another 30 seconds or until the other side is browned. Remove and drain on paper towel.

6 Place the icing sugar in a shallow bowl and, when the biscuits are cool enough to handle, dredge them in the icing sugar.

7 Serve at room temperature with coffee, and perhaps a glass of anise liqueur. Any leftovers will keep in an airtight container for up to a week.

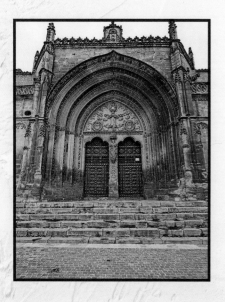

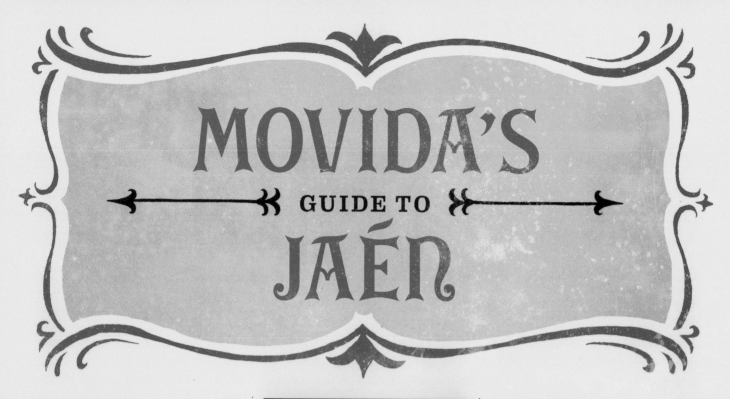

MOVIDA'S

GUIDE TO

JAÉN

Mercado de San Francisco

Calle Álamos 10, Jaén
www.mercadosanfrancisco.es

Don't miss the extensive range of jamón, sausages and preserved meats at this market in the city of Jaén.

Taberna La Manchega

Bernardo López 8, Jaén; tel 953 23 21 92

For a city of its size, Jaén has a lively bar culture, helped along by a large student population. This wonderful old-school bar is in the part of the old town nicknamed 'laneway of the drunks' because of all the bars. Here the liquors are kept in an ice bucket on the bar and you'll find the usual bar snacks such as tortilla, plus perhaps a plate of snails in spring.

El Bodegón

Joaquín Tenorio 4, Plaza del Pósito, Jaén; tel 953 19 00 29

It's as if the kids have taken over granddad's cellar bar, put in a turntable and invited all their friends for a party. A fun and grungy late-night place set in an old bodega and serving decent bar food.

Panaceite

Calle Bernabé Soriano 1, Jaén

With its little terrace on a busy strip, this bar is a rather agreeable place to spend a warm evening. A younger crowd tends to gather here before heading to one of the many late-night bars in town.

Taberna Casa Gorrión

Arco del Consuelo 7, Jaén; tel 953 23 20 00
www.tabernagorrion.es

The thick tapestry-like drape behind the door of this beautiful old bar not only keeps in the warm air, but also adds another layer of privacy. Simple drinks and snacks along the lines of broad beans and salt cod (see page 288) are the order of the day here, but it's worth a visit just to see the 100-year-old jamón preserved in a glass case.

Parador de Jaén ♟ ✕ ⌂

**Castillo de Santa Catalina, s/n Jaén,
tel 953 23 00 00
www.parador.es**

Spend the night in an Arab castle perched
on a narrow ridge overlooking the city. The
views from the rooms across the gorge to the
mountains are stunning and the main salon
is a massive-domed stone structure with
a roof soaring 20 metres above.

Cantina La Estación ♟ ✕

**Cuesta Rodadera 1, Úbeda;
tel 687 77 72 30
www.cantinalaestacion.com**

Channelling the grand era of railway travel,
this bar and restaurant is themed as an Art
Deco train carriage, setting the stage for
modern, produce-driven interpretations
of classic dishes. Start with their excellent
selection of olive oils and a little bread,
then consider the tartare of local trout or
handmade *andrajos* pasta with prawns
and hare.

Panadería Paniceite 🛍 ✕

Calle Real 51, Úbeda; tel 653 68 28 62

This small bakery off the main shopping
strip in Ubéda offers the best pastries from
around Jaén province. Look out for the
light-as-air *hojaldres* puff-pastry treats
and the doughnut-shaped sweet biscuits
called *roscos*.

Monasterio de la Purísima Concepción 🛍 ✕

Calle Montiel 5, Úbeda; tel 953 75 04 03

If you're after convent pastries, look for the
heavy wooden doors in an ancient stone
building down this very narrow street. Push
the bell and, when one of the nuns comes
to the grille, order your pastries, put your
money in the wooden cylinder or *torno* and
wait. Try the *pastas de coñac*, shaped like
a four-leafed clover, or the rich almond-
flavoured sweet treats *pasteles de gloria*
(see page 300).

Oleícola San Francisco ✕

**Calle Pedro Pérez S/N, Begíjar;
tel 953 76 34 15
www.oleicolasanfrancisco.com**

This small family-owned olive oil mill,
located on the edge of a small regional
town to the west of Úbeda, offers tours and
tastings of some rather lovely extra virgin
oils from their olive groves. Call ahead to
book breakfast.

La Finca Mercedes ♟ ✕ ⌂

**Carretera de la Sierra km 1, Parque
Natural de Cazorla, La Iruela;
tel 953 72 10 87
www.lafincamercedes.es**

This hotel and restaurant is run by a
husband and wife team who specialise in
traditional dishes, such as the bean and
handmade pasta stew known as *andrajos*
(see page 278) and game, including tender
wild boar. The dining room overlooks
the rugged peaks of the Sierra de Cazorla
and the olive groves of the foothills, and is
decorated with hunting trophies.

Parador de Úbeda ♟ ✕ ⌂

**Plaza de Vázquez Molina, s/n Úbeda,
tel 953 75 03 45
www.parador.es**

In this renaissance city, perched on a ridge
above a river and recognised by the UN
as a place of cultural significance, is this
state-owned hotel in a magnificent sixteenth
century palace on the historic Plaza de
Vázquez de Molina.

The last rays of sun flood the snowy peaks of the Sierra Nevada with a rich golden glow that rapidly gives way to hues of magenta and violet as the sun finally sets. The lights of Granada blink into life and its monuments are painted yellow by floodlights. The great mountain range soaring nearly 3,500 metres above Granada dominates both the city and its province. It proved the final barrier for the Catholic Monarchs Ferdinand and Isabella to recapture the last Muslim stronghold in Spain. Protected in his palatial yet heavily fortified Alhambra, Emir Muhammad XII, known as Boabdil to the Spanish, held out here until the beginning of 1492. His surrender enabled the Spanish to turn their attentions westward to the Atlantic, starting with Columbus's voyage to the Americas that same year.

Despite the conversion of Granada to a Catholic city, its streets filled with beautiful renaissance and baroque architecture, the sheer power of the Alhambra, rising from a ridge above a gorge, dominates the city. This sprawling complex of intricately carved stone pillars and magnificent archwork, and the constant presence of running water in the gardens of the adjoining pleasure palaces, defines Granada and make it a global drawcard.

The province of Granada has some of the oldest intact Moorish irrigation systems in Europe, still feeding the vegetable gardens of the river plains (see page 329). The harvest of these gardens, combined with game and smallgoods, makes for a rich traditional cuisine of seasonal dishes suited to its colder mountain climate. One of the province's most famous dishes is *tortilla sacromonte*, a thick omelette made with brains or other soft organs. Another hearty dish is *olla de San Antón* – a stew of dried broad beans, white beans, garlic, onions, the ears and tail of a pig, various types of preserved meat and fat, thickened with rice and potatoes. What is counter-intuitive about the cuisine of Granada is the frequent and regular access to fresh seafood. The Mediterranean coast, or Costa Tropical, is only an hour away by truck. But even before fast roads reached the province, dried seafood from the Mediterranean formed a good part of the diet.

The Costa Tropical grows much of Spain's tropical fruit. All over Spain, but especially in the south, fruit is commonly served as dessert, with a fruit basket or platter being placed in the middle of the table and guests helping themselves and peeling fruit at the table. When the Andalusian voyages returned from Central America in the 1600s, they brought back the *chirimoya* (custard apple), and today those grown in Granada have their own protected *Denominación de Origen* status. Also grown here are mangoes, which originally arrived from the former colony of the Philippines, papaya from South America and persimmons from Asia. But perhaps the fruit most readily associated with Granada is the pomegranate, which was introduced to this part of Spain by the Moors. While our English word for the fruit is derived from the old French *pome* ('apple') and *grenata* ('many seeded'), its Spanish name is granada.

SOPA ALPUJARREÑA

ALMOND AND BREAD SOUP WITH SAFFRON

SERVES 6

The Alpujarra is a region of the Sierra Nevada dominated by a string of high-altitude stone villages. Living two kilometres up in the sky is hard work – the daily slog of tending to herds of goats and kitchen gardens is exacerbated by the pull of gravity in these cold, steep valleys. Fed by a constant supply of melting snow, the country is always green, more so for the terraced pastures first built by the Berbers, who settled here in the eighth century. Winters are cold and long, so it is no wonder one of the local favourites is this thick, hearty and delicious soup made from bread, almonds and saffron. Quick and thrifty, it is even better when you use the freshest almonds and the best-quality extra virgin olive and jamón you can afford. This recipe came from Restaurante el Asador, in the town of Capileira.

60 g sourdough bread,
    without crusts
6 garlic cloves, skin on
80 g blanched almonds
sea salt
yolks of 3 hard-boiled eggs
1.6 litres *puchero* stock
    (see page 82) or good
    chicken stock.
good pinch of saffron threads
6 eggs

CROUTONS

120 g two-day-old sourdough
    bread, without crusts
100 ml olive oil
sea salt

1 To make the croutons, cut the bread into 1 cm cubes. Pour the olive oil into a frying pan and place over medium heat. When the oil is hot, add the cubed bread and fry slowly, turning regularly, for 4–5 minutes or until browned and crisp. Using a slotted spoon, lift the croutons out of the oil and drain on paper towel, then season with salt. Reserve the oil in the frying pan.

2 For the soup, you need to start with a *picada*. Return the frying pan to medium heat and, when hot, add the bread and garlic. Cook the bread for 3 minutes or until brown, then turn and cook the other side for 2–3 minutes or until brown, turning the garlic occasionally. Remove the bread and garlic and drain on paper towel. Add the almonds to the pan and cook, stirring occasionally, for 4 minutes or until well browned. Using a slotted spoon, remove the almonds and drain on paper towel. Season with salt.

3 When the garlic is cool enough to handle, squeeze the flesh from the skins into a mortar. Add a pinch of salt and pound to a rough paste with the pestle. Use your hands to crumble the fried bread into the mortar, then pound to break up the bread a little. Add the almonds and pound to a paste, then add the hard-boiled egg yolks and keep pounding to a fine paste.

4 Heat the stock in a large saucepan over medium heat until simmering.

5 Meanwhile, in a small heavy-based frying pan, toast the saffron for a minute or so over medium heat until you just start to smell the aroma. Add a couple of tablespoons of the hot stock to the saffron, swirl it around, then tip the contents of the frying pan back into the pan with the stock.

6 Add the *picada* to the stock, bring back to a simmer and cook for 5–7 minutes to allow the soup to thicken a little.

7 Poach the eggs in the soup by breaking them, one at time, into a cup and sliding into the hot soup. Swirl the soup a little so the egg white wraps around the yolk. Repeat with the remaining eggs, then simmer over low–medium heat for 4 minutes, or until the white is set but the yolk is still a little runny.

8 To serve, ladle the soup into individual bowls with one of the poached eggs and garnish with a handful of croutons.

REMOJÓN GRANADINO

SALT COD, ORANGE AND OLIVE SALAD

SERVES 4-6

This succulent and refreshing salad matches moist morsels of salt cod with tangy segments of orange, counterbalanced with the salty tang of black olives. Bringing it all together is an overarching drizzle of fresh and fruity extra virgin olive oil. It is interesting to think that cod from the Atlantic and oranges from the Middle East would come together to form one of the signature dishes of a landlocked city in the foothills of the Sierra Nevada.

600 g salt cod fillets
100 ml extra virgin olive oil
4 oranges
2 hard-boiled eggs
1 garlic clove, finely chopped
1 tablespoon red wine vinegar
sea salt
1 red onion, thinly sliced
240 g black olives, pitted
a few dried chilli flakes
    (optional)

1 Wash the excess salt off the salt cod, then place in a large bowl. Cover with water and leave to soak for 36 hours, changing the water three times.

2 Preheat the oven to 200°C/180°C fan. Line a baking tray with baking paper and smear with a tablespoon of the olive oil.

3 Place the drained cod on the tray and rub with olive oil. Bake for 20 minutes or until the fish is cooked – the flesh should be creamy white and flake easily when pressed. Remove from the oven and set aside until cool enough to handle.

4 Meanwhile, peel the oranges with a sharp knife, removing all the white pith. Cut crossways into 1 cm thick slices. Peel the eggs and cut into quarters.

5 In a small bowl, mix the garlic with the vinegar, remaining olive oil and a pinch of salt.

6 Arrange the orange slices in a single layer on a large platter or bowl and season with salt. Sprinkle over half the onion and olives, then dress with half the dressing.

7 Using your fingers, gently shred the fish into large, chunky flakes, removing and discarding any bones and skin as you go.

8 Arrange the flaked fish over the oranges, then top with the rest of the onion and olives and the eggs. Finish with the remaining dressing and a few chilli flakes, if desired.

ANCHOAS con TOMATE

ANCHOVIES WITH TOMATO ON TOAST

SERVES 8

Granada is one of the few places in Spain where tapas are complimentary when you order a drink. As a result, there is an intense rivalry between the bars as to which can put on the best tapas. This is a delicious tapa you might find in town – this version is from Bar FM – a piece of toasted bread covered with pulped tomato and garlic, then topped with an anchovy. It was a tapa like this that inspired MoVida's signature dish of a single anchovy laid on a sliver of bread crisped in the oven and topped with a quenelle of smoked tomato sorbet.

2 × 50 g tins Spanish anchovies

2 tomatoes

sea salt

1 baguette

1 garlic clove, skin on

1 Preheat the grill to hot.

2 Drain the anchovies and reserve the oil. Cut the tomatoes in half and grate the cut side against a cheese grater over a bowl to pulp the flesh. Discard the skin. Add the reserved oil from the anchovies and a pinch of salt to the tomato pulp and mix well.

3 Using a bread knife, cut eight 1 cm thick slices of baguette on the diagonal. Grill for 1 minute on each side or until the bread is toasted.

4 Cut the garlic clove in half, keeping the skin on if you can (this will help to stop your fingers smelling of garlic afterwards), and rub the bread with the cut side to infuse the bread with a rich garlic flavour.

5 Spread a tablespoon of the tomato pulp onto each slice of toasted bread, then place two anchovy fillets on top and serve immediately.

BACALAO con TOMATE

SALT COD AND TOMATO

SERVES 6

The water in the Río Monachil runs clear and cold as it passes La Cantina de Diego, a beautiful little restaurant on the edge of the old village of Monachil, not far from Granada. Owner Diego Higueras is passionate about growing as much as he possibly can in his kitchen garden on a patch of fertile ground near the restaurant. Every summer he grows enough tomatoes to preserve for this dish of salt cod covered with sweet, rich tomato sauce. This dish is best made with fresh, very ripe tomatoes in season, or the best preserved tomatoes. The luscious sauce can also be used to cook any fresh fish.

1 kg salt cod fillets

360 ml olive oil

2 brown onions, diced

sea salt

3 garlic cloves, chopped

3 red bull horn capsicums (peppers) or 1 red regular capsicum (pepper), finely chopped

1 green bull horn capsicum (pepper) or ½ green regular capsicum (pepper), finely chopped

1 kg tomatoes, peeled and roughly chopped

1 tablespoon sugar

300 g padrón peppers (see page 380)

1 Wash the excess salt off the salt cod, then place in a large bowl. Cover with water and leave to soak for 36 hours, changing the water three times. Drain, then remove any bones and cut into six thick slices.

2 Pour 100 ml olive oil into a *perol* (see page 380) or wide, heavy-based saucepan and place over medium–high heat. When the oil is hot, add the onion and a pinch of salt and cook, stirring occasionally, for 10 minutes or until the onion is soft and translucent. Stir in the garlic and cook for a minute, then add the capsicum and cook for 15 minutes or until soft. Turn the heat down to low–medium and add the tomato and another good pinch of salt. Mix well, then cover with a lid and cook for 20 minutes, stirring occasionally. Add the sugar, cover again and keep cooking for 25 minutes, stirring occasionally, to make a thick, rich sauce. Remove from the heat and leave to cool for 15 minutes or so, before pureeing with a stick blender. Set aside.

3 Pour the remaining olive oil into a large heavy-based frying pan and place over medium heat. When the oil is hot, cook the pieces of cod, skin-side down, for 2–3 minutes, then turn and cook the other side for 2–3 minutes.

4 Gently transfer the cod to the pan of tomato sauce (keeping the oil in the frying pan), then place over medium heat and simmer, using a spoon to baste the cod with the sauce every now and again, for 10 minutes or until the fish is just cooked through.

5 Meanwhile, increase the heat under the frying pan to medium–high heat. Add the padrón peppers and fry, turning occasionally, for 5–7 minutes or until a little browned and softened. Remove and drain on paper towel, then sprinkle with salt.

6 Serve the cod in shallow bowls, with plenty of the sauce and some of the fried peppers.

PATATAS A LO POBRE

POOR MAN'S POTATOES

SERVES 4-6

This is a simple dish of potatoes cooked with green capsicum. It makes the perfect accompaniment to roast meats, such as the suckling goat that chef José Luis Rosillo Jiménez serves at his Restaurant El Asador in Capileira (see page 337). If you have any leftover *patatas a lo pobre*, gently reheat them and serve with fried eggs, or fold them through beaten eggs to make a tortilla. Alternatively, place a thick layer in a baking dish as a bed for baking a whole fish – the potatoes soak up the cooking juices beautifully, becoming rich and full of flavour.

1.5 kg large waxy potatoes, peeled
1 brown onion
3 green bull horn capsicum (peppers) or 1 green regular capsicum (pepper)
160 ml extra virgin olive oil
4 garlic cloves, thickly sliced
3 fresh bay leaves
sea salt

1 Peel the potatoes, then cut in half lengthways. Cut each half into 5 mm thick slices and place in a bowl of cold water to prevent them from browning.

2 Cut the onion in half lengthways and then thinly slice.

3 Cut the peppers in half lengthways, remove and discard the stalk and stems, then cut each half into quarters.

4 Pour half of the olive oil into a *perol* (see page 380) or wide, heavy-based saucepan and place over medium heat. When the oil is hot, add the onion, garlic, bay leaves and capsicum, then season with a pinch of salt and stir. Cover with a lid and cook for 8–10 minutes, stirring occasionally, until the onion and capsicum are soft.

5 Drain the sliced potatoes and add to the pan, along with a good pinch of salt. Mix well with a wooden spoon, then pour in the remaining olive oil and reduce the heat to low. Cover with a lid and cook, shaking the pan every now and then, for 20 minutes or until the potatoes are tender.

6 Serve warm as a side dish with fish or meat.

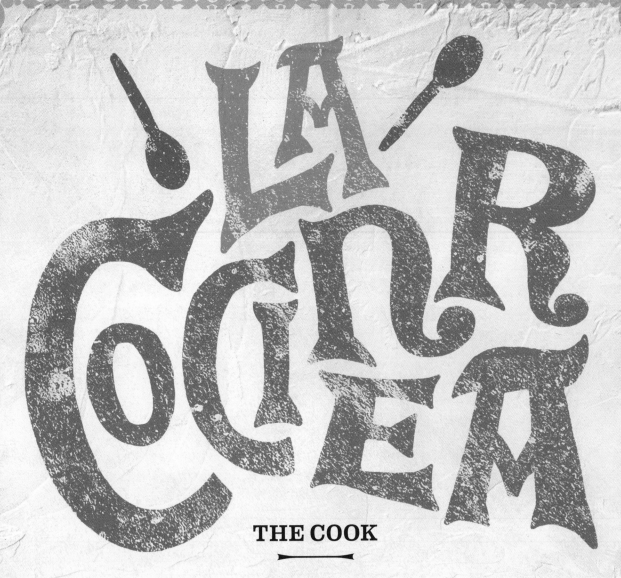

THE COOK

María Moral takes a small armful of asparagus from her *huerta* or kitchen garden and methodically starts to make a dish of pasta, asparagus and prawns cooked together in a rich tomato, garlic and onion *sofrito*. When I ask her about the recipe, she just laughs. 'Recipe? There is no recipe. This is what my mother would cook us.'

Collectively, the women of Spain hold the nation's gastronomic history in their heads, a giant interlinked library of food culture that is passed down from other women – often their mothers, but just as often their mothers-in-law. 'We have to make sure our sons are being properly cooked for,' says María with a smile. Asking women like María for the recipe for a dish is fraught with problems. They measure with their bodies, weighing out rice and beans in cupped hands, detecting temperature with outstretched fingers, judging doneness by touch and smell. Even those who measure out, say, a glass of wine might use a small heavy glass that bears no resemblance to any standard measure.

Like most Spanish housewives, María cuts vegetables in her hands and rarely uses a chopping board. This very simple act gives homemade Spanish food, and food cooked by chefs who cook like their mums, a distinctive taste and texture. Somehow the rough edges created by this method release more flavour from the food. I can personally attest that María's food is some of the tastiest I have eaten.

ALCACHOFAS RELLENAS

STUFFED ARTICHOKES

SERVES 4–6

María Moral takes a freshly picked artichoke and feels its weight. 'Nice and heavy and tight. Good. Good,' she says. She and her husband have worked hard all their lives and are now retired, but choose to tend a large *huerta* or kitchen garden just outside Granada. Using little more than a few simple fresh vegetables from her garden, María makes the most delicious meals. In this dish she stuffs artichokes with a little pork and bread, then thickens the sauce with a hand-pounded *picada*.

juice of 1 lemon
8 large globe artichokes
80 g plain flour

SAUCE

5 ripe tomatoes
60 ml extra virgin olive oil
2 brown onions, diced
sea salt
300 ml white wine
freshly ground black pepper

PICADA

60 ml extra virgin olive oil
3 garlic cloves, skin on
1 slice two-day-old bread
60 g blanched almonds
sea salt

FILLING

2 slices two-day-old bread
125 ml milk
500 g pork mince
2 hard-boiled eggs,
    finely chopped
60 g jamón serrano,
    finely diced
2 garlic cloves, finely chopped
large handful of flat-leaf
    parsley leaves,
    roughly chopped

1 Add the lemon juice to a bowl of water large enough to hold all the artichokes. Clean the artichokes by cutting off the stem at the base, then use a sharp, serrated knife to cut off the top 2.5 cm of each artichoke. Peel away the outer leaves until you get to the softer, paler leaves. Use a paring knife to remove the furry choke from the centre and create a cavity for the stuffing. Place the prepared artichokes in the bowl of acidulated water to stop them from discolouring.

2 For the sauce, cut the tomatoes in half and grate the cut side against a cheese grater over a bowl to pulp the flesh. Discard the skin. Pour the olive oil into a flameproof casserole over medium heat. When the oil is hot, add the onion with a pinch of salt and cook for 15 minutes, stirring occasionally, until soft and translucent. Add the tomato pulp and continue cooking for 10 minutes, stirring occasionally, until the sauce has reduced to a jam-like consistency. Pour in the white wine, scraping the base of the pan to deglaze, then simmer for 2 minutes. Add 1 litre of water, season with salt and pepper and stir. Increase the heat to high and bring to the boil, then remove from the heat.

3 To make the *picada*, pour the olive oil into a frying pan and place over medium heat. When the oil is hot, add the garlic and bread. Cook the bread on each side for 3–4 minutes or until brown and crisp, turning the garlic occasionally. Remove the bread and garlic and drain on paper towel. Add the almonds to the pan and cook, stirring occasionally, for 1–2 minutes or until browned. Using a slotted spoon, remove the almonds and drain on paper towel.

4 When the garlic is cool enough to handle, squeeze the flesh from the skins into a mortar. Add a pinch of salt and pound to a rough paste with the pestle. Use your hands to crumble the fried bread into the mortar, then pound to break up the bread a little. Add the almonds and pound to a very rough paste. (Alternatively, you can do this by pulsing in a food processor – just be careful not to over-process or you'll end up with almond-and-bread butter!)

5 Preheat the oven to 190°C/170°C fan.

6 To make the filling, place the bread in a shallow bowl and cover with the milk. Place another plate on top and leave to stand for 5 minutes. Using your hands, squeeze out as much of the milk from the bread as you can, then tear the bread into small pieces. Place in a bowl with the mince, chopped hard-boiled eggs, jamón serrano, garlic and parsley. Season with salt and pepper, then use your hands to mix everything together.

7 Stuff the cavity of each artichoke with the pork filling so it overflows, covering the top of the artichoke.

8 Return the sauce to a simmer over medium heat. Dust the top of the stuffed end of each artichoke with flour, then sit the artichokes, stuffed-end up, in the sauce. Cook over medium heat for 10 minutes, then gently stir in the *picada* and season with salt and pepper, then bring back to a simmer.

9 Cover and transfer to the oven. Cook for 1½ hours or until the artichokes and stuffing are cooked through.

LA VEGA DE GRANADA

THE OLD VEGETABLE GARDENS OF GRANADA

The sound of water trickling over rocks permeates the garden. Antonio Hurtado raises a plank of wood from a stone-lined channel to send a gentle stream of water flowing into a crop of broad beans. The water flows over the rich soil and quenches the chest-high plants. This simple action has been repeated on this patch of land for more than 1200 years, since the Muslim caliphs living in the Alhambra ordered the channelling of the snowmelt from the Sierra Nevada to be diverted through this high-altitude valley.

Antonio is retired, but for him the call of the land is too powerful to ignore, so he returns from his house in Granada city, just 4 kilometres away, to teach the next generation how to farm. His protégé Nacho Villegas learns how to hoe out the *tasquibas*, an Arabic word still used to describe these ditches. Nacho explains: 'This land is so important that I gave up my job in the city to learn to be a *campesino*.' The ancient tract of land they farm, along with a dozen other farmers, is called *La Vega de Granada*, but much of it is in danger of being engulfed by factories and freeways. 'Farming this land in this way is as important to the culture of the nation as the historic buildings on the hills,' Nacho says, pointing to the Alhambra. He takes pride in being a member of the next generation of *campesinos* or peasants: 'We "people of the land" are part of Andalusia's living history, a culture that keeps on growing as long as there are people still farming the land.'

PULPO SECO

DRIED OCTOPUS

SERVES 8-10

Every now and then you'll see hanging in the markets what looks like a fleshy kite with eight tails. These are *pulpos secos*, octopus that the fishermen catch at sea and then dry in the rigging of their boats, using a handful of seawater to season the octopus as they dry. Sometimes the fishermen hang the octopus on lines stretched out on the beach; some even bring them back home and dry them on the balcony. You can easily dry an octopus in your fridge: the secret is to make sure the tentacles don't touch, otherwise they won't dry properly – and to allow plenty of time, as the process takes up to four days. Pieces of dried octopus, lightly grilled, are among the most delicious snacks I have ever had.

1 medium octopus (about 1 kg),
    head removed
2 tablespoons fine salt
200 ml white wine vinegar
1 iceberg lettuce, leaves
    separated and torn into
    large pieces
1 lemon, cut into wedges

1 Wash the octopus well under running water. Using a sharp knife, cut the octopus from the centre (where its head was) outwards, so the tentacles are no longer in a circle and you can spread them out.

2 Mix the salt and vinegar together in a small bowl. Place the octopus in a large bowl and rub well all over with the salt and vinegar.

3 Take a wire coathanger and, using bamboo skewers, spread the octopus over it so the tentacles hang down, piercing its skin where necessary to secure the octopus to the wire and separate the tentacles so they are not touching.

4 Make space in the fridge so the octopus can hang freely. Hang the octopus, still on the coathanger, in the fridge for 4 days to dry, making sure the tentacles don't touch each other. (Alternatively, if you have a dehydrator, place the octopus in it at 70°C overnight making sure the tentacles are separated and not touching.) If you want to store uncooked dried octopus, wrap individual tentacles in plastic film and freeze for up to a month, then thaw in the fridge and cook as follows.

5 Once the octopus is dried, cut off the ends of each tentacle and discard, as they will be too tough to eat. Cut off one tentacle at time, then cut it on the diagonal into 2–3 mm thick slices. The slices tend to curl, so place each slice on a board and lightly tap with the flat of your knife to flatten it out a little.

6 Place a dry heavy-based frying pan over extremely high heat. Once the pan is very hot, place 10–12 octopus slices in the pan, then place a heavy weight (I use another pan) on top of the octopus to keep it flat and in contact with the heat. Cook for just 60–90 seconds until well browned, then turn over and cook the other side in the same way. Repeat with the remaining octopus.

7 Serve warm on iceberg lettuce, with lemon wedges on the side.

CABEZADA DE PULPO

OCTOPUS HEAD TERRINE

SERVES 6-8

We sell a lot of octopus at MoVida. But we only sell the tentacles. I'd never really known what to do with the heads – until I met Rosa Macías at Bar FM in Granada. In true Spanish style, nothing is ever wasted, and she has created a dish that turns octopus heads into the most delicious terrine, simply by mixing the chopped octopus heads with seasoning and then stuffing them into a single octopus head. To make her recipe more accessible to the home cook, we have adapted it to use just one whole octopus.

1 medium octopus
   (roughly 1.2 kg), head on
2 slices two-day-old bread,
   crusts off
250 ml milk
3 garlic cloves, chopped
2 tablespoons chopped flat-leaf
   parsley, plus extra to serve
sea salt and freshly ground
   black pepper
slices of baguette and extra
   virgin olive oil, to serve

STOCK

1 onion, quartered
2 garlic cloves
4 fresh bay leaves
12 black peppercorns
⅛ lemon, sliced
handful of parsley stalks
40 ml white wine vinegar
60 ml extra virgin olive oil

1 Using a sharp knife, cut the head from the octopus. Remove the beak and guts if any and discard. Rinse thoroughly inside and out and drain well.

2 Cut the tentacles from the octopus, then cut each tentacle into 2–3 mm thick slices; there should be about 800 g of tentacles. Rinse and leave to drain in a sieve. Place the two-day-old bread in a bowl and cover with the milk, pushing it down so the bread soaks up the milk.

3 Place the sliced octopus tentacles, garlic and parsley in a stainless steel bowl and season with salt and pepper. Using clean hands, squeeze out the bread to remove as much of the milk as you can, then crumble the bread into the bowl and mix everything together. Stuff this mixture into the head of the octopus, leaving some room for the filling to expand during cooking. Use a bamboo skewer to firmly secure the opening.

4 For the stock, place all the ingredients in a stockpot or large saucepan and cover with 4 litres of water. Bring to the boil over high heat, then reduce the heat to medium and simmer for 5 minutes.

5 Carefully lower the octopus head into the stock and simmer gently for 1 hour and 10 minutes. Remove the octopus from the pan and leave to cool slightly before refrigerating for at least 4 hours or until completely cold.

6 To serve, take a very sharp knife and cut the octopus into 1 cm thick slices. Place on slices of baguette, then drizzle with a little extra virgin olive oil and sprinkle with salt and finely chopped parsley.

CHOTO ASADO AL AJILLO

BAKED SUCKLING GOAT WITH GARLIC

SERVES 6

Walk into the only roasting house (*asador*) in the Alpujarran town of Capileira, high in the Sierra Nevada, and the cold mountain air is overwhelmed by the warmth of the kitchen, as the aromas of holm-oak smoke and roasting meat fill the dining room. Here chef José Luis serves huge portions to cater for the large appetites generated by cold weather. His suckling goat cooked in a charcoal-fired oven is superb: wonderfully crisp on the outside, sweet and lip-smackingly sticky on the inside. Ask your butcher for the front legs of a young goat, ideally between three and six months old. This is delicious served with *Patatas a lo pobre*, or Poor man's potatoes (see page 323), as in the photo here.

150 g pork lard or
   150 ml olive oil
2 tablespoons sea salt
2 front legs young goat,
   about 1 kg each
3 garlic bulbs, cut in half
   horizontally

1 Preheat the oven to 160°C/140°C fan.

2 Rub the lard or olive oil, then the salt all over the goat legs so they are evenly coated.

3 Place the garlic bulbs, cut-side up, in the base of a large roasting tin. Place the goat legs on top and pour 500 ml of water into the tin.

4 Place the tray on the centre shelf of the oven and roast for 3 hours, turning the legs over every hour. Remove from the oven and leave to rest for 15 minutes before serving.

MOVIDA'S GUIDE TO GRANADA

El Mercado de San Agustín 🛍️✕

Calle San Agustín S/N, Granada

Just a block north of the cathedral, Granada's San Agustín Market displays the Granadinos' love of game, with all parts of wild boar and birds in feather on offer. You'll also find a lively culture of ready-to-eat artisan meals well embedded – it seems the urbane city folk still hanker for great rustic dishes like snails in almond sauce or tripe and pork stew. Look out for local sheep's milk cheeses and *morcilla blanca* – white pork sausage (see page 290).

Ladrón de Agua 🍷✕🏠

**Carrera del Darro 13, Granada;
tel 958 21 50 40
www.ladrondeagua.com**

Charming hotel with a stunning location on a cobbled laneway by the banks of the Río Darro, which flows directly beneath the Alhambra.

Santa Isabel la Real 🍷✕🏠

**Calle de Santa Isabel la Real 17, Granada;
tel 958 29 46 58
www.hotelsantaisabellareal.com**

Occupying a sixteenth-century mansion house, this quaint and comfortable family-run hotel is tucked away in the historic Albaicín quarter, a short walk from the city centre.

Bar FM 🍷✕

**Avenida de Juan Pablo II 54, Granada;
tel 958 15 70 04**

In this little brightly lit bar with maritime décor, set on a busy street in suburban Granada, Francisco 'Paco' Martín and his wife Rosa Macías make and serve some of the most delicious dishes. Try the grilled dried octopus or the terrine-like stuffed octopus (see page 333).

La Fábula/Villa Oniria 🍷✕🏠

**Calle San Antón 28, Granada;
tel 958 25 01 50/958 53 53 58
www.restaurantelafabula.com
www.villaoniria.com**

Set in a rather luxurious hotel, Villa Oniria, the food in this restaurant sits comfortably in the modern Spanish tradition of using good natural and seasonal ingredients and transforming them into delicious dishes, such as red prawn carpaccio and a dish of local vegetables from the traditional gardens that surround the city (see page 329).

Abades Nevada Palace 🍷✕🏠

Calle Sultana 3, Granada; tel 902 22 25 70
www.abadesnevadapalace.com

Modern, large and quiet, with views over
the Sierra Nevada, this is perfectly situated
for those who prefer to park a little way
out of town and avoid Granada's maze of
mediaeval streets.

La Cantina de Diego 🍷✕

Paseo del Río, Esquina con Callejón de
Ricarda 1, Monachil; tel 958 30 37 58
www.restaurantelacantinadediego.es

In the small village of Monachil, not far
from Granada, is this charming riverside
restaurant serving modern versions of
classic Granada dishes. Chef and owner
Diego Higueras grows much of the produce
served here. One of the specialities of the
house is *chuletones*, rib-eye steak from the
local rare breed of cattle called Pajuna.

El Asador 🍷✕

Barranco de Poqueira 16, Capileira;
tel 958 76 31 09

High in the Sierra Nevada, in a stunning
little town called Capileira, is this renowned
roasting house where chef José Luis serves
classic dishes from the Alpujarra and great
roast meats such as goat and pork cooked in
the vast wood-fired oven.

Barceló La Bobadilla 🍷✕🏠

Finca La Bobadilla, Carretera Salinas-
Villanueva de Tapia (A-333), km 65.5,
Loja; tel 958 32 18 61
www.barcelo.com

Five-star luxury in a hacienda in the hills
and olive groves of Loja, about 45 minutes'
drive from Granada.

The restaurant owners stand, arms folded, watching the catch come into the central market. The fish are so fresh that they are still contorted with rigor mortis, the fat red prawns still twitching. To prove a point, the fishmonger prods a squid in a box and its skin erupts in iridescent waves of colour. Almería's fishing fleet is moored just a few blocks down from the avenue named after poet Federico García Lorca. Here the boats work the rich waters surrounded by the stunning volcanoes that form Cabo de Gata. 'We have more names for the hills and valleys under the water than shepherds do for the hills and valleys,' says an old fisherman, the father of one of the fishmongers.

Overlooking the port and the city itself are the walls and lookouts of La Alcazaba, the Moorish castle built by Calipha Abd-ar-Rahman in the tenth century. Back then it was called the watchtower or, in Arabic, *Al-Mariy-yat*, which was Hispanicised to Almería. At the time, it was the largest castle in Andalusia, second only to the Alhambra in Granada. Earthquakes and civil wars have since destroyed much of the Moorish architectural heritage in Almería, yet you can still taste the flavours of the Moors in the dishes the *Almerienses* cook today.

To get a sense of the climate and terrain of Almería, picture a young Clint Eastwood in the Sergio Leone spaghetti westerns. Much of the footage for these films and many others, including *Lawrence of Arabia* and *Cleopatra*, were shot in the semi-arid hills and valleys of Almería. With its mountains, dry vegetation and plains dotted with agave plants it made a perfect double for the American south-west. The sets built during the filming of *The Good, the Bad and the Ugly* still stand, and were back in the spotlight recently, when they were used as the backdrop for an episode of *Doctor Who*. Open to the public as Mini Hollywood, these filming locations do a brisk trade in re-enactments and memorabilia of the halcyon days when hundreds of films were made in the province each year.

The cuisine of this dry part of Almería, with its bare mountains and stark yet beautiful windswept landscapes, is dominated by goat and lamb, animals raised for their meat and milk. Then there's the food of the coast, which is dotted with scores of fishing villages, some prosperous with state-of-the art fleets, others left behind by modern trawling techniques. Here there are dishes that celebrate squid and cuttlefish, but also the small fish that run the Mediterranean coast, cooked with Moorish spices such as saffron.

MIGAS

CRISP PORK AND FRIED BREAD

They call it *la cocina de pobre*, 'the food of the poor', and it is this cuisine that dominates Andalusia, a region for centuries dogged by poverty and scarcity. But from necessity came delicious inventions. This dish of crisp, roughly hand-torn breadcrumbs with sticky pork, garlic and chorizo could be a breakfast for workers heading out into the fields or a lunchtime feed for a hungry family, washed down with rustic red wine. When making *migas*, some pieces of bread should be torn small, with others slightly larger, so that some will become crisper than others. In Spain this is made in a *perol* (see page 380), but feel free to use a large wok with a flat base.

400 g pork belly
30 g rock salt
450 g two-day-old bread,
    without crusts
sea salt
170 ml olive oil
3 chorizo sausages
    (350 g in total), cut into
    1 cm thick slices
12 garlic cloves, skin on
2 teaspoons smoked sweet
    Spanish paprika
roasted green bull horn
    capsicums (peppers) and
    dried ñora or choricero
    peppers (see page 379),
    to serve

1 Using a very sharp knife, cut the pork belly into roughly 1 cm cubes. Place in a bowl with the rock salt and mix well, then cover and refrigerate overnight.

2 Break the bread into pieces with your fingers, pulling apart the bread into rough crumbs – aim for a mixture of sizes and shapes – and place in a large bowl.

3 In a small bowl or jug, dissolve 1 teaspoon of sea salt in 180 ml of water and sprinkle over the bread by dipping your fingertips into the salted water and flicking it over the bread. Mix well, cover with a clean tea towel and leave in a cool place for 12 hours.

4 Rinse the salt off the diced pork, then place in a large *perol* or flat-bottomed wok over low–medium heat. Add 200 ml water, bring to a simmer and cook, covered, for 15–20 minutes, or until all the water has been absorbed.

5 Add the olive oil and increase the heat to medium. Cover and cook for 25–30 minutes, stirring occasionally to prevent sticking, until the pork is crisp and well browned. Remove from the pan and drain on paper towel. Season the pork with sea salt.

6 Drain and reserve the oil, then wipe the pan clean. Pour 40 ml of the reserved oil back into the pan and place over medium heat. Add the chorizo and garlic and cook, stirring occasionally, for about 10 minutes or until the chorizo is browned and the garlic is tender. Use a slotted spoon or tongs to lift out the chorizo and garlic, then drain on paper towel and season with sea salt.

7 Pour the oil from the pan into a heatproof measuring cup or jug, then top up with enough of the reserved oil to make 200 ml. Pour this oil back into the pan and place over high heat. Once it is very hot,

add the bread, stirring constantly with a wooden spoon and tossing the pan frequently. After a couple of minutes, season with salt and 1 teaspoon of the paprika. Continue cooking over high heat for a total of 12–15 minutes, frequently tossing and stirring, until the bread is lightly toasted and slightly crisp – be careful it doesn't burn. Return the crisp pork, chorizo and garlic to the pan and continue cooking for a couple more minutes.

8 To serve, place the *migas* on a plate, sprinkle with the rest of the paprika and garnish with the roasted capsicums and pieces of dried pepper.

BOQUERONES AL LIMÓN

FRIED LEMON ANCHOVIES

SERVES 4-6

Eating anchovies is as Andalusian as going to bullfights, drinking fino and wearing black hats and riding boots – so much so that many Andalusians are called *boquerones* in a friendly, yet slightly derogatory way. You know a good bar when you see *boquerones* cooked *al limón*, because in a good bar, freshly caught anchovies are fried to order. Delicious. Come day two and a good cook will do the honourable thing and liven the anchovies up with a quick marinade to give them a second chance. And what a chance! Crisp, salty and slightly tangy, these are sensational with ice-cold beer or a glass of fino. If you can't find fresh anchovies, use small sardines.

30 fresh anchovies or small
   sardines
juice of 4 lemons (200 ml)
4 garlic cloves, finely chopped
1 teaspoon oregano leaves,
   chopped
sea salt and freshly ground
   black pepper
1 litre olive oil, for deep-frying
200 g fine semolina
lemon wedges, to serve

1 Remove the heads and guts from the anchovies. This is done by taking the head in your fingers and pulling it away from the body towards the tail, taking the guts with it. Rinse.

2 Place each anchovy belly-side down on a board. Using your thumb, apply enough pressure along its spine so you can feel the central bones coming away. Remove the anchovy from the board and, using your fingers, pull out the spine, snapping it close to the tail. Place all the prepared anchovies in a shallow glass or ceramic tray, skin-side down.

3 Pour the lemon juice into a small bowl and add the garlic, oregano, a pinch of salt and 200 ml water. Mix well, then pour over the anchovies. Cover and allow to marinate in the fridge for 1 hour. Do not let the anchovies marinate for longer than this, or the lemon juice will turn their flesh to mush.

4 Pour the olive oil into a heavy-based saucepan or wok and heat to 170°C or until a cube of bread dropped into the oil browns in 15 seconds.

5 Put the semolina into a shallow bowl and season with salt and pepper.

6 Working in batches of 10, shake the excess marinade off the anchovies, dust them in the semolina, again shaking off any excess, then deep-fry for 2–3 minutes until lightly golden. Remove and drain on paper towel. Repeat with the remaining anchovies. Season with salt and serve immediately with lemon wedges.

CALAMARES en ACEITE

CALAMARI COOKED IN OLIVE OIL

SERVES 4–6

The rain had settled in, and the dirty streets of Almería's old town glistened like gold in the last light of the day. Not far from the wharves, in a nondescript bar called Casa Joaquín, a small commotion was playing out as José Mercé, one of Spain's most-loved flamenco singers, was in town and had dropped by to try the *calamares en aceite*. The owner, Joaquín López, tried not to look excited as he presented a little plate of the most tender pieces of super-fresh calamari, gently poached in olive oil with a little garlic and served with a sauce of the juices it had released during cooking. When he had finished eating, Mercé looked up to López, gave him the warmest of embraces and walked out with his entourage into the night.

2 × 500–600 g calamari
250 ml extra virgin olive oil
2 garlic cloves, cut in half
sea salt

1 Ask your fishmonger to clean the calamari for you, reserving the tentacles. (And ask for calamari by name, as they are more tender and delicious than their close cousins that are simply known as squid). Alternatively, to clean the calamari yourself, pull the tentacles from the body. Cut the tentacles off below the eyes and discard the head, beak and guts. Using your fingers, remove any remaining guts and the clear cartilage or 'quill' from inside the calamari and discard. Rinse the tentacles and body, but try to keep the skin on the calamari.

2 Cut each calamari body widthways into two even pieces. Place the olive oil in a large frying pan over low–medium heat and add the garlic cloves. When the oil is warm but not hot, place the calamari, including the tentacles, in the pan and cover with a lid. Cook for about 5 minutes, then remove the lid and turn the calamari. Cover again and cook for another 5 minutes, shaking the pan occasionally so the calamari doesn't stick. Remove the lid, season the calamari with salt, then stir. Cover again and cook for 5 more minutes.

3 Transfer the calamari to a chopping board and cut into 1 cm thick slices. Place on a serving plate and drizzle with a few tablespoons of the olive oil and cooking juices from the pan. Season well with sea salt and serve straight away.

HABAS con GAMBAS y CHOCOS

BROAD BEANS, PRAWNS AND CUTTLEFISH

SERVES 6

The first flush of broad beans coincides with the start of the prawn season, when the prawns are quite small and don't need much cooking. If you're using larger prawns, you may want to cook them for a little longer. The idea is to gently cook the cuttlefish to release its flavour, but not toughen it, and then the prawns are cooked in the juices. There is no need to peel the outer skin off young broad beans, as the skins don't develop bitterness until later in the season. This surprisingly rich dish is delicious with light red wine.

1.8 kg young broad beans
    in pods
fine salt
80 ml extra virgin olive oil
800 g cuttlefish, cleaned
    (see page 65) and cut
    into 2 cm squares
3 garlic cloves, finely chopped
800 g raw prawns, peeled
    and deveined
sea salt and freshly ground
    black pepper
80 ml dry white wine

1 Pod but do not peel the broad beans. Place a medium saucepan of salted water over high heat and cover. When boiling, add the broad beans and cook for 5 minutes or until tender. Drain immediately.

2 Heat the olive oil in a large *perol* (see page 380) or flat-bottomed wok over medium heat. Add the cuttlefish and cook for 2 minutes, stirring frequently. Add the garlic and cook for 2–3 minutes, stirring constantly so it doesn't burn. Add the prawns and cook for a further 2–3 minutes, stirring occasionally, until they are just cooked through. Season with salt.

3 Pour in the white wine, scraping the base of the pan to deglaze. Bring back to a simmer, then increase the heat a little and cook for 5 minutes or so until almost all the liquid has evaporated. Add the broad beans and cook for 1–2 minutes, then season to taste with salt and pepper.

4 Serve immediately on small plates.

LOS PESCADRES

THE FISHERMEN

◄——►

A cluster of ramshackle boats is beached on the sand by the village of Cabo de Gata. Pushed ashore at the peak of the incoming tide, by daybreak they are high and dry. Standing on the deck of one of them is Juan, a young fisherman tending his fishing gear. He is one of the old breed of fishermen who set out from the shore in these little wooden boats and use hand-baited hooks, as opposed to the indiscriminate trawl of the nets. His boat – shared with his brothers – is called *7 Hermanos*, or 7 Brothers.

Juan says that in the old days, before he was born, the most important fish were the *salazones*, small fish that could be easily salted and dried: 'Every family would salt and dry their own fish. Before refrigeration arrived, people would catch the small prawns and eat them raw with lemon and salt. They were delicious. Back then people made a lot of stews. Now with refrigeration everyone wants john dory, hake and especially the big prawns.'

Ironically, Juan and his like may be on the comeback. The big steel boats that work the ports can go out longer and catch the fish in the deeper waters. But they are expensive to run, and as fish in the Mediterranean become more scarce, old-fashioned fishing operations like Juan's are seeing a resurgence.

GAMBAS A LA PLANCHA

PRAWNS GRILLED ON THE HOT PLATE

SERVES 4-6

Down by the old docks at Garrucha, wiry old men pierce scraps of bait onto fishing hooks. Too old to go to sea, they set the hooks as they wait for their sons to return. One by one, the fleet comes in and half the town gathers to watch the action as they unload their catch. Boxes of squid, ray, hake and the fattest, reddest prawns you have ever seen are carted straight into the wholesale market next door. What unfolds is a cross between a Dutch auction and a game of chicken, as buyers watch the numbers on the screen roll down, then press a button when it reaches their desired price. The local red prawns, *gambas rojas de Garrucha*, can sell for up to 100 euros a kilo. Wholesale! The old men look on from the sidelines, watching the prices and watching the prawns go out into restaurant vans. The locals think there is only one way to cook good prawns and that is on a screaming-hot grillplate – *la plancha*.

18 large raw prawns, shell on
2 tablespoons coarse sea salt
50 ml extra virgin olive oil

1 Place the prawns in a bowl and season well with some of the salt.

2 Preheat a chargrill pan or the flat grillplate on a barbecue until very hot. Remember that the hotter the grill, the less cooking time needed and the juicier and tastier the resulting prawns will be.

3 When it's hot, evenly drizzle the pan or barbecue grillplate with a little olive oil, then spread out the prawns on the hot plate. Cook for a minute or so, depending on the heat of the grill.

4 When the prawns are ready to be turned, the shells will change colour and there will be an intense aroma of cooked shellfish. Season again with coarse salt, turn and cook on the other side. Drizzle over a little more olive oil, season this side as well, then cook for a further minute or so. When done, the flesh just behind the head will be firm to the touch.

5 Remove from the grill and place on a plate with more coarse salt and serve straight away. Enjoy with cold beer – and remember to suck the juices out of the prawn heads.

Fresh seafood, straight from the boat, is lunch at a rustic *chiringuito*

PESCADO en ESCABECHE

PICKLED FISH IN SAFFRON

SERVES 4-6

Nestled in the dunes on a lonely beach on the outskirts of the city of Almería, well within an engine's roar of the airport, are a handful of shacks that look out onto a cluster of small fishing boats carefully beached on the sand. By lunchtime every day one of these shacks is ring-barked by BMWs, as the wealthy from town come to this little *chiringuito* that serves light fish meals and plenty of drinks to wash them down with. In their old-fashioned boats, the fishermen around here are only capable of catching the little shore fish, but the chef inside knows exactly what to do with them. He fries up a few and serves them fresh. The rest he fries and leaves to marinate in this fresh, aromatic blend of wine, vinegar, herbs and spices. Originally a way of preserving fish in a strong vinegar solution, *escabeche* has now become much lighter-tasting.

80 ml extra virgin olive oil

1 garlic bulb, broken into cloves

4 fresh bay leaves

400 ml white wine

400 ml good-quality white
   wine vinegar

pinch of saffron threads

8 red mullet, cleaned

200 g plain flour

sea salt and freshly ground
   black pepper

1 litre olive oil, for deep-frying

1 To make the marinade, place the extra virgin olive oil, garlic cloves and bay leaves in a saucepan over medium heat. Cook gently for a minute, then add the white wine, vinegar and 400 ml of water and bring to a simmer.

2 Meanwhile, in a small heavy-based frying pan, toast the saffron over low heat for a minute or so until you just start to smell the aroma. Add 2 tablespoons of the marinade to the saffron, swirl it around, then tip the contents of the frying pan back into the saucepan. Bring the marinade to the boil over high heat, then reduce the heat to low and simmer for 10 minutes. Allow to cool.

3 Cut the heads from the fish. Using scissors, remove the fins and tail. Cut the larger fish in half, but leave the smaller ones whole. Rinse the fish under cold running water, then dredge in seasoned flour, shaking off any excess.

4 In a heavy-based saucepan or wok, heat the olive oil to 170°C or until a cube of bread dropped into the oil browns in 15 seconds. Fry the fish in several batches for about 8–10 minutes, turning occasionally, until golden brown. Remove and drain on paper towel. Season with salt, then leave to cool.

5 Arrange the fried fish in a single layer in a large, glass or ceramic dish. Pour over the marinade, cover and place in the fridge for several hours for the flavours to infuse the fish.

6 Place several pieces of fish on each plate and spoon over some of the liquid. Serve chilled with beer or white wine.

THE TOMATOES

From the air, southern Almería appears to have been hit by a massive snowstorm, with great swathes of the coastal flats and the surrounding hills covered in white. For almost 200 kilometres, from the border with Granada to the city of Almería, the province has been taken over by *invernaderos* or plastic hothouses. In these grow a great proportion of not only Spain's but Europe's fresh vegetables, especially tomatoes.

Spaniards are passionate about their tomatoes, and one of their favourites is the Raf tomato. Although a relatively new variety,

it has already been described as the *pata negra* of tomatoes, a reference to the top-notch jamón made from the *pata negra* or black-footed Iberian pigs. A rich and delicious tomato, the Raf is generally served at room temperature – never chilled – simply sliced and dressed with a little salt and olive oil. What is even more tempting is when a tin of *conservas de pescados* or preserved fish is opened and flaked over the tomatoes. In Spain only the best is put in a tin, and when tinned mackerel or tuna is served with tomato, the taste combination is far greater than the sum of the parts.

CUAJADERA DE JIBIA

CUTTLEFISH BAKED WITH POTATOES

SERVES 6

There is a bar-cum-restaurant by the docks at Garrucha where the buyers wait for the boats to come in. There's good money in fish, and the buyers know value for money when they see it – which is why this bar is always packed. Come lunchtime the chef serves up dishes traditional to the area. Out come great plates of fish stew and this dish of cuttlefish and chunks of potato baked with onion, capsicum, bay leaves and white wine. Cheap and fast, it is delicious with a glass of white wine.

3 green bullhorn capsicums (peppers) or 1 large regular green capsicum (pepper)
2 red capsicums (peppers)
130 ml extra virgin olive oil
4 white onions, cut into 1 cm dice
3 fresh bay leaves
sea salt and freshly ground black pepper
4 garlic cloves, finely chopped
1 tablespoon thyme leaves, chopped
1.1 kg waxy potatoes, peeled and cut into wedges
200 ml dry white wine
2 kg medium-sized cuttlefish, cleaned and cut lengthways into 1 cm strips
2 tomatoes, roughly diced

1 Remove the stems and seeds from the capsicums. Cut the flesh into 2.5 cm × 1.25 cm pieces.

2 Pour 80 ml of the olive oil into a large heavy-based saucepan over medium heat. Add the onion, bay leaves and a good pinch of salt and cook, stirring occasionally, until the onion has softened and become translucent. Stir in the garlic and cook for a further 3 minutes. Add the capsicum and thyme and cook for 20 minutes, stirring occasionally, until the capsicum is soft. Add the potato wedges, mix in well and season with salt, then pour in the white wine, scraping the base of the pan to deglaze. Cover and simmer over low–medium heat for 30 minutes.

3 Meanwhile, preheat the oven to 200°C/180°C fan.

4 Place the cuttlefish strips in a roasting tin and sprinkle with a good pinch each of salt and pepper. Drizzle over the remaining olive oil and mix well, then spread the cuttlefish evenly over the roasting tin.

5 Add the tomato wedges to the saucepan with the potato mixture and stir through. Pour the contents of the pan evenly over the cuttlefish in the roasting tin, but do not mix through. Sprinkle with salt, then bake in the oven for 40 minutes or until the cuttlefish is cooked and the potato wedges are crisp and brown.

6 Serve at the table, straight from the roasting tin.

EL CABRERO

THE GOATHERD

High in La Sierra de los Filabres, a mountain range that soars 2000 metres above the Almerian coast, a young goatherd called Rubén Sánchez tends to his animals. Here the country is so steep that even the almond trees struggle to stay upright. Some of the hillsides are terraced, offering a little wild pasture among the olive trees where his herd of milking nannies graze, the bells around their necks ringing out every now and then. They each produce about four litres of milk, which is sent down to a cooperative cheesery in the nearby town of Filabres.

Although Rubén has the gentle nature of a good shepherd, tending to his herd with care, like most Spaniards he is business-like about livestock and sends young goat carcasses to the best restaurants around Spain: 'That is the reality of food. We all must eat.'

CHOTO AL AJILLO

FRICASSEE OF GOAT RIBS

SERVES 4

The Sierra de Baza is the source of some of the best goat meat in the country. Traditionally, young goats, surplus to the requirements of sustaining herd numbers, were dispatched while their mothers continued to produce milk for cheese. Once food for the poor, *choto al ajillo* is now a speciality of the Parador de Mojácar, one of Spain's renowned state-run resorts, where the chef cooks this traditional peasant dish for wealthy tourists from northern Europe and America. Either way it is lip-smackingly delicious. You should be able to find goat cutlets at farmers' markets or good butcher shops, especially those serving Indian, Middle Eastern or Mediterranean communities.

80 ml extra virgin olive oil

1 kg suckling goat cutlets

3 garlic cloves, peeled and
   cut in half

4 fresh bay leaves

sea salt and freshly ground
   black pepper

6 young garlic shoots
   or garlic chives

1 Heat the olive oil in a large heavy-based frying pan over medium–high heat. Fry the cutlets on one side for a few minutes, then add the garlic and bay leaves, season with salt and continue cooking for 4–5 minutes until well browned on the first side. Turn the cutlets over and cook on the other side for 5–7 minutes until well browned.

2 Add the chopped young garlic shoots or chives, season well with salt and pepper, and serve immediately.

RAYA AL PIMENTÓN

STINGRAY IN SAFFRON AND CUMIN SAUCE

SERVES 4–6

Antonio Zapata is a journalist who has spent his life telling the stories of the *Almerienses*, the people of Almería. 'As the young people leave the land and the seaside villages for the cities, they forget their traditional food and how to cook it,' says Antonio. Over the decades he has compiled books of recipes from around the province to help preserve them for future generations, so he was only too glad to welcome us into his home and show us how to cook this stingray with a saffron and cumin sauce. Surprisingly easy to make, it is quite rich and delicious.

3 green bull's horn capsicums
  (peppers) or 1 large regular
  green capsicum (pepper)

2 medium onions, peeled
  but left whole

sea salt

600 g skate wings, skinned
  but bone in

4 medium-sized potatoes,
  cut into 3 cm pieces

5 dried red choricero peppers
  or 3 fresh red bull's horn
  capsicums (peppers)

1 ripe tomato

5 sun-dried tomatoes, not in oil

2 teaspoons cumin seeds

large pinch of saffron threads

4 garlic cloves, peeled
  but left whole

½ teaspoon freshly ground
  black pepper

3 tablespoons roughly chopped
  flat-leaf parsley

80 ml extra virgin olive oil,
  plus extra to serve

1 Turn a gas burner on high. Using metal tongs, hold the green capsicum over the flame, turning every so often, until the skin is blackened and the flesh is soft. (Alternatively, cook on a very hot barbecue or roast in a 220°C /200°C fan oven on a baking tray with a sprinkle of salt and a drizzle of olive oil for 30 minutes.) Allow to cool, then rub off the charred skin and remove the seeds.

2 Place the onions in a large saucepan, cover with 2 litres of water and add a teaspoon of salt. Bring to the boil over high heat, then reduce the heat to medium. Ease the skate into the water and simmer for 10–12 minutes or until cooked through (the flesh should flake easily). Remove the skate and set aside. Add the potato, peppers or capsicums, fresh and sun-dried tomato to the onion stock and cook over medium heat for 15 minutes or until the potato begins to soften, then take off the heat. Using a slotted spoon, remove the onions, peppers or capsicums, fresh and sun-dried tomato (reserving the stock and potato in the pan). When they are cool enough to handle, use a small knife to scrape the flesh away from the skin of the peppers or capsicums, then discard the skin and seeds. Remove the skin from the fresh tomato and discard.

3 Once the skate is cool enough to handle, remove the cartilage with your hands, then break the flesh into large pieces and set aside.

4 Heat a small heavy-based frying pan over medium heat, add the cumin seeds and toast for 1–2 minutes, stirring occasionally, until lightly browned and fragrant. Transfer the seeds to a pestle and mortar and set aside. Add the saffron to the pan and lightly toast until aromatic, then remove from the heat and add 2 tablespoons of the hot stock from the saucepan.

5 Pound the cumin seeds to a fine powder using the pestle and mortar. Add the garlic and black pepper, then pour in the saffron

liquid and keep pounding until you have a smooth paste. Spoon the paste into a food processor or upright blender, then add the onions, dried and fresh tomato and the flesh from the peppers or capsicums, along with the parsley, and blend until smooth. Add the olive oil and 300 ml of the stock from the saucepan and blend again to make a thick puree.

6 Bring the potato and the remaining stock in the saucepan back to a simmer, add the puree from the food processor or blender and simmer for a few minutes to combine the flavours and warm through.

7 Serve in a bowl, garnished with pieces of skate and strips of the roasted green capsicum.

Raya al pimentón is a traditional Almeriense dish, here prepared by journalist and food historian Antonio Zapata

EL COCINERO

THE CHEF

Antonio Carmona is a staunch traditionalist. While other chefs in Spain were turning their backs on the lesser-loved food of their region in favour of a homogenised blend of dishes found across Spain and known as *La Cocina Nacional*, Antonio Carmona continued to cook the dishes that had been passed down through his family.

Back in the 1930s, Terraza Carmona was an outdoor cinema in the small town of Vera that also sold food. 'My *abuela* (grandmother) did all the cooking,' says Antonio, pointing to an old photo on the wall of her in the old al fresco cinema, 'She didn't go to cooking school, so she simply cooked the dishes her mother taught her – the food of our town.' Over time, the outdoor cinema became a bodega, which became a restaurant, which became a hotel.

Antonio trained as a chef and now has a team of fifty, catering for baptisms, weddings and other family events. But at the core of his business is a stately dining room based around the organic form of a traditional whitewashed fireplace. Here he still celebrates not just the food of Almería but dishes unique to his home town, including eggplant stuffed with anchovies and prawns and *olla de trigo almeriense*, a hearty stew of blood sausage, beans and grains. One of his specialities are biscuits made with dates from the palms descended from those planted by the Arabs. 'We keep cooking the food *abuela* cooked. This is the heart of our business.'

TARTA BORRACHA DE LOS PADRES MÍNIMOS

DRUNKEN MONKS' CAKE

SERVES 9

Antonio Carmona, the chef at Vera's Terraza Carmona, holds a framed letter from a brother of the Padres Mínimos, an Italian order of monks that lived and worked in the region until the 1950s. Despite renouncing so many worldly desires, it seems the brothers couldn't give up their sweet tooth and continued to make a rich sponge cake, filled with custard and candied melon, soaked in rum syrup and coated in chocolate. The letter stipulates that Antonio's father is allowed to use their recipe to make the dessert *Tarta borracha de los Padres Mínimos* (*borracha*, or drunkard, refers to the fact that the sponge is soaked in alcohol). Thankfully, Antonio Carmona has let us share this treasured recipe.

8 eggs, separated
200 g caster sugar
finely grated zest of 1 lemon
200 g plain flour

CUSTARD FILLING

1.1 litres milk
zest of ½ lemon, in wide strips
zest of 1 orange, in wide strips
1 cinnamon quill
1 egg
100 g caster sugar
165 g plain flour
300 g 'angel hair' (see page 379)
    or orange marmalade

RUM SYRUP

250 ml white rum
100 g caster sugar

GANACHE

125 g couverture chocolate
    (70% cocoa)
100 g icing sugar
60 g butter

1 Preheat the oven to 200°C/180°C fan. Grease a 20 cm square cake tin and line the base and sides with baking paper.

2 Whisk the egg whites with half of the sugar 'to the point of snow', until soft peaks form. In another bowl, beat the egg yolks with the rest of the sugar and lemon zest until smooth and creamy and increased in volume. Sift the flour into the egg yolk mixture, stirring it through.

3 Using a spatula or metal spoon, gently fold the egg yolk mixture, a third at a time, into the egg white mixture, trying to keep as much air in the batter as possible.

4 Pour the batter into the prepared tin and bake the cake on the middle shelf of the oven for 30 minutes, rotating it after 20 minutes so it bakes evenly. When it is ready, a skewer inserted in the centre should come out clean. Remove from the oven and allow the cake to cool in the tin for 5 minutes, then up-end onto a wire rack and leave to cool completely.

5 To make the custard filling, pour the milk into a saucepan and add the strips of lemon and orange zest and the cinnamon quill. Bring to a simmer over medium heat, then remove and leave to infuse. When the milk is cold, strain to remove the rinds and cinnamon quill.

6 In a bowl, mix the egg with the sugar and flour. Slowly add the infused milk and mix well, then pour into a saucepan and cook over low heat for 20 minutes, stirring constantly with a wooden spoon. (Although the custard will thicken after 6–7 minutes, it needs the extra time over the heat to cook out the raw taste of the flour.) Allow to cool to lukewarm, then add the angel hair or jam and gently stir through. Leave to cool completely.

7 For the rum syrup, place the rum, sugar and 500 ml of water in a small saucepan and stir over medium heat until it reaches boiling point. Remove from the heat and allow to cool.

8 To make the ganache, break the chocolate into a double-boiler saucepan (or a heatproof bowl set over a saucepan of hot water). When the chocolate has melted, add the icing sugar, followed by the butter, mixing thoroughly with a spatula. When the ganache is smooth, remove from the heat and stir in 2 teaspoons of cold water, then refrigerate until you are ready to coat the cake.

9 Carefully slice the cake horizontally into three equal layers. Place the cake layers on a clean bench, cut surfaces facing upwards, and drizzle with the rum syrup. Place the bottom layer of the sponge onto a serving plate. Stir the custard with a whisk and, using a spatula, spread half of it over the bottom layer of the cake. Top with the middle layer of cake, then spread with the other half of the custard. Finish with the final layer of cake.

10 Using a spatula warmed in a jug of hot water, spread the ganache over the top of the cake. Return to the refrigerator for several hours until the ganache has set.

11 Cut into nine equal squares and serve chilled.

MOVIDA'S GUIDE TO ALMERÍA

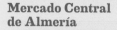

Mercado Central de Almería 🛍✕

Calle Circunvalación del Mercado, Almería; tel 950 25 84 53

Perhaps one of the most exciting markets in Spain, the nineteenth-century shell of this magnificent and lively market has been given a multimillion-euro renovation, yet the ancient art of salting fish and drying octopus is alive and well here. What really sets this market apart, though, is the freshness of the seafood.

Barraquilla del Alquián 🍷✕

Playa del Alquián, Almería; tel 950 52 01 71

A utilitarian white shed on a shabby beach by the airport doesn't raise expectations. But this is a popular rustic lunchtime spot for the wealthy of Almería. A handful of small boats moored on the beach supply this very popular *chiringuito* shack with fresh fish. Order the prawns in salt. Sensational. As are the octopus and fish, both pickled in escabeche (see page 358).

Bar Casa Joaquín 🍷✕

Calle Real 111, Almería; tel 950 26 43 59

When you ask for the menu here, owner Joaquín López points to the refrigerated glass case behind the bar, which is packed with locally caught super-sweet red prawns, twitchingly fresh sardines and still-vibrant squid – all are cooked to maximise their potential in this refreshingly honest bar-cum-diner. The calamari (see page 348) is a winning dish.

Hotel Catedral Almería 🏠

**Plaza de la Catedral 8, Almería; tel 950 27 81 78
www.hotelcatedral.net**

Four-star accommodation in the historic heart of this gritty city. The luxurious large rooms in this nineteenth-century edifice look out onto the palm-tree-lined plaza by the cathedral.

Hotel MC San José 🏠

**Calle El Faro 2, San José, Parque Natural Cabo de Gata; tel 950 61 11 11
www.hotelesmcsanjose.com**

This fresh, contemporarily-styled hotel is close to the dramatic coastline of Cabo de Gata, with easy access to beaches and harbourfront walks.

Hotel Valhalla Spa

**Calle Mojácar 14, Carboneras;
tel 950 13 04 44
www.hotel-valhalla.com**

The coastal resort of Carboneras is
somewhat overshadowed by a recently built
power station, but this comfortable hotel
is conveniently located for exploring the
rugged volcanic coast of Cabo de Gata.

Parador de Mojácar

**Paseo del Mediterráneo 339, Mojácar
www.parador.es**

Paradors are state-owned hotels that often
occupy former castles and other historic
buildings, but the parador in Mojácar,
a sleepy seaside town of white houses
perched on rocky hills, is a purpose-built
resort. One of the key aims of restaurants in
paradors is to serve local dishes: try *arroz a
la Garruchera*, a local rice dish; *gambones de
Garrucha*, grilled prawns from the nearby
port; *choto al ajillo*, fricasee of goat ribs (see
page 366); and *tarta de manzana*, a rich apple
tart.

El Almejero

**Explanada del Puerto S/N, Garrucha;
tel 950 46 04 05
www.restauranteelalmejero.com**

Anticipation of the fishing fleet coming
to shore brings relief to the wives of the
fisherman – and excitement from the
restaurateurs and fishmongers that there's
money to be made. They wait at this urbane
bar near the docks, and if it's lunchtime
they enjoy some of the best seafood dishes
in Spain, cooked simply and well. Wait with
the townsfolk and, while you're doing that,
order the *Cuajadera de jibia*, or cuttlefish
baked with potatoes (see page 362).

Terraza Carmona

**Calle del Mar 1, Vera; tel 950 39 07 60
www.terrazacarmona.com**

At the heart of this hotel complex, based
around an old outdoor cinema in a small
inland town, is a dining room serving dishes
from this part of Almería. The dining room
features a traditional hearth, which, with
its curved lines, looks like something from
Middle Earth. The food here is hearty and
delicious – try the *ajo colorado*, a rich dish
of potatoes and red peppers – so you'd
best stay the night in one of the simply
decorated rooms.

Anchovies

Boquerones

Chorizo

Dried choricero peppers

INGREDIENTS, EQUIPMENT AND BASIC RECIPES

◀━━▶

The Spanish kitchen is based around the produce of the season, which many home cooks and professional chefs still source daily from the market. Spanish cities still have markets in each barrio or neighbourhood from which really good fruit, vegetables, meat, poultry and fish are purchased. The recipes in this book have been formulated using ingredients available in Australia, including appropriate substitutes where necessary. These are given below, along with details of some specific techniques used in the Spanish kitchen.

Anchovies – *anchoas*

In Spain anchovies are first and foremost highly prized fresh oily little fish. They are also consumed pickled and salted. Fresh anchovies are hard to find at Australian fishmongers and markets, so if you're making a recipe that calls for fresh anchovies, look for very small fresh sardines or larger whitebait. *see also* **Boquerones**

'Angel hair' – *cabello de ángel*

Strands of candied *cidra* melon available in jars from specialist Spanish food stores. Use marmalade as a substitute.

Bay leaves

I find that dried bay leaves often have little flavour. If you can't find fresh ones, just leave them out.

Boquerones

Cured anchovies called *boquerones* are popular across Spain. Look in specialist food stores for products labelled 'marinated anchovies'.

Brandy

As brandy casks are essential for maturing sherry, brandy is often used in cooking. There's no need to use your finest aged cognac.

Bull horn capsicums (peppers)

Sometimes called banana chillies, these long green or red capsicums have a better flavour than regular capsicums and are increasingly available in Australia. If you're having trouble finding them, try Middle Eastern grocers.

Chickpeas – *garbanzos*

The Spanish love their chickpeas. They grow different varieties for different dishes and use different-sized chickpeas for different occasions. I prefer the large (about 9 mm in diameter) Australian chickpeas grown in the Ord River region of Western Australia. All chickpeas expand in size and gain weight as they cook: 1 kg dried chickpeas will give you about 2.25 kg of the cooked version.

Chorizo

Chorizo should be full of the flavour of Spanish paprika, garlic and herbs, but good ones are hard to find, and over the past 10 years I have seen some appalling imposters in supermarket fridges. For the real thing, head to a Spanish deli or specialist food store. There are two type of chorizo: fresh and cured. Fresh chorizo acts like a meaty stock cube, infusing the flavour of pork and spices into whatever it is cooked with, while fermented and partially dried cured chorizo is usually served sliced as a bar snack, a nibble with drinks or as a filling in a sandwich to make a *bocadillo*.

'Click' method of cutting – *cascar*

Spanish home cooks rarely use a chopping board to cut vegetables. Instead, they simply hold the vegetable in one hand and the knife in the other, then cut directly into a bowl or pan. It sounds funny, but this cutting technique affects the flavour and texture of the food. Take potatoes: the slight twisting motion of the knife causes the potato to break, leaving a rough and ragged surface, which allows more starch into the cooking liquid, and this in turn thickens the stock.

Dried peppers

The Spanish are not generally into hot food. Go to one of the rare Indian restaurants in a big Spanish city, and you'll find the food there is milder than anything you'd get in an Australian food court. Spaniards do use chilli peppers, but they prefer varieties bred for flavour and not heat. Of these, two of the most common are the sun-dried *choricero* and *ñora* peppers, both of which are available from Spanish grocers and good food stores (soak and scrape away the skin and seeds before use). If you can't find *choricero* peppers, use half a very ripe red capsicum instead; and if you can't find the smaller *ñora* peppers use quarter of a very ripe red capsicum.

Eggs

All the recipes in this book were tested with 55 g eggs. Always use fresh eggs at room temperature; I recommend using free-range eggs.

Fish stock

MAKES ABOUT 2.5 LITRES

1 kg white fish bones and heads
2 brown onions, quartered
5 fresh bay leaves
6 tomatoes
1 garlic bulb, halved horizontally
handful of flat-leaf parsley, leaves and stalks
2 tablespoons black peppercorns

1 Wash the fish bones and heads under cold running water. Place all the ingredients in a stockpot or large saucepan and add 4 litres of cold water.

2 Bring to the boil over high heat, then reduce the heat to low and gently simmer, uncovered, for 1 hour, skimming away any impurities that rise to the surface. Strain the stock into a large bowl, discarding the solids. Use immediately or allow to cool to room temperature, then freeze in 1-litre containers for up to 2 months.

Garlic – *ajo*

Try to use Australian, Spanish or Mexican garlic, and avoid the bleached stuff imported from China.

Garlic mayonnaise – *alioli*

MAKES 480 G

This sharp, garlicky mayonnaise is served with many Spanish foods, from prawns to rice dishes. Use the best garlic and your freshest oil for this. *Alioli* will keep, covered, in the refrigerator for several days.

2 garlic cloves, or more to taste, chopped
2 pinches of salt
2 egg yolks
1 tablespoon Dijon mustard
180 ml extra virgin olive oil
180 ml sunflower oil
2 tablespoons lemon juice

1 Crush the garlic and salt to a smooth paste using a mortar and pestle. Transfer the garlic paste to a bowl set on a damp folded tea towel (this will help to keep the bowl stable while you whisk). Whisk in the egg yolks and mustard, then slowly add the oils, a few drops at a time, whisking continuously and making sure the oil is incorporated before adding any more. Look for a change in consistency – once the mayonnaise starts to thicken, whisk through the rest of the oil.

2 Check for seasoning. If more salt is needed, dissolve it in the lemon juice before adding it, to avoid unattractive white spots in the mayo. Stir through the lemon juice, then whisk in a tablespoon of quite warm water.

Jamón

To Spaniards, jamón is more than the cured hind leg of a pig – it is an object of worship. Top-of-the-range jamón is made from native ibérico pigs that have feasted on autumn acorns in the forest for a season or two, and can be aged for up to 48 months. Called jamón ibérico de bellota, this jamón is very expensive and is generally reserved for special occasions. For general use and for cooking, look for jamón serrano, which is sourced from white pigs that have been raised on farms then cured in the traditional way. In my opinion, good-quality jamón serrano can be better than some jamón ibérico de bellota.

Mortar and pestle

This traditional piece of kitchen kit is very useful for grinding nuts and spices.

Olive oil – *aceite de oliva*

I use good-quality pure olive oil for frying, and extra virgin olive oil for finishing dishes. Spanish extra virgin olive oils tend to be smooth and fruity, and less peppery than their Australian equivalents, although some Australian growers are now producing oils made from Spanish olive varieties such as hojiblanca and picual.

Paprika – *pimentón*

Spanish paprika is made from different varieties of mild chilli peppers that have been dried and ground. In the northern parts of the country the peppers are smoked over open fires and so take on a smoky aroma. In the sunny south the peppers are sun-dried and come from the neighbouring region of Murcia.

Padron peppers – *Pimientos de Padrón*

Like very small capsicums, they are grilled or fried and served as a snack. Mostly sweet, around one in ten is hot. Available from farmers' markets, specialty green grocers and online.

Perol

A wide pan with a rounded base traditionally used to make rice dishes. The best substitute for braising and cooking rice dishes is a wide heavy-based saucepan. For deep-frying, use a flat-bottomed wok.

Piquillo peppers

A large sweet chilli that has no heat, offering instead a lovely rich flavour. Piquillo peppers are roasted, skinned and sold in jars or tins in good food stores and some supermarkets.

Rough puff pastry

SERVES 900 G

Traditionally this pastry would have been made with lard instead of butter; if you decide to do the same, you'll need about 30 g less flour.

500 g plain flour, plus extra for dusting
1 teaspoon fine salt
1 tablespoon sherry vinegar
50 g unsalted butter, at room temperature
350 g cold unsalted butter

1 Sift the flour and salt into a large bowl. Add the vinegar, soft butter and 250 ml of cold water and combine very slowly by hand to form a smooth, elastic dough; do not over-mix. Using lightly floured hands, form the pastry into a ball, then cover with plastic film and refrigerate for 2 hours.

2 Place the pastry on a lightly floured bench and, using a rolling pin, roll into a 30 cm square. Shape the cold butter into a 15 cm square and place in the centre of the pastry. Using a knife, make a cut from each corner of the butter to the nearest corner of the pastry, then fold the pastry over the butter to completely enclose it.

Continued >

Mortar and pestle

Bullhorn capsicums

Jamón

Candied angel hair

Morcilla

Dried ñora chillies

Fideos

3 Using a rolling pin, gently but firmly work the dough and butter into a 45 cm x 15 cm rectangle, keeping the butter between the layers of dough. Fold the dough into thirds as if folding a piece of paper to fit into an envelope. Place on a tray or plate, cover with plastic film and refrigerate for 25 minutes.

4 Place the chilled pastry on a well-floured bench with the folded edge facing you. Again roll out the pastry into a 45 cm x 15 cm rectangle and fold into thirds, then return to the tray or plate, cover and refrigerate for 25 minutes. Repeat this process three more times before using the pastry.

Rondeau

In almost every Spanish kitchen I went to while researching this book, the chef or cook was using a wide, deep heavy-based pan. In France this kind of pan is known as a rondeau, and in Spain is often simply called a cazuela ('cooking pot'). Either way, these pans are the perfect choice for cooking many of the dishes in this book: their heavy base stops the food from sticking, and their width means that food sautés instead of stewing. A large Le Creuset or other enamelled cast-iron pot is the best choice.

Saffron – *azafrán*

Originally introduced by the Moors, saffron is widely used for flavour and colour in Spain; unfortunately, now it is often substituted with artificial *colorante*. Available in good food stores and some supermarkets.

Salt cod – *bacalao*

In the days before refrigeration, salt cod was a crucial part of the diet for Catholics respecting their many fast days. Caught in the northern Atlantic, the preserved cod was traditionally moved around Spain on the backs of donkeys. Today it is still widely eaten, with better cuts used as the star of the meal and lesser parts used for making croquettes and flavouring stews. Look for salt cod in Spanish food stores. To desalinate salt cod, brush off any visible salt crystals, then lay the fish skin-side up in a very large stainless steel bowl and cover with cold water. Refrigerate for 48 hours, changing the water every 12 hours, then remove the skin and bones as directed in the recipe (these can be reserved, along with any trimmings, for making stock).

Servings

In Spain, meals generally don't follow the entree, main and dessert format. Rather the meal might start in a bar with some tapas, followed by a sit-down meal based around one or more shared plates or *raciones*, depending on how hungry you are. In this book, both the tapas and more substantial dishes will serve between four and six people as part of a shared meal.

Spices

After maths, science, architecture and irrigation, the Moors' great legacy to Spain and the rest of Europe were the spices they introduced from the east. Buy spices from food stores or Middle Eastern or Indian grocery stores. When directed, roast spices by spreading on a tray and heating in an oven preheated to 180°C/160°C fan for 5 or so minutes until the kitchen is filled with their aroma.

Sterilising jars

Sterilise jars and lids in a dishwasher on a hot cycle or by placing them in a large saucepan of cold water and simmering for 10 minutes.

Tomatoes – *tomates*

In Spain fresh tomatoes are almost universally used in cooking, rather than canned. Where a recipe calls for peeled and seeded tomatoes, score a cross in the base of each tomato, then place in a heatproof bowl and cover with boiling water. Leave to stand for 30 seconds before removing the tomatoes with a slotted spoon and plunging them into in a bowl or sink of cold water. Starting at the cross, peel off the skin – it should come away easily (if not, return the tomatoes to the hot water for another 30 seconds), then cut each tomato in half and scoop out the seeds.

Vinegar

In Andalusia different grades of sherry vinegar and red and white wine vinegar are used. As a rule, the better the vinegar the better the end result.

Wide heavy-based pan

see perol; rondeau

Wok

Although not found in the traditional Spanish kitchen, a flat-bottomed wok works well for deep-frying.

Cazuela

Paella pan

Perol

Rondeau

GLOSSARY

Aceite – Olive oil.

Ajo – Garlic.

Almadraba – Ancient annual tuna hunt in which tuna are corralled in an underwater maze.

Amontillado – A nutty, dry fortified wine from the Jerez D.O. (sherry) that's perfect with almonds, cheese and jamón.

Anchoas – Anchovies.

Anís – Aniseed-flavoured liqueur. Use pastis as a substitute.

Arrieros – Mule drivers. Pre-industrial revolution counterpart of truck drivers.

Asador – A restaurant that specialises in wood-fired grills and roasts. Also the name of the one who does the roasting.

Atún – Tuna.

Bacalao – Salt cod.

Bellota – Acorn. Famously used to feed pigs for jamón production, acorns are also ground into flour for *la cocina de pobre* ('the food of the poor').

Boquerones – Pickled anchovy. Also a colloquial name for the stereotypical Andalusian flamenco-singing, sherry-drinking, football-loving male.

Borracho – Drunkard.

Café con leche – Coffee with milk, usually served for breakfast. Something to dunk pastries into.

Caldo – Broth. The first course of a *puchero* meal, as well as the stock poured from *puchero* and *cocido* and used in other dishes.

Camarón – A very small shrimp. Camarón de la Isla was also the stage name of Flamenco legend José Monje Cruz, from San Fernando, Cádiz.

Campesino – Peasant.

Caseta – Temporary structure in which to eat, drink, dance and sing during the many festivals held throughout the year.

Cazuela – Traditionally a terracotta cooking pot, now also made of steel.

Chiringuito – Informal beach shack serving seafood and drinks. Beachwear is often acceptable attire, and sometimes wait staff from a nearby *chiringuito* will even serve you drinks while you sunbathe.

Chocos – Southern Spanish term for large cuttlefish.

Choto – Baby goat, also known as *cabrito*.

Churros – Sweet treats made from lengths of deep-fried dough. Usually served with thick hot chocolate for dipping.

Confit – French term for cooking something in its own fat (*confitado* in Spanish), but also often used to describe slow-cooking in other liquid such as sugar syrup.

Confitería – Confectionery shop/cafe.

Conservas – A general term for preserved food, but often associated with seafood. In Spain, traditionally only the best of the season is preserved.

Costillas – Ribs of any animal.

Croquetas – Deep-fried croquettes (a great way to use up leftovers).

Dehesa – Over 2 million hectares of oak forest covering the south-west of Spain and parts of Portugal, used extensively for fattening pigs for jamón production.

D.O. (Denominación de Origen) – Protective status conferred on food and wines from a specified region.

Embutidos – Smallgoods or charcuterie.

Encebollado – Rich onion sauce.

Escabeche – Traditionally a way of preserving food in wine and vinegar, but these days more of a flavouring.

Espetos – Fish cooked on canes in front of a fire.

Estofado – Slow-cooked meat and vegetable dish.

Feria – Traditionally an agricultural show, but now an excuse to dress up in traditional costume and eat, drink, dance and sing into the early hours of the morning. Lots of fun, but not a lot of sleep.

Fideos – Thin, short noodles.

Fino – This pale dry sherry plays a huge part in the eating and drinking culture of Andalusia. If you ask for wine down south, this is what you'll get. Makes tasty food even tastier.

Gaditano – The term for both a resident of the city of Cádiz, and the slang they speak.

Gambas – Prawns.

Gandinguera – The woman of the village entrusted with keeping the recipes for the *matanza* ('slaughter day').

Habas – Broad beans.

Hispania – Ancient Roman name for the Spanish colonies.

Hojaldres – Puff pastries.

Huerta – Vegetable garden.

Jerez – Sherry. This term refers exclusively to the wines made in the Jerez–Xeres D.O. region, near the city of Jerez de la Frontera. Other wines are made in a similar fashion in Andalusia, but only those made in the designated region can be called Jerez or sherry.

Jibia – Cuttlefish.

Lomo – Loin.

Loncha – Perfectly sliced, bite-sized piece of jamón.

Lonja – Market. Often refers to a wholesale fish market, which is an arena for intense transactions and amateur dramatics.

Manzanilla – Dry sherry from the town of Sanlúcar de Barrameda. Confusingly, this is also the name of a variety of olive, and the Spanish word for chamomile.

Marismas – Salt marshes. Also a specific name for the wetlands of the lower Guadalquivir.

Matachín – The man who butchers the pig at *la matanza* ('slaughter day'). An important role handed down to those most capable.

Matanza – 'Slaughter day'. After raising their pig for a year, the family and their neighbours will get together to kill and butcher it – a time of celebration for the family, but not the pig.

Migas – Traditionally a festive dish that makes use of leftover bread, *migas* is often cooked in the open air over coals, and its ingredients can vary from pork to sardines.

Majada – An Andalusian term for the practice of pounding bread, nuts or other ingredients to enrich a dish. In other parts of Spain this is called *picada*.

Mojama – Salted and air-dried tuna loin. Often dubbed 'the jamón of the sea'.

Montilla–Moriles – Besides Jerez and Málaga, this is another D.O. region of southern Spain producing fortified wines, here made using the Pedro Ximénez grape variety instead of Palomino.

Moors – Generic term for the Muslim peoples who conquered the Iberian Peninsula in medieval times.

Morcilla – Blood pudding. Also *morcilla blanca*, made with spiced pork meat and fat but no blood.

Morcón – A nuggety pork sausage made with pork neck meat flavoured with paprika.

Olla – Cooking pot, traditionally ceramic.

Oloroso – Nutty, mahogany-coloured fortified wine made in Andalusia. Perfect with savoury dishes such as game and mushrooms.

Parador – State-owned resort. These are often located in historic monuments, and their restaurants specialise in dishes of the region.

Parrilla – Charcoal grill.

Pastelería – Pastry shop.

Pata negra – Literally 'black foot', a reference to the black hooves of the ibérico pigs so prized in jamón production, this term has now been appropriated to mean any other top-shelf product.

Patatas panadera – Slow-cooked potatoes, traditionally baked in the baker's oven.

Pedro Ximénez – The name used for both a grape variety and the sweet dessert wine made from it.

Pimentón – Spanish paprika made from dried peppers. In Andalusia cooks traditionally use the sun-dried *pimentón* from neighbouring Murcia.

Pimientos – Capsicums or peppers.

Pinchos/pinchitos – Pinchos are skewers/pinchitos are little skewers.

Polvorones – Incredibly short biscuits made with nuts and lard. Named for their powdery texture, they are especially popular at Christmas.

Porra/porras/porro – Don't get these confused. *Porra* is a thick cold soup. *Porras* are thicker versions of the deep-fried lengths of dough called *churros*. A *porro* is, apparently, a marijuana cigarette.

Prueba – Literally meaning 'the test' or 'the proof', this term originally referred to a sample of spiced sausage meat that was cooked to check the seasoning before it was put into casings. Now it is a dish in itself.

Puchero – A rich stew that in other parts of Spain is called *cocido*.

Pulpo – Octopus.

Queso – Cheese.

Rabo de toro – Oxtail (*rabo* means tail, and *toro* means bull).

Ración – A dish to share.

Raya – Skate or stingray.

Riñones – Kidneys.

Rosco – Doughnut or similar-shaped roll or pastry.

Secaderos – A drying room. Often refers to the rooms used for drying jamón.

Sobrasada – A soft cured pork sausage.

Sofrito – A stew of slow-cooked vegetables such as onion, garlic, tomato and sometimes capsicum that becomes the basis for a dish.

Tapas – A bar snack, sometimes served free with drinks, but more often costing a few euros these days. A Spanish culinary and social phenomenon.

Tartessos – The name of the ancient civilisation that existed in the lower Guadalquivir valley around 500BC, as well as the broader cultural community associated with it.

Torno – An upended barrel-shaped device suspended on pivots that allows it to spin. With an opening on one side, it is spun around to allow contactless financial transactions between nuns with cakes and sweetmeats to sell and their customers.

Tortilla – A thick flat omelette, most often made with potatoes but also sometimes with other ingredients such as brains.

THE AUTHORS WOULD LIKE TO THANK THE FOLLOWING:

IN SPAIN

Anna G. Álvarez y las Hermanas Clarisas de Carmona, Miguel Ángel López, Chelsea Anthon, José Antonio y Manuel Jiménez, José Antonio Romero, Arturo Barbero, Jesús Barquín, Mapi Bosch, Iñigo Caño Arbaiza, Reyes Cantarero y Ildefonso Guerrero, José Carlos García, Pilar Plá y María del Carmen Borrego, Antonio Carmona, Charo Carmona, Chema Casero, Cesc Castro, Manuel Contreras, Salvador Cuña, Melanie Denny, Juan Diego, Mireia Dot, Domingo y Manuel Eíriz, Xanty Elías, Antonio Garijo, Loli Gómez, Manuel Gómez, Luis González y María Eugenia Galán, Diego Higueras y Maria José Ruiz, Antonio Hurtado y Nacho Villegas, Keko Hurtado, Manuel Iglesias, Celia Jiménez, José Jiménez, Sor Teresa, Sor Clara, Sor María José y las Hermanas Clarisas del Convento de las Bernardas, Ángel León, Javier López, Jesús y Pablo López, Joaquín López, Luismi López y Adela Ortiz, José Luis y Francisco Paradas, Juan Luis Fernández, Pilar y José Luis Rodríguez, José Luis Rosillo, Fernando Magaña, Anne Manson, Juan María Rodríguez, José Maria Vázquez, Juan y Laura Márquez, Francisco Martín, Paquí Martín, José y Antonio Melero y José Manuel Núñez, Anna y Juan Miguel Ramos, Laura Montes, Luís y Jose Morón, María Moral, Dori Moya, Lourdes Muñoz y David Oliva, Maria Muñoz, Pepi Navarro, Pepe Oreja, Carmen Orta, Miguel Palomo, Francisco de Paula Medina, Rosa Pavón, Jesús Peña, Fidel Pernía, Paqui del Pino, José Ramón Navarrete y Mercedes Castillo, Antonio Reyes, Carlos Ríos, Gonzalo Rojo, Fernando Rueda, Manuel Ruiz, Manuel Ruiz Torres, Rubén Sánchez, Curro Sánchez Noriega y Mario Ríos, Begoña y Montserrat Sauci, Antonio Sorgato, Carlos Teruel, Antonio Torres, Eugenia Torres, Inmaculada Torres y el GDP Levante Almeríense, José Vicente, Manuel Villamuela, Antonio Zapata, Kisko García, Córdoba Tourism, Bishop of Córdoba, Albacor, People of Castro Del Río, People of Aguilar de la Frontera, Toro Albalá

IN AUSTRALIA

Vanessa Hodge, Pepe Camorra, Hugo Camorra, Steve Rogers, Andy McMahon, David Roberts, Ewan Crawford, James Campbell, Liz Carey, Louisa Biviano, Juan and Charo Camorra, Cristina Teijelo, Monica Brun, Susan Wright – Q Strategies, Casey Death, Susan Healy, Tiffany Treloar, Ginger Cornish Treloar, Sunday Cornish Treloar, Prue Acton, Robyn Cornish, Mike and Judy Treloar, Max and Sophie Allen, Adrian and Dianne Kortis, Cherry Ripe, Anita Symon (thanks for the loan of the house to write the book), Nina Rousseau, Mary Ellis, Jane Lawson, The Essential Ingredient, Kylie Walker, Raul Moreno Yague, Raw Materials, Andrew O'Hara, Alan Benson, Julie Gibbs, Daniel New, Alison Cowan, Rachel Carter, Katrina O'Brien, Cass Stokes, Sarah O'Brien, Elena Cementon.

IN SINGAPORE

Spain Tourism: Angela Castaño Cabañas, Vien Cortés, Mapi Bosch Jordà and Arturo Ortiz Arduán; Turkish Airlines: Cengiz Inceosman.

El equipo! The crew (from left): Frank Camorra, photographer Alan Benson, co-author Richard Cornish and researcher Cesc Castro

The research for this book was carried out with assistance from Spain Tourism.

The authors would also like to thank Turkish Airlines for their assistance.

INDEX

CLEARVIEW

First published under the Lantern imprint in Australia in 2014
by Penguin Group (Australia)
Penguin Books is part of the Penguin Random House group of companies
whose addresses can be found at global.penguinrandomhouse.com.

This edition first published in the UK in 2015 by Clearview Books
22 Clarendon Gardens, London W9 1AZ.

ISBN: 978-1908337-269
A CIP record for this book is available from the British Library.

Cover design by Clearview Books
Internal design by Daniel New © Penguin Group (Australia)
Chapter opener illustrations by Daniel New
Typographic illustrations by Freda Chiu and Amy Golbach
Map by Freda Chiu
Photography by Alan Benson
Additional prop styling by Sarah O'Brien
Typeset in Eames Century Modern and GEronto Bis by
Post Pre-Press Group, Brisbane, Queensland
GEronto Bis designed by Smeltery
Colour separations by Splitting Image Colour Studio, Clayton, Victoria
Printed and bound by C&C Offset Printing Co. Ltd

www.clearviewbooks.com